Project-Based Learning

Project-Based Learning

An Integrated Science, Technology, Engineering, and Mathematics (STEM) Approach

Robert M. Capraro
Texas A&M University

Scott W. Slough
Texas A&M University

SENSE PUBLISHERS
ROTTERDAM / TAIPEI

A C.I.P. record for this book is available from the Library of Congress.

ISBN 978-90-8790-637-5 (paperback)
ISBN 978-90-8790-638-2 (hardback)
ISBN 978-90-8790-639-9 (e-book)

Published by: Sense Publishers,
P.O. Box 21858, 3001 AW
Rotterdam, The Netherlands
http://www.sensepublishers.com

Printed on acid-free paper

TABLE OF CONTENTS

TABLE OF CONTENTS

PREFACE

The actual "doing" of Project-Based Learning (PBL) within STEM (science, technology, engineering, mathematics) classrooms at the secondary level is the primary focus of this book. However, that focus does not explain why a group of faculty and graduate students at Texas A&M University have become involved in STEM PBL. It is possible to achieve both equity and excellence in all K-12 schools, regardless of who the students are who attend these schools. By equity, we mean schools that do not have achievement gaps based on race, ethnicity, language or culture, ability, income level, or gender; by excellence we mean that virtually all children can reach high standards. Although equity and excellence are not reality for the majority of schools nationwide or statewide in Texas, this is known from widespread research (Elmore & Burney, 1997; Scheurich & Skrla, 2001; Scheurich & Skrla, 2003) that it is possible to create high performing schools for any group of children.

Furthermore, we also deeply and strongly believe that the quality of schools, that is, the equity and excellence that exist in schools, is the work and responsibility of the adults who run them (e.g., teachers, school leaders, etc.) and the adults in the communities served by the schools (e.g., parents, grandparents, business people, other community members, etc.). In contrast, we do not believe in blaming students, though they certainly must be taught skillfully by adults to take personal responsibility for their learning and school behavior. Nonetheless, it is the adults who plan, organize, teach, and lead the schools, and thus it is the responsibility of adults to create schools that are successful with ALL children.

Developing practical, workable, applicable, powerful classroom tools to accomplish equity and excellence in schools *is* what interested the authors in STEM PBL. Accordingly, we are particularly interested in the tools that can reduce the achievement gaps for those student groups on the bottom side of that gap by driving up achievement for those student groups. In other words, we are interested in developing and implementing classroom tools that significantly improve learning for the lower-scoring student groups, while also being of positive benefit to higher-scoring students. Additionally, the research clearly supports PBL as such a tool (Barron et al., 1998; Blumenfeld, Soloway, Marx, Krajcik, Guzdial, & Palincsar, 1991; Schneider, Krajcik, Marx, & Soloway, 2002).

Traditionally, when mathematics or science courses are taught in secondary schools, they are taught almost exclusively through abstract thought. That is, students are taught formulas or laws, and then the students are tested on those formulas or laws. The real-world connections or importance of those formulas or laws are rarely taught, and even when they are included, they are generally just mentioned in the textbook or by the teacher. These real-world connections are rarely at the center of teaching and learning.

The result of an abstract textbook approach is that students must memorize the formulas or laws without ever understanding their connection to the real world or their application to the "engineered" world. In fact, they have no idea that those formulas and laws are a basis for all of the many technologies students like so much, such as cell phones, iPods, computers, automobiles, television, cable services, wireless computer networking, and many more. Indeed, students appear to love the array of technology that science, mathematics, and their integration through engineering has created without having any clear sense that it was those abstract formulas and laws that made these technologies possible.

The point, then, of PBL is to reverse this relationship by engaging students in real world projects to learn those mathematics and science formulas and laws upon which the world is increasingly built. No matter whether schools have low-achieving students or high-achieving students, a high percentage of students find working with real-world projects to be exciting, engaging, fun, satisfying, and meaningful. Additionally the research indicates (Schneider et al., 2002) that through this method, students learn at a deeper level (failing to learn at a deeper level is one of the weaknesses of the U.S. educational system nationally [Dart, Burnett, Boulton-Lewis, Campbell, Smith, & McCrindle, 1999; Tobin & Gallagher, 1987]) than they learn through traditional teaching methods. Thus, PBL is one of those powerful tools that educators can use in the classroom to increase both equity and excellence throughout U.S. education.

Another reason this team is engaged in this work is due to STEM education. We believe that a curriculum revolution is just beginning in the U.S. educational system. For example, the primary second language to learn was Latin when one of the authors (Scheurich) went to high school, so Scheurich took four years of Latin. Decades ago, Latin mostly disappeared from the U.S. curriculum. Even earlier, high school diplomas were not common, but now of course, diplomas are required, and some postsecondary education is increasingly being seen as necessary for everyone. Consequently, the educational system is always evolving, and now the educational system is experiencing another such evolution—the necessity to be STEM educated.

The curriculum revolution is that science and math will increasingly be taught in an integrated fashion along with technology, just as it is used in the real world, and that engineering will become a common course of study at the high school and maybe even the middle school levels. In other words, as Latin left the standard curriculum offerings, engineering is entering the curriculum. This will happen here, there, and everywhere over the next decade or so until it has become standard in secondary education.

Certainly, one reason this revolution is happening is the national paranoia about the U.S. economy, which is deeply dependent on engineering, being superseded by other economies, like those of China and India. Currently, very few high school students graduate with the idea of becoming an engineer on their minds, even though the field of engineering is where many of the best paying and most satisfying jobs exist. Currently, the U.S. simply does not have an educational system that poses engineering as a paramount choice for college or university study, though school leaders certainly ought to be communicating this to secondary students.

A larger and more important reason this curriculum revolution will happen is the role of STEM in the world. The rate of technological innovation and change has been tremendous over the past 10 years, and this rapid increase will only continue. Ten years ago, cell phones and the Internet were not widespread; now they are world-altering. The next 10 will only bring much more technological innovation. In other words, daily life will be more and more deeply inside of, or interactive with, technology. Even now some are discussing that what it means to be human will become some sort of dynamic integration of people with technology or, more accurately, with STEM. That is, our being as humans will include our integration with technology. This may seem farfetched to some, but how does the world operate differently with iPods, cell phones, and the Internet? These have certainly changed how and how much people communicate with others, and communication is central to being human. Thus, the STEM curriculum revolution is but one part of the larger, worldwide momentum of technological change or the human-built world.

As a final note, the state of Texas is at the forefront of this revolution in many ways, including ongoing work on creating engineering as a high school subject. Our part of this effort is what is called Texas STEM Centers. Two years ago, creative, visionary people at the Texas Education Agency (TEA) and others at the Texas High School Project (THSP, one of many projects of the Communities Foundation of Texas, a private non-profit funded largely by Bill Gates) partnered to create several STEM centers across Texas. Each of these centers had to be partnerships among universities, school districts, private business, workforce organizations, and public institutions, like science museums, and several of these Centers are located primarily in universities.

The goal of this effort was to bring together key players to promote STEM education. In addition, these centers are obligated to become self-sustaining after the state funding is gone. Although starting one of these centers from the ground and building complex partnerships with this array of organizations, all of whom have different discourses and different discourse methods, has sometimes been a difficult struggle, the members at the Texas A&M University-based NTSTEM Center are strongly committed to the original TEA-THSP vision for building STEM education, and this book is an important element of the effort to build this future.

Finally, to return to the beginning, equity and excellence in ALL schools with ALL children is the Center's vision, goal, and challenge. It is possible, and an equitable democracy requires it. Educators have the responsibility to make this happen. The authors of this book are working on the dream, and hoping you are, too. The people at the NTSTEM Center expect that this book will provide key tools for working on the dream.

REFERENCES

Barron, B. J. S., Schwartz, D. L., Vye, N. J., Moore, A., Petrosino, A., Zech, L., et al. (1998). Doing with understanding: Lessons from research on problem- and project-based learning. *The Journal of the Learning Sciences, 7*, 271–311.

Blumenfeld, P. C., Soloway, E., Marx, R. W., Krajcik, J. S., Guzdial, M., & Palincsar, A. (1991). Motivating project-based learning: Sustaining the doing, supporting the learning. *Educational Psychologist, 26*, 369–398.

Dart, B., Burnett, P., Boulton-Lewis, G., Campbell, J., Smith, D., & McCrindle, A. (1999). Classroom learning environments and students' approaches to learning. *Learning Environments Research, 2*, 137–156.

Elmore, R. F., & Burney, D. (1997). *School variation and systemic instruction in community school district #2, New York City.* Unpublished manuscript.

Scheurich, J. J., & Skrla, L. (2001). Continuing the conversation on equity and accountability. *Phi Delta Kappan, 83*, 322–326.

Scheurich, J. J., & Skrla, L. (2003). *Leadership for equity and excellence: Creating high achievement classrooms, schools, and districts.* Thousand Oaks, CA: Corwin.

Schneider, R. M., Krajcik, J., Marx, R. W., & Soloway, E. (2002). Performance of students in project-based science classrooms on a national measure of science achievement. *Journal of Research in Science Teaching, 39*, 410–422.

Tobin, K., & Gallagher, J. J. (1987). What happens in high school science classrooms? *Journal of Curriculum Studies, 19*, 549–560.

James Joseph Scheurich
Department of Educational Administration & Human Resource Development,
Texas A&M University

Kristin Huggins
Department of Educational Administration & Human Resource Development,
Texas A&M University

ROBERT M. CAPRARO AND SCOTT W. SLOUGH

1. WHY PBL? WHY STEM? WHY NOW?
AN INTRODUCTION TO STEM PROJECT-BASED LEARNING: AN INTEGRATED SCIENCE, TECHNOLOGY, ENGINEERING, AND MATHEMATICS APPROACH

INTRODUCTION

Science, Technology, Engineering, and Mathematics (STEM) Project-Based Learning (PBL) integrates engineering design-principles with the K-16 curriculum. This infusion of design principles enhances real-world applicability and helps to prepare students for post-secondary education, with an emphasis on making connections to what STEM professionals actually do on their job.

This book discusses STEM PBL and establishes a set of expectations for implementing PBL in the K-16 classroom. Readers may want to skim chapters, reading those chapters that hold promise to answer questions they already have and reserving some chapters for questions they encounter as they implement PBL in their own classroom. As an edited book, it has some overlap that should provide context within each discrete chapter but hopefully no redundancy. This brief chapter will outline some of the vocabulary, discuss the basic tenets of STEM PBL, and familiarize readers with what to expect from implementing PBL in their school.

CHAPTER OUTCOMES

When you complete this chapter you should better understand:
- the nature of PBL
- STEM PBL concepts and terminology
  When you complete this chapter you should be able to:
- communicate using STEM PBL terms
- explain the basic tenets of STEM PBL
- make informed decisions about which chapters to read first

OVERVIEW OF STEM PBL

Why PBL?

Project-Based Learning has been around for many years, and it has been undertaken in medicine, engineering, education, economics, and business. Project-Based Learning is often shortened to PBL, but this acronym is often confused with

R.M. Capraro and S.W. Slough (eds.), Project-Based Learning: An Integrated Science, Technology, Engineering, and Mathematics (STEM) Approach, 1–6.

problem-based learning. The two terms are not synonymous. In this book, the authors endeavour to keep problem-based learning in lower case to help the reader differentiate the two. PBL is broader and often composed of several problems students will need to solve. PBL provides the contextualized, authentic experiences necessary for students to scaffold learning and build meaningfully powerful, STEM concepts supported by language arts, social studies, and art. PBL is both challenging and motivating. PBL requires students to think critically and analytically and enhances higher-order thinking skills. PBL requires collaboration, peer communication, problem-solving, and self-directed learning. PBL adds rigor for ALL students.

Why STEM?

The idea of PBL is not new; however, what is new is the emphasis on STEM education and a focus to link secondary education with post-secondary practices. It is common in post-secondary institutions for students to be required to work in groups to solve complex problems situated within larger projects. Although problems and projects do not necessitate convergent solutions, students are required to explain their solutions and be able to justify the suitability of a proposed solution to the specifications of the PBL. Commonly, this process has been termed problem-solving and is often expected to be taught in mathematics or engineering classes. However, STEM professionals all engage in complex problem-solving and in most cases, there are multiple possible solutions, each with strengths and limitations. Therefore, it is important for secondary students to develop the broad knowledge that allows them to be successful on high-stakes tests but to also develop the depth of knowledge that allows them to reflect on strengths and weaknesses of their solutions. The process develops critical thinkers who will be more likely to succeed in post secondary institutions where these skills are essential.

An additional advantage to integrating STEM and PBL is the inclusion of authentic tasks (often the construction of an artifact) and vocabulary through the inclusion of design briefs. After identifying the learning goals, the teacher develops expectations for the authentic task to be completed or artifact to be constructed along with the necessary constraints to establish boundaries for the learning. The constraints are often included in the design brief and are the most basic of requirements often considered essential. Therefore, not meeting the constraints would indicate an inadmissible attempt. The design brief contains both the constraints and the criteria informed by knowing exactly which objectives or standards students will be expected to master. The criteria are measurable. These criteria help students know how they are progressing on the tasks and it is these criteria that inform assessment. In fact, it is the criteria that form the basics of all assessments used throughout the PBL.

Why Now?

We define STEM PBL as *a well-defined outcome with* an *ill-defined task*. Well-defined outcomes include clear expectations for learning connected to local, state, and national standards and clearly-defined expectations and constraints for the completion of the task. The ill-defined task requires multiple solutions, which are often constrained by the teachers so that simplistic or trivial solutions are not possible. STEM PBLs engage students in authentic tasks that result in specific learning, essential in the current standards-based educational model, while connecting K-12 education and post-secondary education and addressing the future workplace learning needs.

Building a Common Language

It is important to understand what is meant by somewhat common terms in relation to PBL. For example, *brainstorming* is commonly used to signify simply generating ideas and not engaging in the evaluation of any particular one. In addition, *PBL brainstorming* is used as a pedagogical technique to establish teams and encourage a common focus. It is during brainstorming sessions that teams develop shared knowledge and a group dynamic that will serve as the incubator for their work together and eventually will lead to the groups' solution. The term *relevance* has to have many meanings: the usefulness of the education to life-long learning, meaningfulness to self, importance to society, real-world applicability, and finally, the formation of moral decision-making. In PBL, relevance is not an oversimplification of these ideas, just a prioritization that is used to align learning with formal standards or student expectations. So in PBL educators talk about educationally relevant, and it is this educational relevance that facilitates the development of rigorous and challenging experiences for students.

An important factor when considering PBL is that of the interdependent nexus of learning objectives, assessment, and student learning. It is common to refer to student objectives. The phrase "student objectives" has come to be interpreted in behavioristic terms. STEM PBL would be considered polar opposite to behavioristic paradigms of teaching and learning, therefore, educators use the term student expectations or SEs. The term SEs is not laden with prior notions but still conveys the message that teachers must use some form of national or state standard, objective, learning goal, or performance expectation in order to align teaching, learning, and assessment in this era of accountability. So rather than be stereotyped into a specific paradigm, the perspective of this book is to accommodate many views, and regardless of personal perspective, one can fit those views for describing what students will learn into PBL.

Given the importance of establishing SEs, it is essential also to use some form of assessment to determine the extent to which students master the learning goals. PBL is well suited to rubric assessment but NOT to the exclusion of other forms of assessment. It is important to have a mix of assessments and to build student experience with as many forms as possible.

Many schools that adopt PBL also establish a professional learning community (PLC). A PLC can be an important and very productive school-based initiative that provides for and sustains PBL. The formation of a PLC facilitates discussion about roles and responsibilities, establishes group norms, and sets expectations for everyone involved in the PLC. Often PLCs have stakeholders from across the continuum but it is just as common for school-based PLCs to have representation from a more limited set of stakeholders.

The Flow of the Book

The book contains chapters that address major topics specific to STEM PBL, including special education and a focus on the personal perspective of implementing PBL as a school-wide initiative. The succeeding chapters address the *Who, What, Where, and When of Implementing PBL*, a discussion about making the decision to explore PBL in addition to present practices. The *Theoretical Basis for PBL* explores the theory behind PBL, its reasons for success, and an understanding of when it does not work. *Design Principles* make thinking visible, facilitate metacognition, and develop collaborative learning settings. In *Integrating Content through STEM PBL*, the interrelated and interdependent nature of PBL is discussed along with enlisting collaborator assistance as teachers move along the continuum from partial to full implementation.

The book is designed to provide a modern STEM approach to PBL that is informed by research. It covers the typical major topics but also includes a historical perspective, a modern perspective on assessment that works in symbiosis with high-stakes testing, and insights into the formation of PLCs and their impact on sustaining school change. It is not written as a prescription or novel in the hope that readers select chapters as they journey from dabbling in PBL to its mastery. Because the book was not intended to be read sequentially but by individual need, the overlap in content is purposeful and intended to assist the reader in making transitions and connections between and among the chapters.

Vocabulary for Reading the Book

Constraint. Parameters established as part of the project to structure the deliverables of a PBL event. Constraints are placed on the design process and the product. Constraint is not synonymous with criteria. A constraint could be that a presentation must include research and contain a marketing component that lasts no more than three minutes, no two puzzle pieces can be the same, the boat must float two minutes, or materials cannot be cut. All constraints must be met to have an admissible project.

Criteria. Items written to support specificity that can be ranked or demonstrate the continuum between expert and novice knowledge of the learning outcome. Generally, it is these criteria that function as part of the assessment component.

Designer-defined criteria are used to select among plausible designs and may include wow factor, personal insights, complexity, novelty, or cost.

Design Brief. The parameters for a project-based lesson. The design brief contains the constraints, establishes criteria, may or may not establish evaluation standards, clearly communicates the deliverables, and outlines the conditions under which the project-based inquiry occurs.

Problem-based learning. Problem-based learning for the purposes here is the use of a problem statement that both guides the learning and any resultant activities to explore the topic. Generally, problem-based learning is context rich but textually and informationally impoverished. The focus of the learning is on individual and groups to (a) clearly identify what information they need to solve the problem and (b) identify suitable resources and sources of information.

Professional Learning Community (PLC). Communities of practitioners, students, administrators, community stakeholders, and district personnel whose mission is to facilitate the teaching and learning process where the goals are to establish common language, expectations, and standards and to facilitate increased student outcomes. It is also not uncommon to have a more limited set of stakeholders depending on the level of district commitment.

Project-Based Learning (PBL). A well-defined outcome and ill-defined task. PBL for the purposes here is the use of a project that often results in the emergence of various learning outcomes in addition to the ones anticipated. The learning is dynamic as students use various processes and methods to explore the project. The project is generally information rich but directions are kept to a minimum. The richness of the information is often directly related to the quality of the learning and level of student engagement. The information is often multifaceted and includes background information, graphs, pictures, specifications, generalized and specific outcome expectations, narrative, and in many cases, formative and summative expectations.

Relevance. Refers to the real-world connections that should be fostered in each PBL; it is also associated with facilitating student development of a personal connection to the project and fosters "buy-in" for solving individual problems presented in the project.

Rubric. May be co-developed with the students before the project starts and provides clear criteria that rank the extent to which a team or individual meet the expectations. Multiple rubrics can be developed to assess cooperation, collaboration, presentation, content, completeness, language, visual appeal, and marketing. The evaluator can be the individual, peers, teacher, administrator, or external stakeholder.

Small Learning Community (SLC). Formed by ensuring that all the content area teachers (mathematics, science, social studies, reading/language arts) teach the same students and have common planning, behavior management plans, and common performance expectations. SLC affords teachers the opportunity to become better acquainted with students and improves communication among teachers about student progress on common issues.

Student Expectations (SEs). Specify learning goals where the focus is on the verbs. Clearly defined student expectations facilitate the alignment of teaching, learning, and assessment.

Robert M. Capraro
Department of Teaching, Learning and Culture,
Texas A&M University

Scott W. Slough
Department of Teaching, Learning and Culture,
Texas A&M University

LYNN M. BURLBAW, MARK J. ORTWEIN,
AND J. KELTON WILLIAMS

2. FROM THE PROJECT METHOD TO STEM PROJECT-BASED LEARNING: THE HISTORICAL CONTEXT

INTRODUCTION

Project-Based Learning (PBL) has been a long tradition in America's public schools, extending back to the 19th century and to the work of Francis W. Parker and John Dewey. As a method for general education, the idea of project-based classroom instruction was co-opted from agriculture and the industrial arts and, after first being applied in the elementary schools, was extended to all grade levels. Initially focused on "real-world" problems with tangible, measurable outcomes, the project method was quickly adopted and applied to any activity of interest to students, however transient and/or insignificant. Hampered by the lack of a succinct definition for the project method prevented the assessment of the successfulness, regardless, the "method" became the "current" model of instruction in all subjects for all students, often failing to meet the needs of children, teachers, or society. The project method, as a descriptive term for school practice, was replaced with child-centeredness and the activity curriculum. After a period of near obscurity, PBL has been reclaimed by educators to educate 21st-century students.

CHAPTER OUTCOMES

When you complete this chapter you should better understand:
- the origins of the idea of the Project Method
- the early applications of the Project Method
- the reasons why the Project Method failed to have a lasting influence in 20th-century education practice
  When you complete this chapter you should be able to:
- explain the origins of the Project Method
- identify some of the major proponents of the Project Method
- explain how the lack of a clear definition of the Project Method contributed to its decline in the public schools
- Explain how the idea of the Project Method changed into the ideas of child-centeredness and the activity curriculum

R.M. Capraro and S.W. Slough (eds.), Project-Based Learning: An Integrated Science, Technology, Engineering, and Mathematics (STEM) Approach, 7–18.
© 2008 Sense Publishers. All rights reserved.

In this chapter, the authors present (1) a brief history of the project method, both before and after Kilpatrick's widely read and cited article and (2) some of the issues related to the application of the project method in public school classrooms. We also examine the definition of "project" and how that definition was applied to the use of the project method in the school.

When William Heard Kilpatrick published "The Project Method" in the *Teachers College Record* in September of 1918, he started the piece saying, "The word 'project' is perhaps the latest arrival to knock for admittance at the door of educational terminology" (p. 319). He also posed the following two questions:

> . . . is there behind the proposed term . . . a valid notion or concept which proposes to render appreciable service in educational thinking? Second, if we grant the foregoing, does the term "project" fitly designate the waiting concept? (p. 319)

Kilpatrick (1918) encompassed the whole range of issues related to the "project method," both its history and application to practice. Over the next five years, many authors offered definitions and explanations for the project method and how it should be enacted in schools. However, the definitions were diverse enough to encompass almost any instruction and failed to give teachers specific criteria against which they could measure their practice and, in the end, satisfied neither the theorists nor the practitioners.

ORIGINS OF THE "PROJECT METHOD"

Kilpatrick (1918) readily acknowledged that he was a latecomer to the use of the term project and that he was unaware of its heritage, but he saw value in using the term:

> I did not invent the term nor did I start it on its educational career. Indeed, I do not know how long it has already been in use. I did, however, consciously appropriate the word to designate the typical unit of the worthy life. (p. 320)

Noyes (1909) traced the idea of learning situated around a project to as early as 1875 with the "Swedish" or "Sloyd" system of manual training, which emphasized domestic projects for the purpose of building neatness, accuracy, carefulness, and a respect for labor in a social context. Authors from diverse disciplines used the term in agriculture, manual training (wood and metal shop), and domestic science (homemaking and cooking) classes (Horn, 1922), whereas others traced the evolution of the term and practice to John Dewey at the University of Chicago and Teachers College Columbia University. von Hofe (1916) wrote:

> The sixth-grade pupils in the Horace Mann School are studying science regardless of every artificial division. The class chooses a project, something that has attracted attention and in which they are vitally interested. The teacher then presents the information to follow not the so-called logical

development found in textbooks but the trend of thought of the pupils. (pp. 240-241)

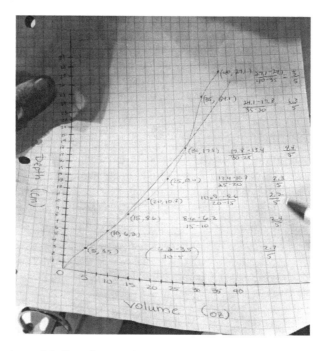

Although not labeling the practice as a "method," von Hofe (1916) described a pedagogical practice that became popularized as the project method. The project method was not rote or recitative learning but learning with a purpose; it was a purposeful act directed by student and teacher interest.

A MODEL OF PEDAGOGICAL PRACTICE

Kilpatrick's (1918) goals were to describe the pedagogical and psychological learning principles on which the idea of the project was based and to provide guidance to teachers. He wrote that behaving in a purposeful way was the basis for a worthy life:

> man who is master of his fate, who with deliberate regard for a total situation forms clear and far-reaching purposes, who plans and executes with nice care the purposes so formed. A man who habitually so regulates his life with reference to worthy social aims meets at once the demands for practical efficiency and moral responsibility. (p. 322)

Kilpatrick, following the idea of Dewey and others that school is not for life but is life, continued to explain the value of a purposeful act:

> As a purposeful act is thus the typical unit of a worthy life in a democratic society, so also should it be made the typical unit of school procedure... education based on the purposeful act prepares best for life while at the same time it constitutes the present worthy life itself. (p. 323)

Seldom in the many articles and books that followed to explain the method of the project does one find either the connection between the purposeful act (the project) and preparation for democratic life or that education is life; the first seemingly is ignored, the second seemingly a given.

A CONCISE DEFINITION

But just what constituted a project remained, and does to this day, somewhat problematic. Despite his best efforts to establish clarity and conformity in describing the project method, Kilpatrick (1918) contributed to the uncertainty of what a "project" was when he wrote:

> [T]he richness of life depends exactly on its tendency to lead one on to other like fruitful activity; that the degree of this tendency consists exactly in the educative effect of the activity involved and that we may therefore take as a criterion of the value of any activity—whether intentionally educative or not—its tendency to directly or indirectly lead the individual and others whom he touches on to other like fruitful activity. (p. 328)

In this statement, Kilpatrick did not see the activity as an end in itself but as something that contributed to a student's growing abilities. However, his next sentences bring confusion:

> It is the special duty and opportunity of the teacher to guide the pupil through his present interests and achievement into the wider interests and achievement demanded by the wider social life of the older world...Under the eye of the skillful teacher the children as an embryonic society will make increasingly finer discriminations as to what is right and proper...The teacher's success— if we believe in democracy—will consist in gradually eliminating himself or herself from the success of the procedure. (pp. 329-330)

Kilpatrick sets the stage for the removal of the teacher from the process of choosing activities. But, according to Kilpatrick, this only occurred after the child had developed the skills and knowledge necessary to choose wisely. By the mid-1920s, student choosing had become the major criterion for selecting projects.

Parker (1922) provided the briefest definition of teaching using the project method by writing, "A pupil project is a unit of practical activity **planned by the pupils** [emphasis added]" (p. 335). This definition was a summary of a much longer position on project-method teaching:

> The central element in project teaching is the planning by pupils of some practical activity, something to be done. Hence, a pupil-project is any unit of activity that makes the pupil responsible for such planning. It gives them

practice in devising ways and means and in selecting and rejecting the method of achieving some definite practical end. This conception conforms with the dictionary definition of a project as "something of a practical nature thrown out for the consideration of its being done"...Furthermore, it describes with considerable precision a specific type of improved teaching that has become common in progressive experimental schools since 1900. (p. 335)

Parker (1922) placed the interest and planning of action by the student as the central tenet of the project method. He defined practical as "not theoretical" but did not ground the practical in utility or social purpose beyond that desired by the student. One example was where fifth-grade students, to understand life in medieval times, constructed a castle from cardboard and wrote a play. However, Ruediger (1923) later criticized this project-method example as producing something with no inherent significance, but Parker justified his example because he believed it had high motivational value.

Kilpatrick chaired a symposium on the project method where several scholars spoke on the issue. This synergy led to a published article where his commentary has become an important component in Science, Technology, Engineering, and Mathematics (STEM) PBL:

> . . . any unit of purposeful experience, any instance of purposeful activity where the dominating purpose, as an inner urge, (1) fixes the aim of the action, (2) guides its process, and (3) furnishes its drive, its inner motivation. The project thus may refer to any kind or variety of life experience which is in fact actuated by a dominating purpose. (Kilpatrick, Bagley, Bonser, Hosic, & Hatch, 1921, p. 283)

Thus, this broad definition was deemed to describe most any type of educational activity that either motivated students or that students said motivated them to learn, without concern for the social utility of the product produced, the ability of students to socially benefit from the activity, or the usefulness of the project in developing additional skills.

A PLAN FOR ALL SUBJECTS

Another difficulty adopters of the project method encountered was questions about the applicability of a method used in manual training and agriculture to non-manual (i.e., academic) subjects (Ruediger, 1923). Several authors questioned the appropriateness of the method for academic subjects. Horn's (1922) criticism of the project method was directed at its appropriateness for academic subjects and its influence on motivation. The statement that "the most serious confusion in recent years has resulted from the teaching of those who define the 'project' as a wholehearted, purposeful act . . . by children" (p. 95) showed Horn's concern about the lack of preciseness, relationship to social utility, and greater purpose. He claimed that the original purpose of the project method, social utility and the teaching of skills for learning, had been ignored, and students' interest and choice had become guiding principles.

Ruediger (1923) argued against using the project method for academic subjects:

> The fact that the project idea in its original meaning is not applicable to the teaching of academic subjects has given rise to a number of interesting yet confusing developments. As used in agricultural education, the project has reference to the use of productive activities for teaching purposes...something of objective significance is produced. A genuine vocational activity, somewhat circumscribed perhaps, is used for educative purposes. When we come to the academic subjects, this idea of a project is not so easily realized. In reading, in arithmetic, in geography, and in history, it is not easy for the pupil to produce something of inherent significance, something that society values regardless of personal sentiment. (p. 243)

As educators struggled to adapt the project method to academic subjects, some argued that real world applicability was paramount:

> The worth of such 'projects' [referring to traditional projects such as baking a cake, raising a plot of corn, building a bookcase] was measured by the degree to which they duplicated projects and activities found in life, by the degree to which they used the best materials and best methods, and by the degree of success that resulted. These "projects" may be defined as highly practical, problematic activities taken in their natural setting and involving the use of concrete materials, usually in a constructive way. They are to be distinguished, in general, from other school activities in that: (1) they are organized more directly about the activities of life outside the school; (2) they are more concrete; and (3) they afford a better test of working knowledge. (Horn, 1922, p. 93)

For some, urgency to define for the project method was less of an issue than the adoption of the philosophy of the project method and the focus on children's interests. Hosic and Chase (1924), contended that there was a limit to the quantity of abstract theory teachers could assimilate and apply and that regardless of imperfections in the implementation or definition of the project method, it is a useful concept for living, learning, and teaching. They concluded by offering their own definition and parameters for which the project method could be expected to contribute results:

> [T]he Project Method means providing opportunity for children to engage in living, in satisfying, worth-while enterprises—worth-while to *them;* it means guiding and assisting them to *participate* in these enterprises so that they may reap to the full the possible benefits. ... The Project Method, then, is a point of view rather than a procedure. (Emphasis in original, p. 7)

A concise definition of the project method never emerged from the literature. However, a new term began to be used along with the word project, one which might possibly have made the project clearer but which ultimately did little to clear up misunderstandings. That emerging term was *problem teaching*.

THE INTERSECTION OF PROJECT AND PROBLEM METHODS

Freeland (1922), once a student-teacher supervisor and principal of the teacher training school at Colorado State Teachers College, used the terms project and problem but made little distinction between them and tried to explain their relatedness by first defining the problem method and then the project:

> The problem is used to appeal to and develop the child's thought...The project may be defined in relation to the problem as something the child is interested in doing and which may involve thinking, but need not always do so. . . If it involves much thinking, it may contain problems. . . [T]he project is different from the problem in that its essential feature is the provision of something to organize, investigate, or accomplish, rather than to stimulate thought. It may be a problem or part of a problem, and it may embrace problems. The more good problems a project affords the better it is for educational purposes. To afford something to do, the project must necessarily arise from the interests of the children. (pp. 6-7; p. 45)

The exact relationship is not clear; a project may include problems, or it may be part of a problem. Whatever label is given to the activity, the activity must arise from the interests of children.

As a pedagogical practice, Freeland (1922) saw an advantage to the project method. "The distinct advantage of the project method over the old topic or question and answer method is that it provides for continuous work on the part of the pupil rather than assignment from day to day" (p. 46). Today, STEM projects are designed so that students participate in sustained, multi-day learning activities.

Some authors, though, considered the difference between problem and project as significant. Douglass (1926) devoted separate chapters to Problem Teaching (Chapter 10, pp. 295-322) and Project Teaching (Chapter 11, pp. 324-356), making a clear distinction that projects could include problems and that problems could, at some point, become projects (pp. 324-325). Douglass, although making a distinction, saw the classification of an activity as a "problem" or a "project" as something teachers should not spend a lot of time on:

> The underlying principles of procedure for problems and projects are essentially the same. Problems and projects possess very much the same values, and the merits of them as teaching procedures are based on the same psychological facts. It is not necessary or desirable even if possible, to attempt here to draw a sharp distinction between the two. (p. 324)

Although carefully defining an activity as problem or project might be possible, the classification would not guarantee quality experiences for students.

> Teachers are inclined to waste much valuable time in quibbling over what technically constitutes a project and what does not. An activity may technically constitute a project and yet be a very inferior educational activity. Merely being a project does not necessarily carry with it merit. A good problem, yes, even a good, old-fashioned, arbitrary, autocratic, daily assignment and recitation, is a much better teaching procedure than a poorly managed project. Not much good can come from merely learning the definition of a project. What is important for teachers is to appreciate the psychological principles which lie behind the project, and which account for its merit and effectiveness. (Douglass, 1926, p. 326)

A little over 20 years later, in another version of the text, Douglass and Mills (1948) devoted only 8 pages to the project method as part of a chapter about teaching units of learning and 9 pages to problem teaching as part of a chapter about questions and problems in teaching. The authors cited Douglass's 1926 definition of project when describing a project: "The project as used in teaching is a unit of activity carried on by the learner in a natural and lifelike manner and in a spirit of purpose to accomplish a definite, attractive, and seemingly attainable goal" (Douglass, 1926, p. 325; Douglass & Mills, 1948, p. 209).

Although, early in his 1918 article, Kilpatrick emphasized the connection between a whole-hearted, purposeful activity and the social environment in which the activity takes place (p. 320), the ideas of whole-hearted and purposeful came to dominate the defining attributes of the activity.

A UNIFIED PERSPECTIVE

In 1918, Kilpatrick emphasized the importance of individualized, self-directed motivation on the part of the student in choosing the purposeful activity and said little about the role of the teacher in the selection process. By the time he wrote his 1925 book, *Foundations of Method*, Kilpatrick had accepted the fact that the teacher may have a role in the planning and encouragement of interest in the project:

> We have, so far, not based any argument on the child's originating or even selecting (in the sense of his deciding) what shall be done. So far, all that we have claimed will be met if the child whole-heartedly accepts and adopts the teacher's suggestion. (p. 207)

Douglass (1926) adhered more closely to Kilpatrick's original statement on self-selecting tasks because he included as one of the characteristics of project, "The learner approaches the task in an attitude of purposefulness; it is a self-imposed task, rather than one imposed arbitrarily by the teacher or the course of study" (p. 325). Douglass did not ignore, however, the role of the teacher in planning and assisting students in the selection and management of projects:

> As in the case with any teaching procedure, the project method in itself does not provide a complete educative situation. Merely having students purposing,

planning and executing projects may or may not be good procedure, depending upon what projects are being completed and the nature of the procedure followed. (p. 341)

THE ACCEPTANCE OF THE PROJECT METHOD

By the mid 1920s, the project method, which seemingly offered something for every student and teacher, had been used to justify the child-centered and activity movements where all curricular plans were to begin with the interests of the child. These practices were not missed by those promoting the project method, even as the idea of the project was being developed. It is important to remember that one should not assume that all interests of children were of equal value. "It is the providence of the teacher to select, stimulate, and direct activities whose worth is high in leading forward toward objectives of unquestioned value (Hosic & Chase, 1924, p. 302). The failure of a teacher to provide guidance "results in indulgence rather than direction, in a form of anarchy rather than of orderly procedure" (Kilpatrick et al., 1921, p. 302).

Years later, Hosic and Chase (1924) warned against thoughtlessly turning control of the class over to students:

First, let us observe that the project idea should not be interpreted as a doctrine of *laissez faire*. The fact that the project teacher invites the pupils to assume a large measure of responsibility does not mean that she turns the school over to them. Both the community and the individual are to be served. (p. 86)

However, few listened to the critics and by the late 1920s, child-centered and activity-based learning epitomized the "progressive" model of education.

CHILD-CENTEREDNESS AND THE PROJECT METHOD

The reaction to the student-centeredness of the project method began almost as it was gaining popular acceptance. Curriculum theorists and practitioners were concerned over the lack of direction and purpose of the method. Rugg and Shumaker in their 1928 work, *The Child-Centered School*, wrote, "We dare not leave longer to chance—to spontaneous, overt symptoms of interest on the part of occasional pupils—the solution to this important and difficult problem of construction of curriculum for maximum growth" (p. 118). Reflecting on the time, Tanner and Tanner (1980) wrote, "Surrounding the pupil with materials but not suggesting an end result or a plan and simply letting pupils respond according to whim, was ridiculous" (p. 295).

The project method thus led to the notion that activity on the part of students was a measure of success and critical to learning. By the 1930s, the project method was under attack by the very person who supposedly was one of the originators,

John Dewey. Dewey (1934) was concerned that teachers had abandoned their proper role in education:

It is the business of the educator to study the tendencies of the young so as to be more consciously aware than are the children themselves what the latter need and want. Any other course transfers the responsibility of the teacher to those taught. (p. 85)

Also, by the 1930s, public schools were under scrutiny and attack for their perceived role in either not preventing the Great Depression or not "fixing" the Great Depression once it had begun thus educational innovations began to fade.

In summarizing the failure of the child-centered project method, Tanner and Tanner (1980) wrote:

. . . experience had made it abundantly clear to many educational theorists that a curriculum based solely on the spontaneous interests of childhood was an impossibility. Such a program could have no sequence and no predetermined outcomes, not even predetermined psychological outcomes. Even a play school had to have objectives and a program that was planned to meet those objectives. Otherwise, the child might as well stay home. (pp. 296-297)

Projects, as a form of child-centeredness, again appeared on the educational scene in the late 1930s in the form of the *Building America* series sponsored by the Social Frontier group at Teachers College. Rugg (1933), also a member of the Social Frontier group at Teachers College, identified the project method as a useful method in social reconstruction at the national level. In his book, *Educational Frontier*, Kilpatrick (1933) discussed the social and educational reconstructivist movement of the 1930s. More specifically, Kilpatrick addressed the need to reform the education system to prepare students for life in contemporary society—a society that required collaborative efforts to solve problems. In this book, Kilpatrick offers a societal justification for using the project method in schools: to achieve social reconstruction.

Later, in the immediate postwar period of the late 1940s and early 1950s, in an attempt to meet the needs of a changing society where more students enrolled and graduated from high school, the project method reappeared in the form of the life-adjustment or continuing life-situations movement led by Florence Stratemeyer, also from Teachers College. Just as the project movement had been criticized for its attention to the immediate interests of children, so too was the life-situations curriculum. Stratemeyer and her colleagues acknowledged that not all children's interests were equally valuable but that starting with the perceived needs and interests of students would better prepare them for the rapidly changing, postwar world in the U.S.

The various teaching innovations of the previous 50 or so years came under attack in the 1950s and soon disappeared from classrooms. The project method had a brief revival in the 1960s in response to the perception that education was failing the nation in science and mathematics. Educators again took an interest in the motivation of children to learn, thinking, "that the thrill of discovering scientific concept autonomously would not only result in more effective learning but also instill in children the desire for further, more significant, discoveries" (Tanner & Tanner, 1980, p. 403). However, as Tanner and Tanner wrote, "This time the model was discipline-focused, not social-problem focused. Discover teaching was a disciplinary effort to teach children to think like scientists instead of children" (p. 403).

THE PAST AND THE FUTURE OF PROJECT LEARNING

As a popular method for general education in the early to mid 20th century, the project method borrowed its theory from agriculture and the industrial arts education and applied that theory to all subjects. However, lacking a clear definition, educational leaders and teachers often used their "definitions" to justify classroom activities driven solely by student interest, regardless of the educational value of the activity. Some (e.g., Douglass 1926, Hosic and Chase 1924) tried to prevent the overgeneralization of the term in classrooms, few practitioners listened and the focus became the interests of students. The social upheavals of the Great Depression and World War II refocused parents and leaders on societal needs rather than the wants of learners. Despite the brief activity in the later 1940s of the life-adjustment movement, the project method was thoroughly rejected by educational leaders failing to meet the needs of children, teachers, or society.

In the last 10 years, augmented by research on learning and the effect of the learning environment on the learner, Kilpatrick's goal of explaining the pedagogical and psychological principles of learning has come closer to being realized. The next chapter, the *Theoretical Framework for STEM PBL*, provides guidelines for implementing PBL in today's classrooms. Although the question of applying the project method to academic subjects was never answered in the 20th century, STEM PBL illustrates that the project method is appropriate for academic subjects.

REFERENCES

Dewey, J. (1934). Comments and criticisms by some educational leaders in our universities. In G. M. Whipple (Ed.), *The thirty-third yearbook of the National Society for the Study of Education, Part II The activity movement* (pp. 77–103). Bloomington, IL: Public School Publishing.

Douglass, H. R. (1926). *Modern methods in high school teaching.* Cambridge, MA: Houghton Mifflin.

Douglass, H. R., & Mills, H. H. (1948). *Teaching in high school.* New York: Ronald Press.

Freeland, G. E. (1922). *Modern elementary school practice.* New York: Macmillan.

Horn, E. (1922). Criteria for judging the project method. *Educational Review, 63,* 93–101.

Hosic, J. F., & Chase, S. E. (1924). *Brief guide to the project method.* Yonkers, NY: World Book.

Kilpatrick, W. H. (1918). The project method. *Teachers College Record, 19,* 319–335.

Kilpatrick, W. H. (1925). *Foundations of method.* New York: Macmillan.

Kilpatrick, W. H. (1933). *Educational frontier.* New York: The Century Co.

Kilpatrick, W. H., Bagley, W. C., Bonser, F. G., Hosic, J. F., & Hatch, R. W. (1921). Dangers and difficulties of the project method and how to overcome them. *Teachers College Record, 22,* 283–321.

Noyes, W. (1909). Ethical values of the manual and domestic arts. *Proceedings of the Northern Illinois Teachers' Association*, 6–17.

Parker, S. C. (1922). Project teaching: Pupils planning practical activities. I. *The Elementary School Journal, 22*, 335–345.

Ruediger, W. C. (1923). Project tangentials. *Educational Review, 65*, 243–246.

Rugg, H. (1933). Social reconstruction through education. *Progressive Education, 10*, 11–18.

Rugg, H., & Shumaker, A. (1928). *The child-centered school*. New York: World Book.

Tanner, D., & Tanner, L. N. (1980). *Curriculum development*. New York: Macmillan.

von Hofe, G. D., Jr. (1916). The development of a project. *Teachers College Record, 17*, 240–246.

Lynn M. Burlbaw
Teaching, Learning, and Culture,
Texas A & M University

Mark J. Ortwein
Doctoral Student,
Texas A & M University

J. Kelton Williams
American History Teacher,
Bryan Independent Schools

SCOTT W. SLOUGH AND JOHN O. MILAM

3. THEORETICAL FRAMEWORK FOR STEM PROJECT-BASED LEARNING

INTRODUCTION

Do you remember learning how to ride a bike? Do you remember teaching someone to learn how to ride a bike? Learning to ride a bike or teaching someone to ride a bike is an iterative process where the learner wants to "experiment" too quickly and where the teacher tries to impart his/her wisdom so the learner does not make the same mistakes he/she did. In the end, the learner probably had to repeat many of the same mistakes; most importantly, no one would have pronounced one of the early experiences as a failure because the learner was not ready to ride in the Tour de' France. Learning to teach Science, Technology, Engineering, and Mathematics (STEM) Project-Based Learning (PBL) effectively requires that an individual have some of the patience and techniques required to teach someone to ride a bike, patience to allow learners to take control as they become more experienced with techniques that build upon their expanding experience and knowledge base as a catalyst for accelerated learning. Just as learning to ride a bike—or learning to let the learner learn on his/her own—is not an all-or-nothing process, learning to learn in a STEM PBL environment and learning to teach in a PBL environment are not all-or-nothing propositions.

CHAPTER OUTCOMES

When you complete this chapter you should better understand:
- how implementing PBL in the classroom occurs in stages, over time, and is informed by research on the design of learning environments and the learning sciences

When you complete this chapter you should be able to:
- implement PBL components into your teaching
- read the rest of the PBL Handbook
- discuss the theoretical underpinnings for PBL with other teachers and administrators

PBL is a special case of inquiry. Although the use of inquiry, inquiry-based schooling, and PBL are not new concepts in science and mathematics, PBL's prominence in national educational standards is a more recent, emerging trend (Bonnstetter, 1998). The recent emphasis on inquiry-based teaching and PBL has

R.M. Capraro and S.W. Slough (eds.), Project-Based Learning: An Integrated Science, Technology, Engineering, and Mathematics (STEM) Approach, 19–37.

been informed by research in both the learning sciences (Bransford, Brown, & Cocking, 2000; Goldman, Petrosino, & Cognition and Technology Group at Vanderbilt, 1999) and the design of learning environments (Linn, Davis, & Bell, 2004). The design of learning environments emphasizes: (1) making content accessible, (2) making thinking visible, (3) helping students learn from others, and (4) promoting autonomy and lifelong learning. The learning sciences emphasize the importance of (1) pre-existing knowledge; (2) feedback, revision, and reflection; (3) teaching for understanding; and (4) metacognition.

DESIGN OF LEARNING ENVIRONMENTS

The following design principles impact the design of PBL:
- making content accessible
- making thinking visible, which includes using visual elements to help the learner and using learner-constructed visual elements to assess learning
- helping students learn from others
- promoting autonomy and lifelong learning
- Although these four design principles are presented separately for discussion purposes, they are integrated in practice.

Design Principle – Making Content Accessible

Content is made accessible by allowing learners to engage in problems, examples, and contexts that connect new ideas to personally relevant prior knowledge and is grounded in three pragmatic, pedagogical dimensions: building on student ideas, use of personally relevant problems, and scaffolding inquiry (Linn, Davis & Eylon, 2004). Thus, effective instruction should provide opportunities for students to ask their own questions, refine those questions through the design and conduct of personally relevant investigations, evaluate data and scientific evidence according to their own personal understanding, verbalize their own theories and explanations, and participate in active STEM learning. Scaffolding and feedback are essential supports for inquiry. Scaffolding allows learners to "become more like experts in their thinking" (Krajick, Blumenfeld, Marx, Bass, Fredricks, & Soloway, 1998, p. 5), which allows them to more deeply participate in the inquiry process. Examples of scaffolds include modeling, coaching, sequencing, interacting with more-knowledgeable others, reducing or gradually building complexity, highlighting critical features, modeling/prompting, and using visual tools (Goldman et al., 1999; Krajick, Czerniak, & Berger 1999; Kozma, 1999). Timely feedback is essential to help students analyze their own reasoning, making them less dependent on the teacher to diagnose their problems.

Design Principle – Making Thinking Visible

Making thinking visible is grounded in how ideas are connected (Bransford et al., 2000) and includes three pragmatic pedagogical dimensions: modeling scientific thinking, scaffolding students to make their thinking visible, and providing multiple representations (Linn, Davis, & Eylon, 2004). STEM is often taught by teachers as a body of knowledge with little understanding of the true nature of science. Students are frequently frustrated when their designs are unsuccessful. Modeling the scientific process allows students to "distinguish among their notions, interpret feedback from others, reconsider information in light of experimental findings, and develop a commitment to the scientific endeavor" (Linn et al., p. 57). Helping students scaffold their thinking helps make their thinking visible. It provides opportunities for students to explicitly monitor their own learning, which encourages reflection and more accurately models the scientific process. Providing multiple representations is essential to allow students to actively participate in the interpretive process of STEM (Linn et al.). Computer animations, modeling programs, dynamic representations, and scientific visualizations represent the cutting edge of STEM and make concepts more accessible to the learner. Recall of one type of representation can support recall of another type of representation of the same material (Baddeley & Longman, 1978; Brunner 1994). Making thinking visible makes scientific thinking visible to the learner and thus more accessible. When the thinking is presented in a visible way, it makes student thinking visible and thus affords opportunities to actively build metacognitive skills. The building of metacognitive skills facilitates more effective scaffolds and feedback from the teacher, makes use of multiple representations, and facilitates student interaction between the two worlds of STEM and learning.

Design Principle – Helping Students Learn From Others

Helping students learn from others is grounded in social constructivism (Vygotsky, 1978), cooperative learning (Johnson & Johnson, 1989), and communities of learners (Brown & Campione, 1994; Pea, 1987) and includes four pragmatic, pedagogical dimensions: encouraging listening to others, design discussions, highlighting cultural norms, and employing multiple social structures (Linn, Davis, & Eylon 2004). Students must be trained to listen to others and to think before responding or acting. Reciprocal teaching (Palinscar & Brown, 1984) emphasizes communities of learners observing and learning from role models. Design is often a central component to PBL. When students design, they must discuss. In a design discussion, students must have time to "reflect, incorporate the ideas of others, and compose their contributions carefully rather than formulating imperfect arguments" (Linn, Davis, & Eylon, 2004, p. 62). It is especially important that these design discussions overtly establish the cultural norms of STEM, which requires the inclusion of all ideas—including ideas that are ultimately rejected, justification for ideas/designs/ rejections, and attribution to experts or evidence. Students must be allowed to establish criteria for scientific explanations, evaluate their own progress, analyze the progress of others, describe the connections between their ideas and those of others, and critique connections proposed by others. These processes are facilitated by the creation of social interactions and norms that enable learners to hear ideas in the words of peers, experts, and members of diverse cultural groups.

Design Principle – Promoting Autonomy and Lifelong Learning

Promoting autonomy and lifelong learning is grounded in metacognition and inquiry and includes four pragmatic, pedagogical principles: encouraging monitoring, providing complex projects, revisiting and generalizing the inquiry processes, and scaffolding critique (Linn, Davis, & Eylon, 2004). One misconception about student-centered instruction is that teachers do nothing when in fact, the teacher is more active than in most teacher-centered, didactic, presentation-styled instruction. Too little or too much monitoring and feedback deters student learning (Anderson, 1982). "Optimal instruction balances feedback with opportunities for students to evaluate their own ideas" (p. 66). Complex projects lend themselves specifically to complex learning and generally to the inquiry process. Through these processes, students are empowered to establish personal goals, seek feedback from others, interpret comments, and adjust behavior accordingly. Students must be encouraged to organize ideas, construct arguments, add new evidence, and revisit phenomena in new contexts. Teachers are encouraged to design ways to scaffold students as they devise new explanations and arguments in the context of inquiry.

Summarizing Foundations for Learning and Design Principles

Changes in conceptual understanding(s) occur as teachers engage and problematize students' pre-existing knowledge. Inquiry and PBL allow the teacher an opportunity to engage the prior knowledge, skills, concepts, and beliefs students bring with them to the learning environment. In order for thinking to become visible and therefore shaped, students must be given the opportunity to expose their own thinking through feedback, revision, and reflection with themselves, teachers, and other students. Inquiry and PBL can be structured in a way that provides students with these opportunities. Inquiry and PBL also promote teaching for understanding by allowing teachers to make available many examples of the same concept at work in different conditions. Metacognition, or awareness of and reflection upon one's own thinking, is a skill that allows people to distinguish when they comprehend and when they need more information. Inquiry and PBL may afford students the opportunity to take control of their own learning when teachers situate the learning goals and actively monitor student progress—both academically and cognitively.

Changes in conceptual understanding are facilitated by overt design decisions that build on the foundations for learning. Making content accessible is facilitated by building on preexisting knowledge, student discourse, and scaffolds feedback by allowing learners to engage in problems, examples, and contexts that connect new ideas that are personally relevant. Using visual elements in instruction and promoting student construction of visual elements promote making thinking visual. As students learn from others, they have the opportunity to learn the cultural norms for learning—including the notion that ideas are accepted or rejected based on evidence—through the attribution to experts or evidence (therefore, students should learn to cite experts and evidence). Promoting autonomy and lifelong learning occurs as students learn to devise personal goals, seek feedback from others, interpret comments, adjust behavior accordingly, and evaluate their own ideas.

FOUNDATIONS IN THE LEARNING SCIENCES

The following foundations in the learning sciences impact the design of PBL:
- pre-existing knowledge
- feedback, revision, and reflection
- teaching for understanding
- metacognition
- Although these foundations in the learning sciences are presented separately for discussion purposes, they are integrated in practice.

Preexisting Knowledge

Humans are goal-directed arbitrators of information they receive beginning at birth. This information forms a wide range of knowledge, skills, beliefs, and concepts. This preexisting knowledge influences what humans observe around them; it influences how they organize and make sense of this information. As children are initiated into the formal learning environment and as they continue throughout their academic career, these prior understandings will significantly influence how they make sense of what they are taught (Bransford et al., 2000).

Students develop preconceptions about how the world operates through their daily interactions with people, places, and things. Students develop logical ideas of how and why things operate based upon these experiences. Although prior learning is a powerful support for further learning, it can also lead to the development of conceptions that can act as barriers to learning (Bransford et al., 2000). A powerful example of how students' prior understanding may act as a barrier to future learning in STEM can be found in the Private Universe research project (Schneps & Sadler, 1987). For example, students know that the closer one stands to a campfire, the hotter he or she feels. Students then use this logic to impose a new understanding to every situation where they feel warmer—it is hotter because I am closer to the heat source. This is a logical and acceptable hypothesis. But, a problem arises when the student brings this naïve conception into a formal school setting where a teacher is attempting to teach the causes of the seasons, essentially trying to determine why it is hot in the summer and cold in the winter. Logical interpretations of the students' lived experience imply that the Earth must be closer to the sun in the summer and farther away in the winter. The teacher explains it is direct and indirect sunlight which determine the Earth's seasons with distance from the Sun having little or no influence. If students' preconceptions about distance from the Sun are not directly addressed by the teacher, students are likely to (1) memorize the teacher's explanation of direct and indirect sunlight whenever it is relevant for a test or assessment and revert back to their initial preconceptions of distance once they leave the formal school environment, (2) develop a theory of the cause of the seasons which blends both the teacher's explanation and students' lived experiences into one unusual theory, or (3) never be able to grasp the concepts of the teacher's explanation.

In a PBL on Non-Newtonian Fluids (see Appendix) Mrs. Gonzalez introduces the following ill-defined task while playing with a large ball of silly putty at the front of the class (engagement 5E model):

What effect does %water have on the viscosity of silly putty . . . and how can the general forms of functions help us interpret this relationship?

The students are then given time to explore how to make silly putty, what exactly is viscosity, how is it measured, what is the general form of a function, what do we have at the school that can be used to make silly putty and measure viscosity, and why is Mrs. G using math terms in a science class? The classroom becomes a blur of motion and the noise level increases. As an experienced teacher, Mrs. Gonzalez seems to ignore the noise and student motion. But, closer inspection shows us that she is moving from group to group checking progress, providing suggestions—never "the answer"—and keeping students on-task. After the initial exploration phase (5E model), Mrs. G has the students share ideas with the whole class before full-scale testing occurs.

Figure 1. An IPC vignette.

Students' preconceptions, the naïve theories they bring with them into the classroom, can impose serious constraints on understanding formal disciplines. These preconceptions are often difficult for teachers to change because they generally work well enough for students in their daily real-world contexts. Students' preconceptions must be directly addressed, or they will often memorize content for the classroom but still use their experience-based preconceptions to act in the world (Bransford et al., 2000).

Teaching for Understanding – Factual and Conceptual Knowledge

Similarities and differences between how experts and novices think and how each group approaches problem solving have led to a better understanding of the relationships between factual and conceptual knowledge (Larkin, McDermott, & Simon, 1980; Leinhardt & Smith, 1993; Nathan, Koedinger, & Alibali, 2001). Factual knowledge is a key component of a person's ability to plan, observe patterns, connect concepts and ideas from other disciplines, and develop and deconstruct points of view, arguments, and explanations. Although factual knowledge plays a vital role in teaching and learning these skills, students with only a large body of disconnected facts are not well prepared for post secondary education or the job market. In order for knowledge to become working or usable knowledge, students must be able to place facts into a conceptual framework (Bransford et al., 2000). In order for students to learn with understanding, factual knowledge must be balanced within a conceptual framework.

Mrs. Gonzalez's Ninth Grade IPC Vignette (continued)

Involved in a PBL activity on Non-Newtonian Fluids (see Appendix), Mrs. Gonzalez's class is now fully engaged in the exploration phase to answer the ill-defined task:

What effect does %water have on the viscosity of silly putty . . . and how can the general forms of functions help us interpret this relationship?

It is the second day in a multi-day PBL, and Mrs. G is still working the room. Students have found various recipes for making silly putty, GAK, and a host of other substances on the Internet. Mrs. G has provided a limited set of materials, so the students are forced to chose the recipe that includes glue + borax + water = silly putty. After all of the groups have experimented with the mixture, Mrs. G again has a whole-class discussion to make sure that all of the students are on-task and to remind them how important taking good notes and multiple trials will be in the next phase of data collection.

Mrs. Gonzalez's Ninth Grade Integrated Physics and Chemistry (IPC) Vignette

---

Figure 2. An IPC vignette.

A student learning with understanding is situated within two foundational concepts: (1) understanding requires that factual knowledge is suspended within a conceptual framework and (2) concepts are given meaning by multiple representations that are rich in factual detail (Bransford, et. al., 200). Learning goals, what the student should know and be able to perform at the end of instruction, are built on neither factual nor conceptual understanding alone. A longstanding debate in education has been and continues to be whether factual knowledge or conceptual understanding should be the primary focus of curriculum and instruction. Although these two concepts appear to be in conflict with one another, factual knowledge and conceptual understanding are actually mutually supportive.

Conceptual knowledge is clarified when it is used to organize factual knowledge, and the recall of factual knowledge is enhanced by conceptual knowledge. Experts in any discipline, whether science, technology, engineering, or mathematics, work from a set of core concepts that organize factual knowledge and conceptual understanding. Thus, teaching for understanding overtly emphasizes the organization of these same core concepts to help learners organize factual knowledge and their individual construction of concepts (Clement & Steinberg, 2002; Gilbert & Boulter, 2000; Lehrer & Schauble, 2000; Penner, Giles, Lehrer, & Schauble, 1997; Vosniadou, 1992).

Metacognition

Metacognition is broadly defined as a person's knowledge and skills to be aware of and reflect upon one's own thinking (Brown, 1978; Flavell, 1979). Progress in the learning sciences emphasizes the importance of helping people take control of their own learning. Because understanding should be the goal of curriculum and instruction, people must learn to recognize when they understand and when they need more information (Koschmann, Kelson, Feltovich, & Barrows, 1996). Teaching and learning that emphasizes the metacognitive process is proactive. Students do not passively receive information as others make sense of it for them. Students must proactively engage in the learning process and must determine for themselves how this new information is connected to current understanding. In order for this to occur, students must be aware of and able to reflect upon their own thinking.

The actual and intended goal(s) of education are often disputed, but most would agree that formal schooling should produce self-directed, lifelong learners capable of making sense of new information even after their formal education has ended. The intended goals of education includes fostering the development of meta-cognitive criteria for knowing when one knows and does not know, the ability to assess what needs to be learned in a particular problem context, the ability to identify and use resources efficiently to improve the state of one's knowledge, and the ability to reflect upon the learning process to improve its efficiency and effectiveness (Koschmann et al., 1996). To meet the goal of producing self-directed lifelong learners, (1) students must be explicitly taught metacognitive strategies, (2) reflecting upon one's own thinking should be modeled by the teacher, and (3) opportunities for students to make their thinking visible need to be incorporated into the learning environment.

To better understand the metacognitive strategies to be employed in a successful learning environment, it is useful to narrow the broad definition of metacognition into three classifications: awareness, evaluation, and regulation. Metacognitive awareness relates to learners' understanding of (1) where they are in the learning process, (2) factual and conceptual knowledge, (3) personal learning strategies, and (4) what has been done and still needs to be done to meet cognitive goals. Metacognitive evaluation refers to judgments made regarding one's cognitive capacities and limitations. Metacognitive regulation occurs when individuals modify their thinking (Schraw & Dennison, 1994). Students must be explicitly made aware of their own thinking, taught how to evaluate this understanding, and then given the opportunity to regulate or modify these concepts.

Mrs. Gonzalez's Ninth Grade IPC Vignette (continued)

Involved in a PBL on Non-Newtonian Fluids (see Appendix), Mrs. Gonzalez's class is now fully engaged in the exploration phase to answer the ill-defined task:

What effect does %water have on the viscosity of silly putty . . . and how can the general forms of functions help us interpret this relationship?

It is the third day in a multi-day PBL and the students are wrapping up their explorations and beginning explanation (5E model). Mrs. G is focused today because she knows how critical today's transition is . . . without good data, the students' explanations will be weak. She has really taken a risk by requiring that the students use functions to explain their science, but as she checks the students' notes, she only needs to make gentle reminders because the groups have all recorded good data. As the students begin to analyze data, questions about what type of graph to use and how many points it takes to make a graph and a variety of questions about functions start to permeate the room. After several small group interventions, Mrs. G decides to have a short whole-class review on functions and graphing. She takes the time to find out where each group is at and facilitates an exchange that is largely student driven because she knows where the groups and individuals are in the process. The students return to their groups, work well to complete their analysis, and start with their presentations.

Figure 3. An IPC vignette.

As noted by Bransford et al. (2000), students who are more aware of their own metacognitive learning processes and are provided opportunities to express their own thinking tend to learn better. It is important that these strategies are embedded throughout the instructional framework rather than taught as isolated skills. Making discussions of metacognitive processes a part of daily language urges students to more explicitly attend to their own learning (Pintrich, 2002). Metacognition is often an internal dialogue, and students with no experience making this dialogue external may be unaware of its importance (Vye, Schwartz, Bransford, Barron, Zech, and Cognition and Technology Group at Vanderbilt, 1998).

Metacognition has been shown to predict learning performance (Pintrich & De Groot, 1990). Students with high metacognitive skills outperformed those with lower metacognitive skills in problem-solving tasks, regardless of their overall aptitude. General aptitude and metacognitive abilities appear to operate independently (Swanson, 1990). Integrating metacognition into curriculum and instruction is a component of effective teaching and learning for understanding.

Feedback, Revision, and Reflection

Effective instruction must incorporate opportunities for students to reflect upon their own thinking, to receive feedback from others about their thinking, and the freedom to revise their thinking as a result of this new information. These metacognitive characteristics are critical to the development of the ability to regulate one's own learning (Goldman et al., 1999).

Often "hands-on" activities fail to be "minds-on" because students' understanding is not engaged (Goldman, et. al., 1999). Criticisms of these activities focus primarily on the lack of opportunities for student reflection. Bettencourt (1993) argued that, "unless hands-on science is embedded in a structure of questioning, reflecting, and re-questioning, probably very little will be learned" (p. 46). Typically, in the traditional classroom, these activities (1) do not allow students the appropriate amount of time to make sense of the new information, (2) tend to be taught in isolation and unrelated to one another, and (3) focus on the manipulation of objects and events rather than on the understanding of a phenomenon (Schauble, Glaser, Duschl, Schulze, & John, 1995).

Once learners have reflected upon their own thinking, the next logical step is to make their internal dialogue external—to make their thinking visible to others. Whether through group discussions, concept mapping, or written communication, students need to share their thoughts and understanding with others. This allows learners to acquire feedback on their conceptual understanding. This feedback often supports aspects of their understanding, problematizes other elements, and leads students to proactively change their own thinking rather than act as a passive receiver of information. Effective teachers have students revise their own conceptual understandings to place factual knowledge within a conceptual framework, rather than passively memorizing new information.

The STEM disciplines are made available to learners by allowing them to connect new thinking to preexisting knowledge. Effective instruction should provide opportunities for students to evaluate scientific evidence according to their own personal understanding, to articulate their own theories and explanations, and to participate actively in learning. One would expect to see participants in the learning environment given multiple opportunities to communicate their understanding to others, often engaging in group discussions to solve problems within the context of a project or a problem, and readily able to present their understanding in the same manner as a professional within the discipline.

Mrs. Gonzalez's Ninth Grade IPC Vignette (continued)

Involved in a PBL activity on Non-Newtonian Fluids (see Appendix), Mrs. Gonzalez's class is now fully engaged in the exploration phase to answer their ill-defined task:

What effect does %water have on the viscosity of silly putty . . . and how can the general forms of functions help us interpret this relationship?

It is the fourth day in a multi-day PBL, and Mrs. G is rewarded by students who come to class and immediately start on their projects. Most of the students are focused on completing graphs and placing them in PowerPoint presentations. Mrs. G notices that although the students were able to collect good data and were able to determine the equation of their lines, they really hadn't focused on answering the question. From experience, she had expected this and had planned some extension activities (5E model) that would hopefully prompt the students to think beyond just the graph and to understand how the shape or form of the line was critical to differentiating between linear and non-linear flow. Examples of appropriate extensions include: What would the data for a Newtonian fluid look like? Or how do engineers take advantage of nonlinear flow?

Figure 4. An IPC vignette.

PROJECT-BASED LEARNING AS AN EVOLUTIONARY PROCESS

The national standards for science and mathematics curriculum and instruction are dynamic. As each transforms to incorporate more inquiry and PBL, so too does the emphasis on training teachers and students to define and use these methods appropriately. Bonnstetter (1998) broadly examines inquiry as he opens a dialogue on how to define inquiry, how to determine specific levels of inquiry based upon student-centeredness, and the potential for success when using inquiry in classrooms by teachers and students. Bonnstetter describes inquiry as an evolutionary process across five levels of inquiry: traditional hands-on, structured, guided, student directed, and student research and with six levels of implementation: topic, question, materials, procedures/design, results/analysis, and conclusions. A teacher progresses across the inquiry continuum by facilitating additional student control up the implementation continuum. For instance, the teacher is in control of everything in a traditional, hands-on environment, but in structured inquiry, the student is in control of the conclusion with the teacher and student sharing control of the results/analysis.

In a recent article, Settlage (2007) argues against this model and other incarnations of open inquiry, stating that open inquiry should not be promoted because it is not effective in all school settings, it rarely occurs, and the "examples provided within the National Science Education Standards of inquiry are fictionalized" (p. 465). A common misconception—or myth—about open inquiry is that as classrooms become more student-centered, the teacher becomes less responsive to student needs, when in fact, just the opposite is true. As a class progresses towards open inquiry on the Bonnstetter model, the teacher becomes an active facilitator, not a bystander. Thus Slough and Milam (2007) broadened the scope of this discussion on inquiry by proposing a model that extends the Bonnstetter (1998) model and addresses the Settlage deficiencies by emphasizing the How People Learn framework of the novice, informed novice, and expert learners (Bransford et al., 2000). Slough and Milam's proposed model also adds a level of community-centeredness that is warranted by both the foundations for learning and design principles, creates a standards-based assessment category along with some minor edits to the implementation continuum, and recognizes the importance of time (see Table 1).

PROJECT-BASED LEARNING CONTINUUM

Traditional, Hands-On Lab (Verification of Facts)

The emphasis in the traditional, hands-on lab is on the verification of facts already presented to the learner. The teacher controls the assessment, topic, task, resources, procedure/design, artifacts/analysis, and often, even the outcomes. This type of experience is often dominated by worksheets and fill-in-the-blank forms.

Novice (Factual Knowledge)

The differences between traditional, hands-on labs and novice are subtle. Instead of verifying factual knowledge previously learned, the student is generating factual knowledge which is novel to them. Although the lab and its components have been determined by the teacher, this constructivist approach allows the learner to analyze the data and determine the outcomes. It is important to note that at this novice level, the outcomes and determinations by the student are only factual in nature. For example, if I drop a ball, it falls to the ground. At the traditional hands-on level, this lab would verify previous teachings that when a ball is dropped, it falls to the ground. At this novice level, it is the student who constructs the factual understanding.

Table 1. Project-Based Learning as an Evolutionary Process

	Traditional Hands-On (Verifies Facts)	Novice (Factual Knowledge)	Informed Novice (Understands facts/ideas in context of conceptual framework)	Expert (Adapts conceptual frameworks through transfer)	Researcher (Creates new knowledge and/or conceptual frameworks)
Standards-Based Assessment	State/ Teacher	State/ Teacher	State/ Teacher	State/ Teacher	State/ Teacher
Topic	Teacher	Teacher	Teacher	Teacher	Student/Researcher/ Community
Task	Teacher	Teacher	Teacher	Student	Student/ Community
Resources	Teacher	Teacher	Teacher	Student/ Community	Student/ Community
Procedures/ Design	Teacher	Teacher	Teacher/ Student	Student/ Community	Student/ Community
Artifacts/ Analysis	Teacher	Teacher/ Student	Student/ Community	Student/ Community	Student/ Community
Outcomes	Teacher/ Student	Student	Student/ Community	Student/ Community	Student/ Community

Informed Novice (Understand Facts/Ideas in Context of Conceptual Framework)

At the informed-novice level, chunks of factual knowledge are connected to build a conceptual understanding. Students rationalize the relationships and connections between multiple pieces of knowledge. In the previous example, students determined that when they drop a ball, it falls to the ground. Perhaps in another learning activity, students also learned Newton's Law of Gravity. At the informed-novice level, the purpose of the lab is to connect these two pieces of factual knowledge to form a conceptual understanding. If someone drops a ball, it falls to the ground. Newton's Law of Gravity states that objects with larger mass attract objects of smaller mass. Therefore, the ball drops to the ground because it has a smaller mass than the ground (Earth). Students analyze relationships between facts to develop more complex conceptual understandings.

At this level, the idea of community becomes vital. Students must be given opportunities for discourse with each other, with experts, and with the teacher. Opportunities to dialogue about ideas and naïve theories with one another, to determine what information is valid and reliable, and to decide how factual information is connected in order to form a conceptual understanding, all of which should be community-centered. The community of learners ultimately decides which naïve theories become appropriate knowledge and understanding. The importance of community continues to deepen as the levels of complexity increase.

Expert (Adapts Conceptual Frameworks Through Transfer)

In general, experts are capable of applying their knowledge, their expertise, to new or novel situations. The ability to transfer knowledge to new situations successfully is a crucial assessment component when teaching for understanding. At the expert level, the goal is for students to be able to transfer their understanding of the material to novel situations. There is usually more than one method for solving problems. The student and/or the community must be given more freedom of choice when determining (1) how to approach the problem, (2) what acceptable resources to use, (3) how the data is analyzed, and (4) how the results are interpreted. The teacher and the student must both have experience and success operating with fewer constraints. Therefore, the expert level not only requires deep factual knowledge and a solid conceptual framework, but also the ability to work more independently than in the past.

Researcher (Creation of New Knowledge and/or Conceptual Frameworks)

At the researcher level, the learner is in control of his or her learning. Students are capable of choosing a topic of interest and are well-equipped to make learning happen. This level requires many years of practice, and the learner must be scaffolded at each step. Reaching the researcher level is analogous to obtaining a terminal degree—you have been given the tools to learn independently. This should be the goal of education regardless of subject matter. One cannot expect a student or teacher to effectively operate at this level without proper training and experience. To expect either to move from any previous level to the researcher level without this training and experience is irresponsible—movement must be slow and thoughtful.

IMPLEMENTATION CONTINUUM

The implementation continuum has one major addition and a couple of minor edits to Bonstetter's (1998) original continuum to better match PBL in a standards-based environment. The major addition centers on standards-based assessment. PBL will never be teaching to the test, and it should not be, but it is critical that PBL address specific assessment standards as mandated by the national, state, or local authorities— that is, well-defined outcomes. Additionally, conclusions become outcomes to match the definition—ill-defined tasks and well-defined outcomes— artifacts replace results to highlight the choices that students make as they chose how to demonstrate/interpret data, and resources supplant materials to reflect the incorporation of various types of digital technology available in today's classroom.

Teacher-, Student-, and Community-Centeredness

Perhaps the most important aspect of the new model is the overt design of community. Our definition of community begins in the classroom and expands to the global community as the learner matures. The teacher, students, administrators, parents, businesses, neighborhoods, and churches are all part of community. But community also refers to norms of the learning environment. As students interact with the teacher and each other, are their ideas valued? Do they feel safe to make their thinking visible? Are they properly scaffolded through the process of inquiry? Providing the learner a community-centered learning environment is a component of effectively incorporating PBL into the classroom.

Settlage (2007) posits that open inquiry is rare, fictionalized, and apparently unavailable for all learners. Without a learning community that has been built for the purpose to support PBL, Settlage is probably correct. But, with the purposeful incorporation of community, the teacher can purposively design learning environments that take advantage of foundational knowledge from the learning sciences and design principles. As students become more autonomous from the teacher, they require a larger community in which to interact, especially if the expectation is that all students learn.

TIME

Time is often the forgotten dimension in today's fast-paced environment, but research has shown that it takes three to five years for meaningful changes in curriculum and instructional practices following a professional development experience (Horsley & Loucks-Horsley, 1998). This time (and the time following the experience) must be spent by stakeholders to consistently advocate for and pursue significant change in teacher, student, and community behavior. In short, significant change in teacher, student, and community behavior takes more than resources; it takes time. This has implications on effective implementation of PBL strategies. If a teacher enters a professional development seminar at the most teacher-centered level of PBL, this educator should not be expected to operate at the more sophisticated student-centered levels of PBL immediately. Students from kindergarten to postsecondary levels enter the learning environment at various levels of sophistication and experience with PBL. They, too, should not be expected to work completely outside of their comfort levels. Growth towards a more sophisticated level of PBL should be incremental and within the appropriate zone of proximal development (ZPD) (Vygotsky, 1978) of all participants—teachers, students, and the community. If teachers and students operate beyond their ZPD, failure is likely. Mistakenly, this failure may be blamed upon the PBL itself or on the inability of teachers and students to work within the PBL framework. In actuality, success or failure depends as much on understanding levels of PBL and working within the appropriate ZPD as it does on the teacher's actual ability and knowledge to implement this new technique.

ILL-DEFINED TASKS AND WELL-DEFINED OUTCOMES

An engineer always starts with the outcome in mind—build a bridge to span the Golden Gate in the San Francisco Bay—but is often rewarded for elegance. In this sense of the word, elegance refers more to the unusually effective and simple design of the Golden Gate Bridge, but it is easy to see the secondary meaning of elegance, defined as grace. Just as engineers design towards a known outcome, teachers must design towards a known outcome. Further, just as the engineer is allowed the freedom to purposively design for elegance, the teacher is allowed to design unusually effective and simply elegant educational designs for PBL. Thus, ill-defined tasks allow the teacher to take advantage of all the foundations for learning and design principles while ensuring the well-defined outcomes mandated in today's high-stakes accountability standards occur or are addressed.

REFERENCES

Anderson, J. R. (1982). Acquisition of cognitive skill. *Psychological Review, 89*, 369–406.

Baddeley, A. D., & Longman, D. J., (1978). The influence of length and frequency of training session on the rate of learning to type. *Ergonomics, 21*, 627–635.

Bettencourt, A. (1993). The construction of knowledge: a radical constructivist view. In K. Tobin (Ed.), *The practice of constructivism in science education* (pp. 39–50). Washington, D.C.: American Association for Advancement of Science.

Bonnstetter, R. J. (1998). Inquiry: Learning from the past with an eye on the future. *Electronic Journal of Science Education, 3*(1).

Bransford, J. D., Brown, A. L., & Cocking, R. R. (2000). *How people learn: brain, mind, experience, and school.* Washington, D.C: National Academy Press.

Brown, A. L. (1978). Knowing when, where, and how to remember: aA problem of metacognition. In R. Glaser (Ed.), *Advances in instructional psychology* (Vol. 1, pp. 77–165). Hillsdale, NJ: Erlbaum.

Brown, A. L., & Campione, J. C. (1994). Guided discovery in a community of learners. In K. McGilly (Ed.), *Classroom lessons: Integrating cognitive theory and classroom practice* (pp. 229–270). Cambridge, MA: MIT Press.

Brunner, D. D. (1994). *Inquiry and reflection: Framing narrative practice in education.* New York: SUNY Press.

Clement, J. J., & Steinberg, M. S. (2002). Step-wise evolution of mental models of electric circuits: A "learning-aloud" case study. *The Journal of the Learning Sciences., 11*, 389–452.

Flavell, J. H. (1979). Metacognition and cognitive monitoring. A new area of cognitive developmental inquiry. *American Psychologist, 34*, 906–911.

Gilbert, J. K., & Boulter, C. J. (Eds.). (2000). *Developing models in science education.* Dordrecht: Kluwer.

Goldman, S. R., Petrosino, A. J., & Cognition and Technology Group at Vanderbilt. (1999). Design principles for instruction in content domains: lessons from research on expertise and learning. In F. T. Durso, R. S. Nickerson, R. W. Schvaneveldt, S. T. Dumais, D. S. Lindsay, & M. T. H. Chi (Eds.), *Handbook of applied cognition* (pp. 595–627). Indianapolis, IN: John Wiley & Sons.

Horsley, D. L., & Loucks-Horsley, S. (1998). CBAM brings order to the Tornado of Cchange. *Journal of Staff Development, 19*(4), 17–20.

Johnson, D. W., & Johnson, R. (1989). *Cooperation and competition: Theory and research.* Edina, MN: Interaction Book Company.

Koschmann, T., Kelson, A. C., Feltovich, P. J., & Barrows, H. S. (1996). Computer-supported problem-based learning: A principled approach to the use of computers in collaborative learning. In T. D.

Koschmann (Ed.), *CSCL: Theory and practice of an emerging paradigm* (p.p. 83–124). Mahwah, NJ: Erlbaum.

Kozma, R. B. (1999). The use of multiple representations and the social construction of understanding in chemistry. In M. J. Jacobson & R. B. Kozma (Eds.), *Innovations in science and mathematics education* (pp. 11–46). Mahwah, NJ: Erlbaum.

Krajick, J. S., Blumenfeld, P. C., Marx, R. W., Bass, K. M., Fredricks, J., & Soloway, E. (1998). Inquiry in project-based science classrooms: Initial attempts by middle school students. *The Journal of the Learning Sciences, 7,* 313–350.

Krajick, J. S., Czerniak, M. C., & Berger, C. (1999). *Teaching children science: A project-based approach* (pp. 5–25). Boston: McGraw-Hill.

Larkin, J., McDermott, R., & Simon, D. (1980). Expert and novice performance in solving physics problems. *Science, 208,* 1335–1342.

Lehrer, R., & Schauble, L. (2000). Modeling in mathematics and science. In R. Glaser (Ed.), *Advances in instructional psychology.* Mahwah, NJ: Erlbaum.

Leinhardt, G., & Smith, C. (1993). On understanding the nature of scientific knowledge. *Journal of Educational Psychology, 77,* 247–271.

Linn, M. C., Davis, E. A., & Bell, P. B. (Eds.). (2004). *Internet environments for science education.* Mahwah, NJ: Erlbaum.

Linn, M. C., Davis, E. A., & Eylon, B. S. (2004). The scaffolded knowledge integration framework for instruction. In M. C. Linn, E. A. Davis, & P. B. Bell (Eds.), *Internet environments for science education* (pp. 47–72). Mahwah, NJ: Erlbaum.

Linn, M. C., Davis, E. A., & Eylon, B. S. (2004). The scaffolded knowledge integration framework for instruction. In M. C. Linn, E. A. Davis, & P. B. Bell (Eds.), *Internet environments for science education* (pp. 29–46). Mahwah, NJ: Erlbaum.

Nathan, M., Koedinger, K., & Alibali, M. (2001, April). *Expert blind spot: When content knowledge eclipses pedagogical content knowledge.* Paper presented at the meeting of the American Educational Research Association, Seattle, WA.

Palinscar, A. S., & Brown, A. L. (1984). Reciprocal teaching and comprehension-fostering and comprehension monitoring activities. *Learning Disability Quarterly, 24,* 15–32.

Pea, R. D. (1987). Socializing the knowledge transfer problem. *International Journal of Educational Research, 11,* 639–663.

Penner, D. E., Giles, N. D., Lehrer, R., & Schauble, L. (1997). Building functional models: Designing an elbow. *Journal of Research in Science Teaching, 3,* 125–143.

Pintrich, P. R. (2002). The role of metacognitive knowledge in learning, teaching, and assessing. *Theory Into Practice, 41,* 219–225.

Pintrich, P. R., & De Groot, E. V. (1990). Motivational and self-regulated learning components of classroom academic performance. *Journal of Educational Psychology, 82* (1), 33–40.

Schneps, M. H., & Sadler, P. M. (1987). *Harvard-Smithsonian center for astrophysics, science education department, science media group, A private universe. Video.* Washington, DC: Annenberg/CPB.

Schauble, L., Glaser, R., Duschl, R. A., Schulze, S., & John, J. (1995). Students' understanding of the objectives and procedures of experimentation in the science classroom. *Journal of Learning Sciences, 4,* 131–166.

Schraw, G., & Dennison, R. S. (1994). Assessing metacognitive awareness. *Contemporary Educational Psychology, 19,* 460–475.

Settlage, J. (2007). Demythologizing science teacher education: Conquering the false ideal of open inquiry. *Journal of Science Teacher Education, 18,* 461–467.

Slough, S. W., & Milam., J. (2007, October). *Defending the mythology of open inquiry: A novel conceptual framework.* Paper presented at the SouthWest-Association of Science Teacher Education Conference, Ft. Worth, Texas.

Swanson, H. L. (1990). Influence of metacognitive knowledge and aptitude on problem solving. *Journal of Educational Psychology, 82,* 306–314.

Vosniadou, S. (1992). Mental models of the earth: A study of conceptual change in childhood. *Cognitive Psychology, 24,* 535–585.

Vye, N. J., Schwartz, D. L., Bransford, J. D., Barron, B. J., Zech, L., & The Cognition and Technology Group at Vanderbilt. (1998). SMART environments that support monitoring, reflection, and revision. In D. J. Hacker, A. C. Graesser, & J. Dunlosky (Eds.), *Metacognition in educational theory and practice* (pp. 305–346). Mahwah, NJ: Erlbaum.

Vygotsky, L. S. (1978). *Mind in society: The development of higher psychological processes.* Cambridge, MA: Harvard University Press.

Scott W. Slough
Department of Teaching, Learning and Culture,
Texas A&M University

John O. Milam
Gordon A. Cain Center for Scientific, Technological, Engineering and
Mathematical Literacy,
Louisiana State University

JAMES R. MORGAN, APRIL M. MOON,
AND LUCIANA R. BARROSO

4. DESIGNING ENGINEERING PROJECT-BASED LEARNING

INTRODUCTION

The requirements for a successful career in the 21st century are completely different than they were in the 20th century. With ever-changing technological advances and new problems being identified daily, educators must prepare students for jobs and challenges that possibly do not even exist today. Therefore, students must be equipped with problem-solving skills that enable them to systematically find solutions regardless of the specific problem they face. In addition, the Internet has made information easily and quickly accessible, which has caused a shift from the need for memorization to learning how to acquire valid information and create new information based on observations and analysis. Machines have also decreased the need for unskilled labor, making it vital that students know how to apply concepts instead of merely understanding concepts. These new demands are the reason engineering, Project-Based Learning (PBL), and the design process are now a focus in 21st century curricula.

CHAPTER OUTCOMES

When you complete this chapter you should better understand:
– engineering and its importance in today's curricula
– the design process
– the essential elements needed to define a project
  When you complete this chapter you should be able to:
– adapt projects for different proficiencies
– define, manage, and assess projects

WHAT IS ENGINEERING?

Engineering applies concepts from mathematics, the sciences, and technology to solve complex problems in a systematic manner. While the process is systematic, it does require creativity in the application of scientific principles in order to achieve a solution. Because engineering addresses real-world problems, it provides an excellent context in which to illustrate concepts that otherwise may be difficult for students to visualize. Moreover, because engineering problems are often of real

R.M. Capraro and S. W.Slough (eds.), Project-Based Learning: An Integrated Science, Technology, Engineering, and Mathematics (STEM) Approach, 39–54.

importance to students and society, they have the potential to motivate students to gain deeper understanding of mathematics, science, and technology curricula.

WHAT IS THE DESIGN PROCESS?

Importance of the Design Process

The design process is a systematic approach followed when developing a solution for a problem with a *well-defined outcome*. There are many variations in practice today, but most of them include the same basic steps. Following a well structured design process is important because it provides the structure needed to formulate the best solution possible, and the act of following a design process builds problem-solving skills and logic.

Steps of the Design Prcess

Engineering design can be represented utilizing a six-step process. The process is, by nature, iterative in that engineers almost never work linearly through these steps but, instead, alternate between the various steps until the final design solution is identified and detailed. The six steps, illustrated in Figure 1, are outlined below.

Step 1: Problem and constraints identification

Although this task may seem overly obvious, it is actually of great importance. By identifying the problem, engineers clearly and concisely describe the goal of the planned design work. This provides an opportunity for all individuals involved in the design (engineers, scientists, project clients, suppliers, and consumers) to come to agreement on specifically what needs to be accomplished. However, some project stakeholders do not have a direct voice in the process. For example, product consumers may not be a direct part of the design team and yet will have a critical role in determining whether a product succeeds. Also, society as a whole is impacted by the products developed, particularly in a large scale project such as infrastructure development. Engineers must find a way to incorporate these points of view, possibly through focus groups or town-hall meetings, for example.

In addition to defining the design goal, the team needs to identify all appropriate constraints and criteria. It is possible that in the process an over-constrained problem will result where no solution exists that satisfies all criteria. For example, achieving a desired product durability and reliability may not be possible given the budget constraints. This problem is typical of real-life situations, and the team must work at relaxing some of the constraints in order for a solution to be possible. Sometimes, an under-constrained problem, where multiple solutions are possible, results from this process. Under-constrained problems can also exist from the start of the problem definition. In either case, the design team must work together to balance the conflicting constraints and criteria until identifying a final solution.

Step 2: Research

Background research provides information necessary to formulate and critically analyze design ideas. It is most efficient for engineers to investigate prior work on the specific topic of their design so they may avoid duplicating effort. In addition, engineers need to be familiar with applicable laws, rules, ordinances, local customs, and appropriate industry design standards. As discussed in "Step 1: Problem Identification," some stakeholders do not have a direct voice in the design team. Engineers must research how to best assess and incorporate the perspective and needs of stakeholders. In today's world, most projects involve stakeholders from different countries and diverse cultures, a fact that adds complexity and additional limitations that need to be considered. Finally, environmental issues related to the project must be researched so negative effects can be minimized.

Engineers must fully understand the properties of the materials being used in the manufacture of products or of the materials that may be processed as part of the design process. In understanding the properties of materials, engineers often rely on design and implementation of experiments followed by analysis of collected data. The selection of materials is key for satisfying project constraints, such as limited funds or completion deadlines, while meeting criteria, such as durability. Local access to suppliers, shipping processes and fees, contract terms, negotiated bulk pricing, reliability, and political issues all need to be investigated when selecting a supplier. In addition, if foreign suppliers are *included*, import taxes must be *considered.* Although the selection of a supplier is almost always a step in the design process, it is important to note that engineers are often restricted to materials available from pre-approved vendors and suppliers.

Step 3: Ideation

Effective design involves the generation of multiple solution ideas, and creativity is an essential part of this process. To this end, design engineers often employ brainstorming techniques. Brainstorming is particularly useful for attacking specific (rather than general) problems where a collection of good, fresh, new ideas (rather than judgment or decision analysis) is needed. Therefore, brainstorming techniques should be used to develop a thorough list of ideas for solving the problem and to identify all risks and benefits associated with each idea.

Although many believe they know how to brainstorm, they often have not truly developed it as a skill or realized the value added from proper brainstorming. Brainstorming should be performed in a relaxed environment. If participants feel free to relax and take risks without being criticized, they will stretch their minds further and therefore produce more creative ideas. Creativity exercises, relaxation exercises, or other fun activities before the session can help participants relax their minds in order to enhance their creativity. When team members brainstorm, they are not focused on perfecting or developing their ideas or evaluating whether or not they are even possible. They are simply recording every thought that comes to mind.

The final idea is often a conglomeration of all thoughts, and sometimes the seemingly impossible idea ends up being the best one some amount of refinement. By permitting and encouraging team members to think outside the boundaries of ordinary, normal thought, brilliant new solutions can arise. Brainstorming is often performed in "Think-Pair-Share" activities, which work well for inspiring one idea from a previous one (Johnson, Johnson, & Smith, 1991).

Step 4: Analysis of ideas

After preliminary ideas have been identified during the Ideation step, they need to be refined and more fully developed. Engineering applies math, science and technology principles for this purpose. Mathematical and scientific models are generated that can be used to predict the performance of the different solutions being considered. The results of these models must be analyzed within the context of the project criteria and constraints in order to identify the alternatives with the highest likelihood of success, so that the design efforts may be concentrated in refining and improving those options.

Engineering requires students to grapple with complex systems. Because engineering problems are audience- and context-specific, there are typically many feasible answers that need to be analyzed in order to select the best solution. To sort through possible solutions, students are required to consider multiple goals, criteria, and constraints that frequently conflict within and across audience- and context-specific issues. Engineering design does not address a single correct answer; rather it aims to identify the best solution out of several possibilities.

Identification of the best solution for a design problem requires careful, objective assessment of the top alternatives. This type of exercise requires students to critically evaluate and communicate the various benefits and drawbacks of each design alternative and should be carried out using a systematic process. A table is therefore often used to rank the options that meet all design constraints for a set of defined criteria. The best solution is a function of both the problem criteria as well as how these criteria are weighed. Although two different teams may have identical problem criteria, they may decide to give greater weight to different items. For example, although two teams both have product reliability and adaptability as criteria, one may value reliability more than adaptability whereas the other might place higher value on adaptability. Neither choice is necessarily wrong, nor are the weights given to the criteria constant. Reliability may be highly rated up to a certain level, beyond which any additional gains are no longer of primary importance. For example, a student may want the product to be highly reliable over a period of 10 years, but past that time span it may be acceptable for the reliability to be significantly reduced.

Step 5: Testing and Refinement

After applying mathematics, science, and technology to fully develop the best design idea, an attempt at building a working model, or prototype, should be undertaken. The prototype's performance will be experimentally evaluated and tested under all possible conditions. For each evaluation, thorough documentation should be recorded, including predictions, testing conditions, observations, and results. Although testing conditions should emulate the actual environment of the finished product, these conditions are sometimes not known at this point in the project. In addition, exact simulation of the actual environment is often not possible. Any deviation, as well as factors that may vary from one test to another, must be identified and recorded. Photographs or videos of the prototype from different angles are beneficial in most cases. A common item of known size (so as to provide a sense of scale), the date, and the designer's signature should also be visible in all shots. Finally, during tests, teachers should ensure that detailed observation notes are recorded. For example, in the design of the houseboats, students should test assumptions about the viability of their design. These results, as well the limits under which the design meets the purpose, should all be part of the observation notes.

After testing and observing a prototype, new information will be identified that may improve the design. At this point, it is important to go back to the start of the Ideation phase to brainstorm alterations, analyze and select an updated or new design, build a new prototype, retest, and refine again. It is possible that the engineer will need to revisit problem constraints and objectives based on the new data or research further. This refinement process is cyclical until the final design is selected. However, time and money typically constrain efficiency in projects, which affects the extent of the refinement process.

Step 6: Communication and metacognition

Engineering design requires effective communication. The days of engineers working independently in cubicles with little interaction are a thing of the past.

Now, engineering problems require experience in at least four styles of communication: interpersonal, oral, visual, and written.

Engineering design is most often done in teams to facilitate broad ideation, share workload, and take advantage of diverse individual strengths. This teamwork setting requires significant interpersonal communication and emphasizes the importance of constructive and professional interaction.

Oral communication is often required to receive validation, approval, and funding for projects. Good engineers must develop the skills to explain their design in layman's terms while being able to back it up with technical concepts and terminology. Many great designs go undeveloped simply because designers cannot gain the trust of investors or customers based on their technical explanations.

The use of illustrations, sketches, blueprints, diagrams, graphs, and other visuals are beneficial throughout the design process. They help communicate difficult concepts and undeveloped ideas, and they serve as input for the Build phases of the project. If a physical product is being designed, detailed dimensions are also required. Standard dimensioning practices should be followed to avoid confusion and to allow products to be recreated with precision.

Written communication and documentation are essential to the design process. Engineers typically record all their thoughts, research, rough drawings, detailed sketches, test results, and interactions in a journal. The format of a journal varies with personal preference, but all journals should be bound to ensure pages are not removed or added. It is important to keep documentation in chronological order to accurately represent the progression of design ideas. Reflection on the process and results will help develop the best design possible, but it may take time for everything to come together; thus, recording these thoughts in a journal is critical to the success of a project. Proper journaling will also prove ownership of ideas, which may be needed for obtaining patents. More importantly, this activity will improve metacognition, and thinking about thinking leads to more and deeper learning.

THE PROJECT DESIGN BRIEF, CONSTRAINTS, AND CRITERIA

Key Elements of Project Design Brief

All projects should be introduced to the students with a Project Design Brief. This document includes the design problem, constraints, and criteria. The design problem should be presented in a personal way that excites the project team about taking ownership. A *well-defined outcome* should be provided, but the path to achieving that outcome must be determined by the team. Project design briefs are presented at the start of every project, and a rubric outlining how the project team will be assessed is typically provided concurrently.

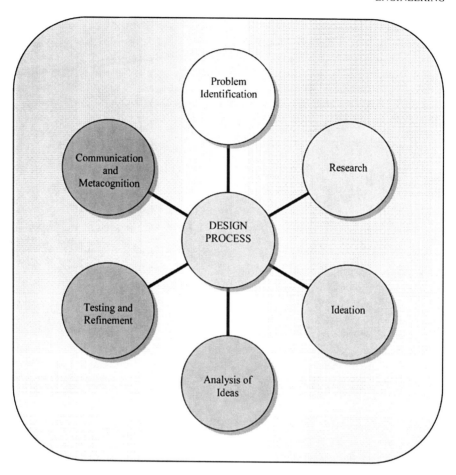

Figure 1. Six-step design process.

Constraints and criteria

Successful engineering considers multiple constraints and criteria that should be satisfied with the final design solution. Each project will have constraints, or limitations, which will often conflict. For example, two common project constraints, low cost and a short implementation timeframe, may be mutually exclusive. Constraints are often focused on the process used when designing a solution or on the limited resources and conditions for the project.

Defined criteria, sometimes referred to as requirements, focus on the desirable or necessary characteristics of the final design. For example, it may be desirable that a product is visually appealing and necessary that it be safe to use. Criteria are typically evaluated on a scale, with a minimum level often being specified, whereas constraints are simply met or not met.

In the classroom setting, criteria and constraints are typically combined in one list provided by the teacher. However, student project teams can and periodically should be required to define or identify constraints and criteria on their own, making explicit decisions as to how the different criteria will be weighed when analyzing their solution, as trade-offs between criteria are inevitable. For example, a solution may be slightly more reliable at a corresponding higher cost; it is important that students explicitly address these trade-offs.

Toaster Design Example
Criteria
- Affordable for target consumer
- Safe to use
- Reliable (consistently toasts bread without burning)
- Multifunctional (works well at light or dark settings)
- Adjustable (slot accommodates different types of bread/pastries)
- Durable (guaranteed to work one year without defects)
- Visually appealing

Constraints (based on process and implementation)
- Time – must complete detailed drawings of prototype design for manufacturer within 20 calendar days and under 300 man-hours
- Project team – two people must work together on the project
- Documentation – all meeting minutes and preliminary sketches, calculations, and notes must be recorded and dated in journal

Constraints (based on business requirements)
- Production cost verses net sales revenue – must generate a minimum 30% profit margin
- Suppliers – must use negotiated suppliers only

Figure 2. Example of defined criteria and constraints.

As an example of possible criteria and constraints, specifications for the design of a toaster are given in Figure 2. Notice that the elements under "Criteria" can all be assessed on a sliding scale. For example, although a toaster must be safe to use, some designs may be safer than others. Additionally, minimum performance levels are defined for some of the criteria. The toaster must operate without defects for at least one year, though better designs will operate without defects for longer time spans. As previously discussed, students may need to research in order to more fully define the criteria listed. Deciding on the target consumer and identifying what is affordable for that person may be part of the project. This can be particularly useful for tying projects to courses outside of math and science; in this case, the teacher could potentially integrate the toaster problem with a social studies or an economics course.

ENGINEERING IN THE CLASSROOM

Benefits

Introducing engineering design into the classroom brings many benefits to the learning process. Engineering:
- Requires higher order thinking
- Provides a realistic context for the application of math and science concepts
- Provides a good structure for breaking down and managing complex problems
- Builds problem-solving skills
- Fosters creativity
- Makes connections between mathematics, science, and technology to real world products and processes
- Increases business sense, identifying connections between different industries
- Promotes ownership based on discovery learning and development of unique solutions
- Cultivates skills required for successful collaboration and teamwork
- Develops a deeper appreciation for and a stronger interest in mathematics, science, and technology concepts
- Provides an environment where metacognition and journaling are of great importance and the purpose of these activities are therefore better understood and appreciated

Process

47

The learning resulting from engineering fits well with accepted learning cycle and instructional models. One widely used instructional model is the BSCS 5E model (Bybee & Landes, 1988), which provides a structured sequence of learning steps. Table 1 summarizes the steps of the 5E model and ties them to steps in the engineering design process. This comparison also could be extended to the Science Curriculum Improvement Study learning cycle (Karplus & Their, 1967) or other models; however, extensive comparisons among learning cycles already are available (Bybee et al., 2006). Regardless of the model used, it is sufficient to say that *engineering supports the learning process.*

Table 1. Alignment of 5E Model with Engineering Design Process

5E step	Design Process step
Engagement	Problem and constraints identification
Exploration	Research
Explanation	Ideation; Analysis of ideas
Extension	Testing and refinement
Extension and Evaluation	Communication and metacognition

Important Points in the Engineering Design Process and the BSCS 5E Model

Engagement/Problem and constraints identification

Before introducing a project to your students, you must capture their interest in the design problem. Brainstorming sessions in combination with class discussions based around what the students already know are a great way to kick off a project. Questions related to the human element and relevance of the design problem are especially important.

In today's classroom, video clips, podcasts, field trips, or guest speakers are effective methods used to engage students. Students typically relate to the problem easier when it is presented with these tools rather than through a traditional lecture. In addition, these methods satisfy most learning styles.

Finally, the Project Design Brief is created or provided during the engagement phase. Be sure to outline clear requirements, constraints, and durations or deadlines. A rubric should also be provided upfront with information on how the projects will be assessed—by the teacher(s), peers, and/or community.

Exploration/Research

During the research phase, it is vital that a purpose is provided for *all* activities. In addition, these activities must model *real world* tasks and be based on discovery learning. During this phase, tasks should be designed so that the students in the class have common experiences upon which they continue formulating concepts, processes, and skills.

Students must consider the "big picture" when creating and communicating their designs. For example, cultural diversity, local environmental issues, and legal requirements may need to be considered.

Explanation/Ideation: Analysis of ideas

Throughout the project, teachers must continually assess student progress, provide feedback, and celebrate successes. It is particularly important to recognize and encourage creative thinking at this stage. Students typically do not associate creative solutions as part of the math and science curriculum and may be particularly uncomfortable that there is not one "correct process or solution" to the project. This challenge also presents a great opportunity to engage students who may otherwise not become engaged in learning math and science.

In addition to validating data, assumptions, and project designs, teachers must evaluate the processes being used to carry out the project and how well project teams are working together. As teachers assess the students, they should provide guidance where needed, but it is important that they do not lay out specific procedures for the students to follow. Often the best guidance comes in the form of questions a teacher poses to the student team.

Throughout the project, teachers should ask themselves questions, such as:
– Can students adequately justify decisions made related to design constraints and alternative selection?
– Can students appropriately apply requisite mathematics, science, and technology concepts that are related to their designs?
– Are the tools and resources used to gather information valid and accurate?
– Are project teams following the design process?
– What are the dynamics of the team? How can they improve efficiency?
– Are the project teams staying on schedule?
– Is detailed documentation being maintained and dated?

Ensure students follow a real-world design process, and always ***allow, demand, and reward creativity and rigor!***

Extension/Testing and Refinement

Discovery learning or problem solving through hands-on tasks is a "must" at every phase of the process. The development of physical prototypes provides a tangible connection to abstract scientific and mathematical concepts. Many students learn best when they:
– have opportunities to acquire information in a context that allows them to see how course material relates to the real world (concrete)
– process information in an environment that allows them to fail safely (active)

Based on testing results, students will refine their design solution. This process requires that they analyze the results based on the problem criteria and objective. In comparing the results of different tests with their predictions, students should think critically about both the strengths and weaknesses of their design. This is one of the most critical parts of the design process. Students' comprehension level tends to increase when making discoveries based on their own unique experiences.

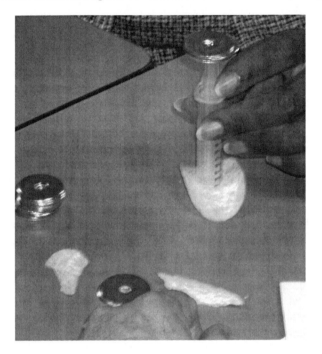

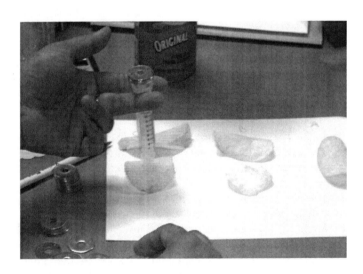

Additionally, students should be encouraged to consider:
- How would a design change if the audience or context were different?
- How would changing the priority of design constraints influence the final design solution?

Students need to be encouraged to revisit previous steps, such as ideation. Initially, students may consider this a step-backwards in the process or even a failure on their part. Teachers need to be conscious of reinforcing that the design process is iterative and not a straight path through the basic steps.

Extension and Evaluation/Communication and Metacognition

A key component of project-based learning is effective and continuous written and oral communication. Students will be required to communicate to both technical and lay audiences. In addition, they must communicate within a team, as a team, and on an individual basis during the different steps of the design process.

The teacher is responsible for providing feedback during all phases of the project and should require the students to communicate to a target audience as much as possible. Peer evaluations, presentations open to the community and school officials, and presentations seeking approval to move forward on the project are a few motivators that a teacher may want to consider when having the students present. Due to the significant time requirement and complexity of each project-group conducting presentations, it is vital that learning continues during this phase. To ensure that this occurs, feedback must be provided not only on the design but also on the project's delivery and students' communication skills. In addition, open discussions should be allowed after each presentation to review and expand on the information learned from each group.

The project team must discover the best means of transmitting its ideas and, in the process, discover or be introduced to domain-specific communication mechanisms. For example, Graphical Management Charts are typical in engineering management as a mechanism to visually organize and keep track of schedules and major project milestones.

At each phase, milestones or progress points should be assessed, and successes should be celebrated. As such, both formative as well as summative evaluations must be part of the process. Rubrics for assessment should be provided up-front, allowing students to have a clear sense of their expected performance.

Formative assessment should focus on the design process and whether the students are conscious of the decisions being made and understand the basic principles being applied. Teachers should ask students to:
- Explain the mathematical and scientific principles used in the development of their product.
- Justify or explain decisions related to design constraints and alternatives analyzed during the design process.
- Discuss various solution alternatives and how well they meet the selected design constraints.

– Evaluate their progress in both completing project tasks and developing new knowledge and skills.

These questions not only provide a basis for the formative assessment, they also can guide students into explicitly developing their metacognition skills. Metacognition, or thinking about thinking, is a vital part of all projects. It must be done continuously, and all reflections should be well documented. It is important to reflect individually and within a team setting.

Metacognition is also important for students to do at the conclusion of each project phase, especially at the end of the project. Considering what they learned throughout the design process, they should identify what changes they would make not only to their design but also within their journey.

Summative assessment includes the evaluation of how well the final product meets all the problem criteria and if it meets the defined constraints. It also evaluates the oral, written, or graphical artifacts prepared during the course of the project. A target audience should be defined clearly by the teachers for all communication artifacts, and the students must gear their presentation to that audience. A presentation that would be suitable for a technical audience would not be the same as one for a layperson. It is beneficial for students to present their work to different audiences so as to develop a broad communication skill set. This can be accomplished without having the students duplicate their efforts. For example, the written report should be directed towards a more technical audience, allowing the teacher to fully assess the rigor of the approach of the student team. The in-class presentation could be designed for a lay audience. The presentation to a lay audience facilitates assessments when students are asked to role-play and sell their idea to potential customers, who could be represented by their classmates.

Adaptations for Different Proficiencies

Engineering projects are easily adapted to meet various levels of proficiency while still holding students accountable for high levels of rigor. Projects can be modified in the following ways.

Providing additional help (Closer Monitoring) of self-management of learning. It can be difficult for some students to manage their time effectively or not get overwhelmed by the size of a project. A teacher can help the students slowly develop the necessary skills by providing frequent and clear feedback on where students should be in the design process.

Breaking down tasks of long duration. Some students can lose their motivation when tasks are of long duration because they do not have a sense of accomplishment. By breaking down long tasks into smaller ones, students more readily see their progress towards meeting the project goals.

Extending deadlines. Most students can meet any criteria and level of rigor given enough time to complete a task. Balancing the time provided to complete tasks against a student's ability is a critical element in developing an appropriately challenging project.

Creative partnering (Group Projects). Team projects can take advantage of the different strengths of the members of the teams. Although you do not want to partner students of such different abilities that the stronger members feel like they need to do all the work in order to achieve the grade they desire, balancing different abilities can lead to deeper learning for all students.

The above modifications are often all that is needed to get any student group to meet the project criteria. When necessary, additional modifications can be made by simplifying project criteria and constraints, such as:

Eliminating some constraints. By eliminating constraints, a wider solution set is available, and students can more easily meet the project objectives. However, a wider solution set can occasionally make it more difficult for the students to select their best design alternative. As a result, they may need more guidance during that phase of the project or a clearer rubric that provides a more detailed mechanism for weighing the various design criteria.

Modifying criteria and rubric. Typically, this modification is tied to changes made to eliminate constraints. More detailed criteria and rubrics can be useful to students that are not yet comfortable making decisions or accepting that multiple solutions may be possible.

These modifications should be a last resort, however, as most students can meet the desired project criteria and constraints if given enough time and support during the process.

SUMMARY

Discovery learning or problem solving is the best way to prepare students for jobs that do not even exist today (Resnick, 1999) As technology and problems evolve at an ever increasing pace, students need to develop the skills to creatively apply fundamental principles to new challenges. Although knowledge of Language Arts, social studies, science, and mathematics have traditionally been the fundamentals of the U.S. educational system, students in the 21st century require an expanded set of basic skills that emphasize thinking and problem-solving. In particular, students must be able to connect knowledge and skills learned in one topic area to another topic area as well as make connections to the real-life application of that knowledge.

Engineering project-based learning inherently addresses these needs, though they are complex in nature and span multiple disciplines. The design process provides a structure for approaching complex problems while encouraging creativity in achieving project goals. Projects are easily adaptable to meet the needs of different student populations by changing project criteria, constraints, and overall project duration. Students with diverse learning styles all benefit from the project, as different stages are more directly related to different learning styles. This allows more students to operate within their comfort zone at least part of the time and can provide an environment that allows them to learn from their mistakes safely. The questioning and analytical elements of the process also serve as self assessments on the state of each student's own learning and understanding. Additionally, projects emphasize teamwork, communication, and problem-solving skills that will be important to all students regardless of their future educational or career goals.

REFERENCES

Abrami, P. C. (1995). *Classroom connections: Understanding and using cooperative learning*. Toronto: Harcourt Brace.

Bybee, R. W., & Landes, N. M. (1988). What research says about new science curriculums (BSCS). *Science and Children, 25,* 35–39.

Bybee, R. W., Taylor, J. A., Gardner, A., Van Scotter, P., Powell, J. C., Westbrook, A., & Landes, N. (2006). *The BSCS 5E Instructional Model: Origins and effectiveness,* A Report Prepared for the Office of Science Education National Institutes of Health, BSCS, June 2006.

Johnson, D. W., Johnson, R. T., & Smith, K. (1991). *Active learning: Cooperation in the college classroom*. Edina, MN: Interaction Book.

Karplus, R., & Their, H. D. (1967). *A new look at elementary school science*. Chicago; Rand McNally.

Resnick, L. B. (1999). Making America smarter. Education Week Century Series, 18(40), 38–40. Retrieved June 30, 2008, from http://www.edweek.org/ew/vol-18/40resnick.h18

James R. Morgan
Zachry Department of Civil Engineering,
Texas A&M University

April M. Moon
Engineering Teacher,
Waxahachie Global High School

Luciana R. Barrosa
Zachry Department of Civil Engineering,
Texas A&M University

MELANIE N. WOODS AND JAMES R. MORGAN

5. ETIOLOGY OF STEM PROJECT-BASED LEARNING: LINKING ENGINEERING AND EDUCATION

INTRODUCTION

Traditional classroom instruction will encounter several changes in the transition to Project-Based Learning (PBL). Therefore, Chapter 5 examines some of the transitions experienced by teachers and students. Specific topics covered are the role of the teacher and the student, designing PBL problems, cooperative learning, and the problem-solving process. The chapter opens with the historical development of problem-based learning in the medical field due to the early adaptation of problem-based techniques in engineering and evolution into PBL. Also included is a comparison chart between problem-based learning and PBL, as well as a diagram of the problem-solving process.

CHAPTER OUTCOMES

When you complete this chapter you should better understand:
- the history of development of PBL in engineering
- the changes in philosophy required to implement STEM PBL
- the changing roles required to implement STEM PBL
- the role of problems in the design of STEM PBL
- When you complete this chapter you should be able to:
- develop PBLs that build on the engineering design process
- develop problems and artifacts for STEM PBL
- develop PBLs that accommodate multifaceted student outcomes

HISTORY AND DEVELOPMENT OF PROBLEM-BASED LEARNING

The origin of problem-based learning began in the medical sciences. In the late 1960s, McMaster University in Canada pioneered a new curriculum designed to make learning medical information more effective for medical students. A new curriculum was necessary because the lecture method fell short in advancing student knowledge at the rate medical procedures were being adopted. The goal of the new curriculum was to present an ill-structured medical problem to drive the problem-solving process. The design of the new curriculum focused on methods to make learning student-centered, as well as make medical students lifelong learners, a necessary attribute for medical practice. Therefore, the learning environment

R.M. Capraro and S.W. Slough (eds.), Project-Based Learning: An Integrated Science, Technology, Engineering, and Mathematics (STEM) Approach, 55–65.

shifted to small group, cooperative, self-directed, self-assessed, and interdependent (Woods, 1996). Through trial and error, problem-based learning was being perfected. Since that time, problem-based learning has been adopted by medical schools across North America, Europe, and Australia and has been adapted to meet the needs of other university disciplines and some K-12 school systems.

Problem-based learning is grounded in constructivism, thus the belief students learn when they are afforded the opportunity to put together information with what they already know; PBL is grounded in constructivism and constructionism, the extended belief that students build knowledge from life experiences and the production of an artifact to display their understanding. Furthermore, the constructed artifact should be shared with others for critique, discussion, examination and questioning. In this way, the student gains insight into how others view the artifact, which deepens the student's understanding of the concept.

Moving beyond the medical model of problem-based learning that focused on specific scenarios with a single diagnosis, higher education colleges of engineering went one step further and began presenting real-world projects to engineering students. The projects centered on actual problems encountered in the workplace to make learning student centered and student driven. The engineering curriculum was driven by problems or tasks, and these problems or tasks increased in intensity with each year as an engineering students' knowledge and skills progressed. Presenting a project to small groups of students put learning in the hands of the students. The intent was similar to problem-based learning except for the addition of brainstorming, selective inclusion of constraints, design briefs, detailed criteria for evaluation, and the production of a discipline-specific artifact. Brainstorming is a critical early step in the PBL process where students focus on discussion of unrestrained ideas, creativity, and examination of alternative views. Constraints are what turn a question into a PBL. Engineers design in the real world and thus constantly deal with constraints on both the process and the product (e.g., a bridge must support a certain weight, span a certain length, be completed in a limited time, and visually blend with local architecture). Design briefs expand upon our notion of a well-defined outcome by presenting the constraints, evaluation standards, deliverables, and objectives. Engineering-based PBLs typically require presentation of the project to the client or professors serving as clients, answer questions related to the project, and receive feedback to justify the findings of the project. Clear criteria for evaluating the entire design process, product, and presentation are a must; students can focus on the learning rather than the assessment.

Project Versus Problem-Based Learning

Although there are many similarities between PBL and problem-based learning, there are also clear distinctions between the two strategies. Both practices are based in constructivism and involve the student taking an active role in the learning process. However problem-based learning has roots in behaviorism because it emphasizes single correct solutions to the specified problem. Differences are listed in the table below.

Table 1. Project Versus Problem-Based Learning

Project-Based Learning	Problem-Based Learning
Student centered	Student directed
Learning method	Teaching method
Learning through experiences	Learning through problems
Produces product	General exploration of the topic
Collaborative and self-directed learning	Cooperative and assigned student roles
Culminates in the end-product	Culminates in the studying of the problem
Well-Defined problems and well-defined outcome	Ill-structured problem
Driven by project	Driven by problem
Undetermined time frame to complete projects	Specific time frame to explore topic
Constructivism and Constructionism	Constructivism and Behaviorism

THE TRADITIONAL TEACHER AND PBL

Transitioning a traditional teacher into the practice of PBL is a complex process. The shift in emphasis essentially redefines most aspects of the teaching and learning process. When the culture and climate have been defined in a classroom, and the role of a teacher and student has been established, a reasonable amount of reluctance can be expected. Nevertheless, the most important challenge the teacher will make involves a change in philosophy and role.

A Change in Philosophy

Teachers of all levels and years of experience are often required to produce a teaching philosophy, a document outlining their objectives, methods of instruction, and student assessment techniques. Preparing a philosophy should give teachers an opportunity to take a critical look at their beliefs about how students learn and incorporate progressively more sophisticated understandings of the teaching and learning process. Whether conscious or subconscious, every teacher operates with a teaching philosophy often constrained by campus, district, and state philosophies (e.g., high-stakes testing). The philosophy provides a framework for the value placed on the teaching and learning processes. Thoughts regarding the objectives, methods, and assessment of teaching are important parts of a teaching philosophy. The objectives speak to what the student knows and is able to do as a result of the learning. For example, although the teacher values the content, the end result of learning the content provides the basis for education. The teacher in a PBL classroom should believe also, at the very least, in students obtaining critical thinking, higher-order, problem-solving, and lifelong learning skills, for these are the transferable skills of the modern workplace.

With clear objectives in place, the methods used to deliver instruction continue to shape student learning. At the heart of PBL instruction is ill-defined problems and well-defined outcomes, and in that way, the method is already established. Embedded within the problems are opportunities for students to develop the critical thinking, higher-order, and problem-solving skills related to the teaching objectives. Above and beyond that, however, the teaching methods change from direct instruction to self-directed learning.

The last issue related to the teaching philosophy causes a change in the assessment of teaching as a measure of student learning. Traditionally, teachers rely on a whole suite of formative and summative teacher-made assessments (e.g., worksheets, checklists, tests) as well as summative district and state standardized tests. In the PBL classroom, tests measuring student learning by multiple-choice answers run opposed to the many solutions garnered from ill-defined problems. Therefore, the teacher should develop a philosophy of assessment intended to measure problem-solving skills through design, transferable skills, and level of performance. The adjustments in philosophy are just beginning in preparing a teacher for PBL instruction.

A Change in Role

A major emphasis of PBL instruction is the problem-solving process. In order for students to begin to see themselves as problem solvers, the teacher acts as a facilitator to guide the learning process. In this position, the facilitator presents a problem, yet remains neutral about how to solve the problem, preferring to guide students through a series of questions to help them through the problem-solving process. Indeed, the goal of education should be to direct students in learning how to think, not what to think, so students become lifelong learners.

Traditionally, the role of the teacher is one who imparts knowledge to students utilizing a variety of instructional practices (e.g., lectures, guided practice, verification labs). The obvious problem with this model is knowledge may be limited to what the teacher knows. Consequently, the students are not able to develop breadth and depth of knowledge; the students will only know as much as the teacher knows. In order for students to be actively involved in the learning process and develop self-directed learning skills, the teacher has to relinquish some authority and allow students to do the work (i.e., read supplementary material, consult field experts, choose strategies) themselves in an effort to strengthen their problem solving skills. PBL instruction requires the teacher to be an expert in facilitation and this is achieved through the scaffold of questions asked by the teacher. The questions should support the metacognitive (i.e., how to think about thinking) strategies for problem solving as well as specified content and processes.

In addition, when teachers use PBL they value and encourage metacognitive thinking to help students understand the problem-solving process. Of equal importance is the teacher should be aware when it is necessary to allow students room to struggle through the learning process. The successful PBL facilitator is also an expert learner. That is to say, aware students are always looking for assistance, the facilitator continuously utilizes visible thinking strategies for the benefit of the students. As students observe the facilitator, they will begin to adopt those strategies and apply them when the learning goal is more self-directed.

The most immediate and necessary change a teacher in a traditional classroom will make with regards to establishing a PBL environment is the teaching philosophy. The philosophy lays the foundation and provides a framework to guide the objectives, methods, and assessment in the classroom. The teacher as a facilitator is vital to success in a PBL classroom. Using effective questioning strategies will help the teacher guide the problem-solving process, and more importantly, make the thinking process visible to help students learn how to think.

THE TRADITIONAL STUDENT AND PBL

Students transitioning from traditional instruction to PBL instruction will experience difficulties similar to that of the teacher. In fact, the dilemma for the student may be a little more overwhelming depending on the environment PBL is replacing. For years, traditional classroom practices have created an image for students of what it means to be a student (passive), how knowledge is transmitted (by the teacher), and even how to learn (memorization of rules and facts). Just as the teacher in a traditional classroom experiences a paradigm shift in philosophy and role, the student in a traditional classroom experiences the same paradigm shift, that is, a change in philosophy and role.

A Change in Philosophy

Rarely, if ever, are students asked to create a philosophy of learning. However, such a philosophy would provide students a framework to transition to the more student-directed learning necessary in a PBL classroom. Similar to the teacher's philosophy, the student in a PBL classroom has objectives for learning. The objectives for the student speak to why learning is important, not just in the classroom, but in general. Further, the objectives for learning should speak to students understanding the differences in types of learning (e.g., Bloom's Taxonomy).

As students begin to establish why learning is important, the next concern is the methods of learning. The PBL teacher's methods of instruction speak directly to the methods of learning. During lesson preparation, the teacher has to emphasize opportunities for multiple learning styles or preferences in all lessons. The student in transition from a traditional classroom is taught more often than not using an auditory method (e.g., lecture). While this method has a place in either classroom (traditional or PBL), the PBL environment calls for learning through various methods, and the student in a PBL classroom should be aware of each method, and how to make each method work best to meet the learning goals of the classroom.

The final part of the student's philosophy of learning should be related to how the student views assessment. In a traditional classroom, assessments are handled by the teacher and are usually in the form of teacher-made assessments used to gather evidence of the student's knowledge of rules or facts, often memorized. The student is not required to do more than regurgitate that which the teacher transmits. In the PBL classroom, the problems are ill-structured (i.e., there are many possible ways to arrive at the answer, if there is one). Therefore, the student has to begin to demonstrate learning far beyond repeated steps to a well-defined problem or exercise. Just as teachers assess learning in many ways, students demonstrate knowing and doing in many ways.

A Change in Role

For students who are accustomed to being passive recipients, the PBL environment will present several significant challenges. Not the least of these challenges will be the way learning is constructed in the classroom. Different from the traditional classroom where the teacher transmits knowledge and the students wait to receive information, in the PBL classroom, learning is intrinsically motivated and self-directed.

Intrinsic motivation, ideal for the PBL classroom, occurs when student feels they have a stake in taking part in the problem-solving activity. One key feature of the PBL problem is authenticity. That is, the problem should relate not only to students' everyday experiences but challenge them to consider how this learning activity will represent itself in future career plans or as an active member of society (e.g., voting decision to support bridge maintenance). Whereas students in a traditional classroom are rarely given an opportunity to make use of the problem beyond a test, the curriculum in a PBL classroom is ideal for motivating students to take the learning activity and make it a transferable skill to take into the 21st century workplace.

The intrinsic motivation students have in a PBL classroom will compel learning to be self-directed. Self-directed learning requires the student take responsibility for what needs to occur to meet the learning goal. Students transitioning from a traditional classroom might find this to be a difficult task as they are comfortable having the teacher guide them directly to what needs to be learned. The teacher, as a facilitator, will help to guide students' thinking during the problem-solving process and encourage critical-thinking skills. The design of the ill-structured problems in the PBL classroom will prevent passivity on the part of the students, especially if the problems are authentic and meet the needs of the students.

A student in the transition from a traditional classroom to a PBL classroom has to reevaluate various parts of the learning process. The well-defined outcomes for learning help students define what it means to learn, the methods of learning help students understand how to learn best, and the assessment helps students measure what was learned beyond traditional testing methods. Intrinsic motivation and self-directed learning play an important role in helping students actively pursue the learning goals, which, with well-designed, ill-structured problems and proper guidance from the facilitator, will make the transition smooth. These together help the student take the initial steps to learn successfully in a PBL classroom.

PROBLEM DESIGN

A key element of the PBL classroom is the problem. Indeed, the problem drives the learning process. For students to be actively engaged, the problem should have characteristics to draw out the natural problem-solving skills all students have by addressing some specific design features. Towards that end, Weiss (2003) suggests PBL problems be appropriate, ill defined, collaborative, authentic, and promote self-directed learning. These criteria are essential for an environment where learning is student centered.

Students are motivated by challenging problems. In order to be challenging, the problem should create a gap in knowledge between what the student knows and is able to do and what the student needs to know and be able to do. The teacher, in this case, should constantly assess student knowledge and skills throughout the PBL process. The students, on the other hand, will be encouraged to make up the difference in learning and not be passive recipients.

Well-defined problems have a place in the teaching and learning of all subjects, perhaps, when the goal is guiding students through steps to solve a problem in mathematics or engineering. However, the goal of problem design for a PBL classroom is making students self-directed and encouraged to find unknown information. Therefore, the problem should have characteristics of those found in the real world, that is, require more knowledge to understand the problem, have more than one way to solve the problem, and require the assistance of another person(s) for additional information and solution possibilities.

In a PBL classroom, discourse between the students is needed to promote higher-order thinking. Therefore, the designed problems should have an element of purposeful collaboration among the students. When students are presented with a problem having multiple solutions, collaboration with group members will be a valued component of the learning process; students will have to listen to other possible solutions and decide where new information fits into their prior experience and also defend their own solution.

Traditional teachers are often told problems should have real-world application. The significance of authentic problems in a PBL classroom cannot be overlooked. First and foremost, students are drawn to problems germane to their everyday life experiences. The teacher is wise not to present problems too theoretical in nature and out of the vision of the students. Likewise, the problem should address future aspirations of the students. Taking a career inventory ahead of time is helpful to identify what the students are interested in after high school.

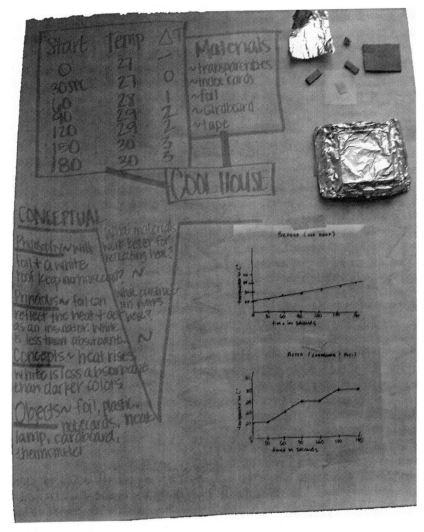

Learning occurs when students have an opportunity to connect prior knowledge and new knowledge. Self-directed students are motivated to learn by the appropriateness of the problem, the varied processes to arrive there, discourse between students, and relevance. These factors considered when designing a problem help students move to higher-order thinking skills.

THE PROBLEM-SOLVING PROCESS

In a PBL classroom, the ill-defined task and well-defined outcome drives the learning process, which is student-centered; however, designing good problems does not develop problem-solving skills. In traditional classroom instruction, problem-solving skills are encouraged by the use of problem-solving strategies (e.g., find a pattern, make a table, work backwards, guess and check). These strategies help students develop the initial skills needed to solve the well-defined problems found in students' textbooks; however ill-defined PBL problems have more involved problem-solving processes. Beginning with metacognitive strategies, the students move on to more rigorous problem-solving strategies designed to identify the source of unknown information.

Metacognition is a higher-order thinking skill and is often defined as thinking about thinking, and in the PBL classroom, this is an important issue for the teacher to support in students. All students come to school with some amount of informal strategies used to solve problems. One responsibility of the teacher is to guide the students into thinking, visibly and often, about the steps and processes used to solve problems. Self-directed learners have the ability to regulate prior knowledge and consider how new knowledge takes shape in order to solve the problem. Regulation is achieved by the teacher asking the students guiding questions before, during, and after to promote reflective thinking about the steps involved in problem solving. Metacognitive strategies are important if traditional students are to become intrinsically motivated and independent problem-solvers.

In order to be successful with PBL, students have to apply metacognitive strategies to the problem-solving process. According to Dochy, Segers, Van Den Bossche, and Struyven (2005) and Hmelo-Silver (2004), the problem-solving process is systematic and involves several steps. In addition to steps introduced by traditional problem-solving strategies (e.g., read the problem, identify givens, and identify unknowns), students need to identify prior knowledge, determine learning goals, have opportunities for independent research, and collaborate with group members to redefine the process. Most parts of the problem-solving process are designed to be collaborative. Students work together to diagnose the problem and more importantly, to determine what needs to be learned. Students' personal learning goals prepare the way for the independent research. During this time, the students have an opportunity to gain a deeper understanding of the problem and possible solutions based on the information found during research.

COOPERATIVE LEARNING

The ability to work with others is a necessary and desired skill for the 21st century workplace. Traditionally, students work independently and have few opportunities to learn from classmates. Cooperative learning is one instructional strategy used by many teachers to not only foster positive social interactions, but also to increase achievement and motivation among students.

Learning is an active and social process; that is to say, students learn not just by being in a group together, but by being provided with an opportunity to hear what others have to say, share what they think, and make some connections to prior knowledge. The process involves more than just putting students in a group; when properly configured, students have an opportunity to develop interpersonal, collaborative, and communication skills. For the traditional student, a self-directed learning environment will take adjusting to and require the assistance of the teacher to demonstrate self-directed learning practices.

It is imperative the teacher, as facilitator, set clear expectations about cooperative learning groups and model appropriate cooperative learning behaviors. It is likely students familiar with cooperative groups will misunderstand the notion of cooperative *learning* groups, i.e., how to participate in a group to ensure individual and group learning take place. With a focus on learning, the facilitator has to establish an environment where the elements of cooperative learning groups are not sacrificed. According to Stahl (1994), some of the areas to concentrate on to achieve successful cooperative learning groups include the promotion of: heterogeneous groups, positive interdependence, individual accountability, public recognition, and readily available resources.

Finally, the facilitator has to exhibit the behaviors expected from the students. As in real-life work environments, suitable behaviors include but are not limited to: active participation, ability to stay-on-task, listening to others, and encouragement. The transition from cooperative groups to cooperative learning groups is vital to the PBL environment. The teacher plays a key role in helping students overcome difficulties and move toward positive learning behaviors.

ASSESSMENT AND EVALUATION

Learning takes place over time and often from a variety of opportunities to engage independently and cooperatively with activities. Therefore, multiple observations and evaluators are useful to determine the level of learning in a PBL classroom. Generally there are two types of evaluations in a PBL classroom: formative and summative. Formative evaluation allows the evaluators (student, teacher, and group) to determine how the student is progressing at various stages of the activity. Individual input from the student gives the student ownership of the learning to occur and an opportunity to self-determine where more emphasis should be placed in the problem-solving process. Formative group evaluation allows the students to focus on all aspects of the activity (e.g., how well the group handles conflict, effective communication among members, too much time spent working independently) and refocus their own efforts to make the cooperative learning experience a success. Ideally, more formative assessments are helpful before the final summative assessment to gauge the overall learning experiences. The summative evaluation can be both qualitative and quantitative depending on the nature of the activity. However, an opportunity for students to demonstrate learning through an authentic assessment will help the teacher understand what areas of the activity and the learning outcome were most effective for the students. For an extended discussion of PBL-based assessments, see chapter 13 in this edition.

REFERENCES

Dochy, F., Segers, M., Van Den Bossche, P., & Struyven, K. (2005). Students' perceptions of a problem-based learning environment. *Learning Environments Research, 8*, 41–66.

Hmelo-Silver, C. E. (2004). Problem-based learning: What and how do students learn? *Educational Psychology Review, 16*, 235–266.

Stahl, R. J. (1994). *The essential elements of cooperative learning in the classroom.* ERIC Digest. Abstract from. ERIC Clearinghouse for Social Studies/Social Science Education, Bloomington IN: ED370 881. Retrieved July 18, 2008, from http://www.ericdigests.org/1995-1/elements.htm

Weiss, R. E., (2003). Designing problems to promote higher-order thinking. In D. S. Knowlton & D. C. Sharp (Eds.), *Problem-based learning in the information age.* (pp. 26–28). San Francisco: Jossey-Bass.

Woods, D. R. (1996). (Ed.). *Problem-based learning: Helping your students gain the most from PBL.* Canada: Author.

Melanie N. Woods
Department of Teaching, Learning and Culture,
Texas A&M University

James R. Morgan
Zachry Department of Civil Engineering,
Texas A&M University

SERKAN ÖZEL

6. W³ OF STEM PROJECT-BASED LEARNING

Who, When, and Where

INTRODUCTION

Science, technology, engineering, and mathematics (STEM) Project-Based Learning (PBL) has the power to enable students, teachers, and administrators to reach out beyond closed classroom doors. Through PBL students take control of their learning and have the opportunities to delve into content in a more direct and meaningful way. Thus, PBL promotes lifelong learning. This perspective of STEM PBL extends the scope of who should implement STEM PBL as well as when and where.

CHAPTER OUTCOMES

When you complete this chapter you should better understand:
- who should implement PBL
- when should PBL be implemented
- where should PBL be implemented
  When you complete this chapter you should be able to:
- decide for whom, when, and where PBL can be implemented

WHO SHOULD DO PBL?

Administrators

Administrators have substantive roles in both the promotion and the imple-mentation of PBL. Because PBL might be a novel instructional approach for many teachers, administrators can provide teachers with the training and support they need to successfully implement PBL in their classrooms (Mathews-Aydinli, 2007). Preparation can be in the form of professional development with experienced, successful teachers in PBL who can share their knowledge and experiences as well as help teachers initiate their first projects. As is necessary with every instructional approach, ongoing professional development will support teachers as they integrate PBL.

Another important role of administrators in the implementation of PBL is providing teachers with necessary resources (Mathews-Aydinli, 2007). The resources can range from traditional classroom equipment (e.g., meter stick, balances, beakers, stopwatches, etc.) to be used during a project to technological

R.M. Capraro and S.W. Slough (eds.), Project-Based Learning: An Integrated Science, Technology, Engineering, and Mathematics (STEM) Approach, 67–78.
© *2008 Sense Publishers. All rights reserved.*

equipment, such as computers, and field trips. For a successful implementation of PBL, administrators need to facilitate timely access to the resources for teachers. Educational technology has important uses in PBL; therefore, administrators need to support their teachers to become proficient users of technology and employ instructional technology specialists.

Administrators can also support the implementation of PBL in classrooms by modifying the expectations for teaching and learning from traditional transmission of knowledge to the facilitation of learning (Mathews-Aydinli, 2007). Administrators can conduct classroom observations to understand how PBL works, what problems teachers encounter, and what needs to be improved. Administrators can provide teachers with constructive feedback as a result of these observations. Administrators are also more likely to support teachers and PBL if they experience the rich learning environment in the classrooms themselves.

Teachers

It is possible to implement PBL in a variety of classrooms including all content areas (e.g., science, mathematics, social studies, language arts) and in every grade from pre-K through college. However, PBL might be a novel instructional approach for many teachers, sometimes substantively different from what they are used to doing. If teachers make the effort to incorporate PBL, they generally think the outcomes are well-worth the effort. Both starting and veteran teachers can implement PBL or at the very least, apply the foundational concepts and ideas of PBL to some extent in their classrooms.

In PBL, teachers act more as facilitators, mentors, or coaches rather than disseminators of knowledge. They guide the learning process by effective questioning and support students to reflect upon the questions rather than providing direct information. As students explore the content and adapt the skills covered within the project, teachers need to provide direction for research and inquiry. They should facilitate learning by monitoring students' contribution and participation, engage students in learning that is personal and cooperative, and encourage students to develop deeper and more meaningful understanding of concepts (Johari & Bradshaw, 2008).

Basically, PBL necessitates that teachers share control of the learning environment with students. This change in roles can be hard for teachers to adapt to or at times confusing when teachers have predominantly taught using traditional teaching approaches. Another factor that may inhibit their adoption of this new learning approach is that most teacher-education programs still rely on traditional lecture formats, so teachers have little or no experience using projects in their own learning. It is difficult for teachers to adopt learning methodologies they have never experienced before (Ward & Lee, 2002). In this sense, administrators can take a role in the PBL and provide teachers with the professional development they need. These professional development opportunities can prepare teachers for developing projects, implementing them in the classroom, generating self-learning environments, and evaluating the various outcomes of PBL through multiple assessment models including ones that are closely aligned with standards-based assessments. In addition to or as a substitute for professional development, teachers can take advantage of online resources that help teachers develop and implement PBL. These online sources include various projects that are fully developed and that were already implemented in classrooms.

Teachers in all subject areas can implement PBL in their classrooms. Most importantly, because PBL is an interdisciplinary instructional approach, teachers from different disciplines can work collaboratively on various projects. At its initial set-up, PBL may require more planning than traditional class preparation. Teachers from each discipline need to know their respective standards and align them with other disciplines and develop projects where they can address these standards efficiently. In addition to content standards, teachers can identify competencies from the Secretary's Commission on Achieving Necessary Skills (SCANS) report that students develop during the project activities. It is often a good idea to include students in the development of the project so that they feel an ownership of the project.

Project-Based Learning has been used in colleges, particularly medical and engineering schools, and today its use has been extended to all levels of pre-K-12 education. Teachers can start using PBL in as early as early childhood education programs. Research in pre-K-5 education shows the positive impact of PBL (Katz, 1994; Chard, 1992). Because in early childhood, students are curious about different aspects of life and have diverse interests, teachers can utilize PBL to engage and challenge them as well as help them develop collaborative learning skills. As students move up to middle and high school, instead of teaching formulas and rules that students memorize and apply, teachers can utilize PBL to help students develop conceptual understanding as well as applications of theoretical knowledge.

Although the transition from the traditional classroom environment and teaching to PBL can be time-consuming and challenging, teachers in general acknowledge that outcomes of PBL are worth the effort. The interdisciplinary approach of PBL helps develop collaborative-learning environments among teachers. Teachers can also develop partnerships with professionals in their communities who are related to and contribute to the projects. In this endeavor, administrators need to provide the support and encouragement that teachers need.

Students

Students from all ages, pre-K to college, have been effectively involved in PBL. After its initial appearance in colleges, students today engage in PBL even in early childhood education contexts. In fact, it is even better to have students experience PBL in early stages of their education to help them develop lifelong, essential skills such as self-directed learning, effective inquiry, and peer collaboration as early as possible. Engaging in PBL promotes a self-directed learning environment, so students need to take control of their learning and develop self-directed learning skills. Students from every grade level learn how to gather and apply knowledge to become lifelong learners. The collaborative working environment in PBL encourages students to work in diverse learning setting with students from different ethnic or socio-economic backgrounds. Different abilities or skills a project may require help students with diverse abilities contribute to the success of the project in various aspects. Therefore, although every student may not be proficient in every content or skill, students feel accomplished with their contributions.

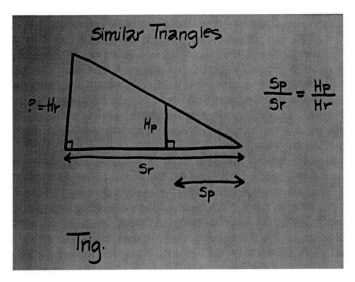

Students have essential tasks in both the development and execution of PBL. Students are recommended to be involved in PBL from the development of the projects to the assessments. Most students have been instructed using the traditional lecture approach before, and they have grown accustomed to the role of the teacher as disseminator of knowledge. It can be stressful and disorienting for students to be required to self-direct their learning or not to be given the answers. However, PBL should not replace traditional instruction completely. There might be times, particularly if students and the teacher are new to PBL, where lecture-style instruction is needed. However, for successful PBL, teachers need to improve their leadership skills to guide students to control their learning, and be confident about asking questions and looking for answers.

Community Partners

Science, Technology, Engineering, and Mathematics professionals from the community are important stakeholders who can contribute to the projects. During project development, application, and assessment, teachers can collaborate with STEM professionals to give projects authenticity. These professionals can be within the school's local community, or today, through the use of the web, even professionals from different parts of the world can participate in PBL. These experts can be of substantive help for teachers in the development of the projects with the insights and up-to-date information they provide. In general, students value STEM professionals' contributions to projects and the outside-school knowledge they bring to the learning environment. When STEM professionals are involved in the evaluation of projects, students feel more motivated to make an impression on them.

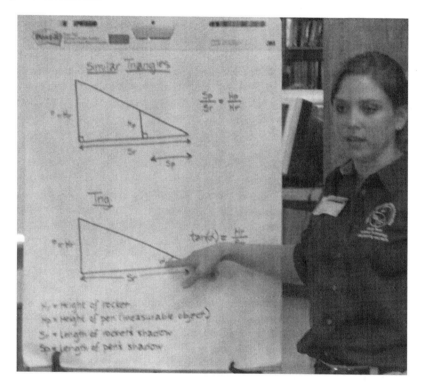

WHEN SHOULD PBL BE IMPLEMENTED?

Two out of three students are bored in school at least everyday according to Indiana University's High School Survey of Student Engagement (HSSSE) survey. Nearly 300,000 students from 110 high schools across 26 different states in the U.S. participated in HSSSE. Two main reasons for students' boredom in school are lack of interesting material and lack of relevant material (Yazzie-Mintz, 2007). When students are bored, they become less engaged in the material taught. Moreover, bored and unengaged students are less likely to learn (Blumenfeld et al., 1991). On the other hand, students are more likely to learn better when they are authentically engaged in meaningful material (Hancock & Betts, 2002).

Many teachers, regardless of their disciplines, ask themselves how they can make their students think (Duch, 2008). The underlying premise of PBL is that "students will develop personal investment in the material if they engage in real, meaningful tasks and problems that emulate what experts do in real-world situations" (Krajcik & Blumenfeld, 2006, p. 649). Thus, PBL challenges students to learn to learn, working cooperatively in groups to seek answers to real-world problems. These problems are used to engage students' curiosity and initiate learning the subject matter. PBL prepares students to think critically and analytically and to find and use appropriate learning resources (Duch).

Problem solving, particularly complicated, everyday problem-solving, has been a major concern in education. One of the essential goals for schools is to educate students who are able to experience the richness and excitement of knowledge about the natural world, who are aware of difficult real-world problems, and who use appropriate processes and principles in making personal decisions (National Research Council, 1996). Students have to learn ill-structured, well-structured, and unstructured problem-solving skills by experiencing various real-life situations in order to make personal decisions.

Ill-Defined Tasks

Ill-defined tasks are the organizing center for PBL. They are complex and messy by nature and have "no simple, fixed, formulaic, right, solution" (Illinois Mathematics and Science Academy, 2004). According to Jonassen (1997), the best solution to an ill-defined problem is "the one that is most viable, that is, most defensible, the one for which the learner can provide the most cogent argument" (p. 81). With ill-defined problems, students start to investigate multidisciplinary elements beyond the boundaries of school settings and learn inquiry skills (Chin & Chia, 2006). A good ill-defined task has no clear and readily available solution. Instead, ill-defined tasks may have many possible solutions since they are complex and ill-defined. Ill-defined tasks—when paired with well-defined outcomes—introduce concepts to students by challenging them to find solutions to authentic, real-world problems. Dealing with real-world problems makes the knowledge relevant and increases the transfer of skills and knowledge from the classroom to the outside world (Bransford, Brown, & Cocking, 2000).

The best way to approach an ill-defined problem is by gathering information about the problem and the setting where the problem occurred. The best solution to an ill-defined problem depends on the priorities underlying the situation. For instance, what is best today may not be best tomorrow. Ill-defined problems require the development of higher-order thinking skills because these problems do not have unique solutions. A critical skill students develop through this distinct learning process is to identify the problem and set parameters on the development of a solution. It is important to note that although problem-solving is an important skill for completing PBL tasks, these tasks are by their nature more complicated, than traditional problem-solving heuristics designed for solving exercises (e.g., do all of the odd numbered problems at the end of the chapter) are not adequate for PBL. However, iStudy (2006) suggests nine steps for solving an ill-defined problem that are applicable to solving many PBL tasks:

- Determine the real problem
- State the real problem
- Identify alternative perspectives
- Determine constraints
- Gather information
- Generate possible solutions
- Choose the best solution
- Plan the steps for implementing the solution
- Adapt the solution

In order to understand the nine steps of the iStudy (2006) approach to solving ill-defined problems, a hypothetical scenario follows. Imagine being a member of a group given the ill-defined task to estimate the height of a very tall building. You do not have the tools to directly measure the height of the building, but you do have a variety of measurement tools (e.g., meter stick, stopwatch, protractor, compass, clinometer, which measures elevation angles about the horizon). The numbered steps show an example of the implementation of the iStudy (2006) approach to solving this ill-defined problem.

- We need to estimate the height of a building.
- How can we estimate the height of an object, if we cannot directly measure it?
- Similar triangles and trigonometry using shadows or time for an object to fall from the top.
- We are constrained because we do not have a tape measure that is long enough or string or other object to directly measure the height.
- We can use objects that we can directly measure to estimate the height of an object.
- We can find an object that we can measure, measure the height of the object, and measure the length of the shadow of the object.
- We can measure the angle of the triangle of the building and its shadow and measure the shadow of the building.
- We can measure the time it takes for an object to fall to the earth from a known height.
- We might end up with multiple solutions to our problem.
  We can form similar triangles with the triangle of the small object and its shadow and the building and its shadow.
- We can form a triangle with the height of the building and the length of the shadow of the building.
- We can use ratios to compare the time for an object to drop from a know height and the time it takes for the same object to drop from the building.
- Depending on tools available, the amount of sun, access to the roof, and preference of the group we can choose any strategy.
- For each strategy we considered, we need to plan the steps for implementation.
- Mark the end of the shadows for the measurable object and for the building. Measure the height of the measurable object. Measure the length of the shadow of that object. Measure the length of the shadow of the building. Use similar triangles to estimate the height of the building.

- Use geometry to measure the angle of the triangle formed by the height of the building and the length of the shadow of the building. Measure the length of the shadow. Estimate the height of the building using trigonometry.
- We can drop an object from a known height and measure how long it takes to fall, then drop the same object from the building and use ratios to estimate the height from the time it takes for the object to hit the ground.
- You can adapt these techniques to estimate the height of a variety of objects that you cannot measure directly.

Group Discussions

The PBL approach fosters collaborative learning approach. Group work is a strategy that promotes participation, interaction, and collaborative work among students. Interaction in groups helps students to develop valuable professional team-working and effective communication skills, which are required qualifications in every professional environment. After graduation, students in their work environments need to work collaboratively with their co-workers and supervisors in order to be productive (Savery, 2006). The format of PBL provides opportunities for students to improve these skills.

Teachers have a role of promoting active student participation in group work by asking open-ended questions that encourage critical thinking and collaboration. These questions to any and all members will ensure teachers that group members shared the information related to the problem (Savery, 2006). Even though students work collaboratively with each other in the group, they have individual responsibilities which increase individuals' motivation (Savery & Duffy, 1995). Collaborative group environments provide students the opportunity to freely express their ideas and critique each other's views (West, 1992). When students are working in a group, they take responsibility not only for their own learning but also for their group mates' learning.

WHERE SHOULD PBL BE IMPLEMENTED?

The roots of PBL lie as far back as the early 1900s in Dewey's Constructivist Learning Theory, which promotes experiential, hands-on, and student-centered learning (Markham, Mergendoller, Larmer, & Ravitz, 2003). Constructivism is a highly-supported learning theory that students construct new knowledge through accommodation and assimilation from their experiences. In constructivist learning, students are actively engaged in doing rather than just receiving information.

PBL has been implemented in K-12 schools as well as universities and professional schools. Promising reports have been revealed about its effective use in K-12 schools; it has yet to be widely adopted by K-12 teachers (Ertmer & Simons, 2006). Not only schools but also government, commerce, and industry seek the high-level competencies and transferable skills that are facilitated by PBL. Thus PBL is implemented where there is need for active learning.

PBL in Elementary School

Educators want students to take responsibility for any kind of problem they may face in their life and become lifelong learners. In order to achieve this goal, students have to gain lifelong learning skills at an early age. Edutopia (http://www.edutopia.org) has several examples of implementation of PBL in K-5 classrooms. An early education center principal, discusses the value of PBL in one of the videos where students are working on a project about a virtual trip to Brazil (Ellis, 2007). The principal says:

> These kids have a very authentic, real purpose for learning...When you want to find something out, what do you do? You go to the computer, you get on the Internet, you get a book. You don't go to an adult and just have them feed you all the information. You have to learn to be a problem solver; you have to learn to be resourceful. So we teach them to be lifelong learners, and you have to keep them excited about the process of learning. (video)

These kinds of student-driven projects help kindergarten students become lifelong learners (Ellis, 2007). Edutopia has several examples and videos about PBL in elementary school. Inquiry Schools (www.inquiryschools.net) also shares quality educational practices in PBL and provides videos about practices.

PBL in Middle School

Middle-school projects can be similar to elementary ones but at a more sophisticated level. The National Science Resource Center (1998) argues that middle graders learn more when they are actively involved in finding solutions rather than selecting from solutions provided to them. Making contributions to real-life problems is highly motivating and inspiring for students. Sharon Campbell, art teacher at Redwood Middle School in Napa, California, provides her students opportunities to learn by touching, feeling, manipulating, and analyzing. For example, in her energy conservation project, she had her students pedal a bicycle to generate electricity for their classroom (see video at http://www.edutopia.org/redwood-energy-conservation-video). In this example, students are able to investigate the transfer of energy from pedaling to electricity as an application of the conservation of energy. Middle graders are interested in being actively involved in real-life problems (Jennings, 1995). Moreover, they feel that they can change the world and find solutions to real-world issues more than students of other age groups (Daniels, 2005). At this age, middle grade students decide about their future plans, education, and careers. Even though PBL requires more time than regular instruction and is not easy to implement, the time spent on projects is worthwhile in helping students make decisions about their lives (Bernt, Turner, & Bernt, 2005).

PBL in High School

In kindergarten students who experience PBL begin the path to becoming self-learners. Throughout elementary and middle school, as they experience increasingly more sophisticated PBLs build the knowledge and skills they will need for high-school success. Continuation of PBL in high school provides opportunities to explore their possible college majors. Even though similar strategies for middle graders will work with high school students, the format of PBL may vary in high school. Most high school students do not want direct supervision by their teachers and prefer to work independently (Lambros, 2004). In PBL, teachers are facilitators and guides, and they will be ready to help when students need guidance from them. Thus, high school students' preference for working individually supports their active engagement in the solution of problems enabling them to deeply learn the concepts.

PBL in Higher Education

Although large college lecture halls may not be optimal for PBL, using different strategies, PBL still can be applied to college classes and can be effective to motivate college students (Ram, 1999). In large classroom settings, multiple PBL groups can be formed, and peer facilitators can be assigned to each group to monitor group processes. With this strategy, the cooperative and collaborative structure of PBL is conserved within the college classroom also (Allen, 2004). Further, recitation, laboratory, and design studios offer the perfect opportunity to implement more creative PBL. Finally, students who are experienced problem-solvers will be successful in a variety of self-directed, high-stakes assignments prevalent in the college environment.

CONCLUSION

Who should do PBL? Everyone should do PBL. When should PBL be used? PBL should be implemented when students need to develop personal investment in learning, when solutions to real-world problems are educationally sound, and when challenging students to do more than repeat and memorize are valued. PBL should be implemented when educators want students to think critically and analytically and find and use appropriate learning resources. PBL should be used often. Where should PBL be used? PBL should be used in all classrooms and learning environments when the teachers and students are ready and where in-depth, authentic learning is valued.

REFERENCES

Allen, D. (2004). *Problem-based learning in undergraduate science: 21st century pedagogies.* Retrieved February 3, 2008, from http://www.pkal.org/documents/Vol4ProblemBasedLearning.cfm

Bernt, P. W., Turner, S. V., & Bernt, J. P. (2005). Middle school students are co-researchers of their media environment: An integrated project. *Middle School Journal, 37*(1), 38–44.

Blumenfeld, P., Soloway, E., Marx, R., Krajcik, J., Guzdial, M., & Palincsar, A. (1991) Motivating project-based learning: Sustaining the doing, supporting the learning. *Educational Psychologist, 26,* 369–398.

Bransford, J. D., Brown, A. L., & Cocking, R. R. (2000). *How people learn: Brain, mind, experience, and school.* Washington, DC: National Academy Press.

Chard, S. C. (1992). *The project approach: A practical guide for teachers.* Edmonton, Alberta: University of Alberta Printing Services.

Chin, C., & Chia, L. (2006). Problem-based learning: Using ill-structured problems in biology project work. *Science Education, 90*(1), 44–67.

Daniels, E. (2005). On the minds of middle schoolers. *Educational Leadership, 62*(7), 52–54.

Duch, B. (2008). *Problem-based learning.* Retrieved June 5, 2008, from http://www.udel.edu/pbl/

Ellis, K. (2007). *Voyages of discovery: Five-year olds explore through PBL.* Retrieved February 3, 2008, from http://www.edutopia.org/beginning-journey

Ertmer, P. A., & Simons, K. D. (2006). Jumping the PBL implementation hurdle: Supporting the efforts of K-12 teachers. *The Interdisciplinary Journal of Problem-based Learning, 1*(1), 40–54.

Hancock, V., & Betts, F. (2002). Back to the future: Preparing learners for academic success in 2004. *Learning and Leading with Technology, 29*(7), 10–14.

Illinois Mathematics and Science Academy. (2004). *What is PBL?* Retrieved June 6, 2008, from http://www.imsa.edu/programs/pbln/tutorials/intro/intro6.php

iStudy for Success! (2006). *iStudy for success.* Retrieved June 6, 2008, from http://istudy.psu.edu/

Jennings, J. F. (1995). School reform based on what is taught and learned. *Phi Delta Kappan, 76,* 765–770.

Johari, A., & Bradshaw, A. C. (2008). Project-based learning in an internship program: A qualitative study of related roles and their motivational attributes. *Educational Technology Research and Development, 56,* 239–359.

Jonassen, D. H. (1997). Instructional design models for well-structured and ill-structured problem-solving learning outcomes. *Educational Technology Research and Development, 48*(4), 63–85.

Katz, L. G. (1994). *The project approach.* (Rep.ort No. EDO-PS-94-6). (ERIC Document Reproduction Service No. ED368509)

Krajcik, J. S., & Blumenfeld, P. (2006). Project-based learning. In R. K. Sawyer (Ed.), *The Cambridge handbook of the learning sciences* (pp. 317–334). New York: Cambridge.

Lambros, A. (2004). *Problem-based learning in middle and high school classrooms: A teacher's guide to implementation.* Thousand Oaks, CA: Corwin Press.

Markham, T., Mergendoller, J., Larmer, J., and& Ravitz, J. (2003). *Project based learning handbook.* Hong Kong: Buck Institute for Education.

Mathews-Aydinli, J. (2007, April). Problem-based learning and adult English language learners. Center for Adult English Language Acquisition *(CAELA) Brief.* Retrieved June 5, 2008, from http://www.cal.org/caela/esl_resources/briefs/Problem-based.pdf

National Research Council. (1996). *National science education standards.* Washington, DC: Author.

National Science Resource Center. (1998). *Resources for teaching middle school science.* Washington, DC: National Academy. Retrieved June 20, 2008, from http://books.nap.edu/books/0309057817/html/

Ram, P. (1999). Problem-based learning in undergraduate education: A sophomore chemistry laboratory. *Journal of Chemical Education, 76,* 1122–1126.

Savery, J. R. (2006, Spring). Overview of problem based learning: Definitions and distinctions. *The Interdisciplinary Journal of Problem-based Learning, 1*(1), 9–20.

Savery, J. R., & Duffy, T. M. (1995). Problem-based learning: An instructional model and its constructivist framework. In B. Wilson (Ed.), *Constructivist learning environments: Case studies in instructional design* (pp. 135–148). Englewood Cliffs, NJ: Educational Technology Publications.

Ward, J. D., & Lee, C. L. (2002). A review of problem-based learning. *Journal of Family and Consumer Sciences Education, 20*(1), 16–26.

West, S. A. (1992). Problem based learning: A viable addition for secondary school science. *Problem Based Learning, 73*(265), 47–55.
Yazzie-Mintz, E. (2007). *The HSSSE 2006 report: Voices of students on engagement.* Retrieved April 20, 2008, from http://ceep.indiana.edu/hssse/pdf/HSSSE_2006_Report.pdf

Serkan Özel
Department of Education Psychology, Educational Technology,
Texas A&M University

Z. EBRAR YETKINER AND ROBERT M. CAPRARO

7. FACTORS INFLUENCING THE IMPLEMENTATION OF STEM PROJECT-BASED LEARNING

INTRODUCTION

In the development as well as the implementation of Science, Technology, Engineering and Mathematics (STEM) Project-Based Learning (PBL), national, state, and local standards need to be addressed. Teachers need to establish what knowledge students are expected to learn, and tie that into state/national standards, and devise a project that will meet these goals. In addition to curriculum-based national, state, and local standards, PBL can accommodate standards for the workplace, namely the Secretary's Commission on Achieving Necessary Skills (SCANS). Through involvement in PBL, students can develop essential workplace skills such as working collaboratively within groups, effective peer communication, problem solving skills, and self-directed learning. The ill-defined task that the project will address and the end product should incorporate these standards and skills. The effectiveness of PBL should be evaluated to determine if benchmark knowledge and skills have been gained using formative and summative assessments throughout the learning process. The authentic assessment model used in PBL allows the evaluation of these various student expectations.

CHAPTER OUTCOMES

When you complete this chapter you should better understand:
– the role of national, state, and local standards in PBL design
– the role of tasks and artifacts in PBL design
  the role of student expectations in PBL
  When you complete this chapter you should be able to:
– develop PBL that accommodates national, state, and local standards
– develop questions and artifacts that address national, state, and local standards and essential real-life skills
– develop PBL that accommodates multifaceted student outcomes

THE ROLE OF NATIONAL, STATE, AND LOCAL STANDARDS

Standards are a major force in today's educational environment. In response to the Department of Education's *No Child Left Behind* Act, whereby all states and schools must have clear and challenging standards of achievement and

R.M. Capraro and S. W. Slough (eds.), Project-Based Learning: An Integrated Science, Technology, Engineering, and Mathematics (STEM) Approach, 79–89.

accountability for all children and effective strategies for teaching those standards, national education organizations and state departments of education have implemented standards in virtually every subject area. Education World TM's website (http://www.education-world.com/standards/index.shtml) offers quick access to national and state standards in major subject areas. States have adopted standards that follow the National Council of Teachers of Mathematics' (2000) standards, national science standards, as well as those standards for reading and social studies.

In standards-based education, "clearly defined academic content standards provide the basis for content in instruction and assessment" (U.S. Department of Defense Domestic Dependent Elementary and Secondary Schools, n.d., ¶ 1). Standards guide instruction to focus on student learning by providing clear and well-defined learning goals for all students. Therefore, standards act as references for teachers to know what they are expected to teach and as a basis for what will be assessed on state accountability instruments. Standards also guide students in their learning as they know their learning objectives. In an age of accountability, standards are used as benchmarks against which student achievements are measured in state accountability systems. Because standards are the basis for content and are used as benchmarks to assess student learning, they should be integrated into every aspect of PBL from the development of projects to assessments.

When developing a project, one guiding principle should be to start with the end in mind. Teachers need to know what knowledge and skills students are expected to learn and tie these expectations to national, state, and local standards, devise a project that will meet these goals, and then determine the most useful and thoughtful assessments to determine the extent to which students met the expectations. It is important to make PBL central to everyday instruction and not attempt to add PBL on top of everything else that is currently being done. Instead of PBL being an add-on to an already packed curriculum, PBL is a vehicle for conveying the curriculum the teacher already teaches, and it incorporates well-defined outcomes that are clearly tied to national, state, and local standards. When teachers know the standards, they have control over the curriculum, which facilitates management of the learning event.

The design of the project, the specific classroom activities, the direct instruction components, and the assessment should be aligned with curriculum standards. That is, if the project is self-contained within one teacher's class and does not incorporate any other content, then the standards are those specific to that one set of curriculum standards. However, one tenet of PBL is that it incorporates and necessitates knowledge from other content areas. For instance, it would be uncommon to write a project report without building on the content learned in English class. It is the intersection of the content areas in which PBL is situated. Therefore, a great deal of collaboration among the various content-area teachers is desirable in the design of the projects, classroom activities, instruction, and assessments to ensure alignment with various content standards.

The link between standards across the contributing content areas is essential. It is this link between the standards from across the curriculum that maximizes learning and provides an applied context as a purpose for learning. When all aspects of the activity are aligned with specific curriculum standards from different disciplines, students benefit from knowledge learned in distinct curriculum content, and so the learning is maximized. Sometimes it may even be possible to modify PBL to incorporate a specific learning expectation from a content area that is critical. For instance, students break potato chips in the Food Texture PBL (Appendix) to assess texture and freshness. This activity can be easily modified to incorporate important writing standards. For example, a marketing plan can be developed that is specific to the characteristics for each tested chip. This writing link can serve two purposes: (1) students have to synthesize the information gathered during experimentation, and (2) students need to consider how to best convey the information to a consumer. In essence, the link between the standards across different subjects is as important as links within any subject area.

Selecting a Project

Choosing the project is important especially when it will likely impact teachers in other content areas. Integrating the national, state, and local standards into a project may require more planning time and effort on the part of teachers, and at times teachers might feel like PBL is time consuming. However, once the project plan is developed and implemented carefully, PBL covers every aspect of standards – the procedural as well as the conceptual knowledge as students experience the application of the content underlying the standards. The nature of PBL creates high concentrations of standards within a short period of time. The power of PBL is that it addresses standards covered previously as well as the ones currently being learned and creates an applied environment where students can see the importance of their learning across disciplines. In general, teachers appreciate the outcomes of PBL and think the results are well-worth the effort.

In addition to curriculum-based national, state, and local standards, PBL can accommodate standards for the workplace, namely SCANS (2000). Through involvement in PBL, students can develop essential workplace skills such as working collaboratively within groups, effective peer communication, problem solving, and self-directed learning. To reinforce the development of SCANS skills, teachers can make these skills part of the assessments rubrics. As students are involved in rubric development, they become aware of the expectations from the SCANS report as part of their learning progress.

Standards expressed as learning goals can help students improve their metacognitive skills. When students are involved in project development, in addition to developing an ownership of the project, they witness the integration of the standards into the project and thereby think about expected learning objectives. Therefore, teachers should involve students in project development and make the standards and learning objectives clear in different aspects of PBL so that students can reflect upon them and become cognizant of their learning progress.

THE ROLE OF QUESTIONS

Every STEM PBL starts with an ill-defined task that the project will address. Greenwald (2001, ¶ 5) described an ill-defined problem as being "unclear, and [it] raises questions about what is known, needs to be known, and how to find out. This opens the way for finding many problem possibilities, the nature of which are influenced by one's vantage point and experience." Therefore, ill-defined problems are similar to the problems students encounter in their everyday lives. In everyday problem-solving situations, they are faced with developing solution strategies for novel problems. Individuals come up with strategies based on their experiences or knowledge. The nature of learning through PBL has students confront complex problems before instruction rather than after, as compared to traditional instruction. Using PBL embraces learning and problem solving in real life, where an ill-defined problem initiates the learning (Gallagher, Stepien, Sher, & Workman, 1995).

The ill-defined task is at the heart of the PBL in that it "serves to organize and drive activities; and these activities result in a series of artifacts, or products, that culminate in a final product that addresses the driving question" (Blumenfeld, Soloway, Marx, Krajcik, Guzdial, & Palinscar, 1991, p. 371). Therefore, the construction of the ill-defined task is very important and requires careful consideration of standards, learning objectives, resources, time, and student characteristics. Tasks underlying the projects should address the national and state standards and direct students to learn a set of essential concepts and ideas of a discipline or two or more disciplines. Interdisciplinary projects are one of the basic tenets of PBL; therefore, teachers from different areas can co-construct questions that support connections among different subjects and that will incorporate learning objectives from various disciplines. Having standards and learning the objectives that will be addressed by solutions to ill-defined tasks set up at the onset will help teachers to control student learning as students work on their projects.

The ill-defined tasks need to be complex and require students to critically analyze the situation and devise a plan as they work on developing a solution. Thus these questions set a context for students to improve their critical thinking and analysis skills, communicate as they share ideas about the problem situation, endorse their problem-solving and research skills, and give opportunity to use their creativity. Ill-defined problems are open-ended and thus can be solved in multiple ways, which is similar to the problems encountered in real life and different than well-defined problems that require standard procedures. There is not one right answer to an ill-defined task but rather reasonable answers at varying levels. This property of ill-defined tasks support critical-thinking skills, which Beyer (1995, p. 8) defines as meaning "making reasoned judgments." Students need to critically analyze the problem situation to develop their best answer with empirically-based justifications for the steps they take.

Because there are multiple plausible answers for an ill-defined task, teachers do not evaluate if the solution strategies are distinctively right or wrong but develop rubrics to evaluate the degree of the feasibility of the answers. The lack of a distinction between right and wrong answers might be ambiguous for students who are used to multiple-choice assessments with one right answer. Teachers can overcome this difficulty by involving students in rubric development to help them understand how their learning and projects will be evaluated. Because students are expected to develop novel solutions, ill-defined problems support their creativity in problem-solving situations, which is a desirable skill in the workplace.

Although ill-defined tasks need to be complex and challenging to reinforce higher-order thinking skills, they need to be doable given students' characteristics, time, resources, and constraints. Therefore, as teachers construct the ill-defined tasks, they need to give careful consideration to these components. The questions should require new knowledge and skills but an appropriate zone of development for students needs to be chosen. Also, teachers should provide students with necessary information to guide the students in their inquiry so that they will not feel lost in the problem situation. For example, teachers can provide students with resources, which can be websites or communication with professionals outside-of-school. The professionals can talk with students about how they deal with similar problems in their workplace. When PBL is a completely new approach for the students, teachers might prefer to structure the ill-defined tasks to ease the transition for students from traditional, well-defined questions to open-ended and complex problem-solving situations.

In addition to the ill-defined tasks that inspire the projects, teacher questioning in the classroom during the project should also be effective. Teachers need to guide the learning process by asking questions and reflecting upon them rather than always providing direct information. The questions need to promote higher-order thinking skills and should not be constructed in a way to lead to the correct answer. Thus in PBL, teachers act as facilitators of learning and co-constructors of knowledge. This does not mean, though, that student-directed learning will completely replace direct instruction; there will be times in PBL when teachers need to carefully incorporate didactic instruction (Yetkiner, Anderogul, & Capraro, 2007).

Teachers can adapt a lot of real-life problems and use them as ill-defined questions in their classrooms with appropriate accommodations. There are also numerous websites on PBL where teachers from different disciplines share their ideas and ill-defined questions that they implement in their classrooms. Online resources about how to develop an effective ill-defined question are also available. Once teachers are exposed to some examples of these open-ended, complex questions and use them with their students, they can start developing their own questions that will lead to effective projects.

THE ROLE OF ARTIFACTS

The main characteristic of PBL that differentiates it from other inquiry-based learning approaches is PBL is centered around a clearly defined artifact (e.g., build a bridge with the following constraints). The artifacts are chosen from the real-world, and the project process, from the development to the presentation of the artifacts, needs to be authentic. The fact that students reflect in the classroom what professionals do in the workplace is one of the attractive aspects of PBL for students. It is highly recommended that professionals in the particular field of the artifact are involved in the PBL starting from the development of the project until the evaluation of the artifacts. Professionals can help teachers in the choice of an artifact in that they are more up-to-date in regards to the different types of artifacts and different methods or technologies used in the production or development of artifacts. Thus teachers and professionals can work collaboratively to adjust the artifact to students' special needs and the classroom environment in a way that reflects real life but also is doable within the constraints of students' knowledge, skills, resources, time, and other classroom constraints. From the students' perspective, working with professionals makes the process more authentic and helps them recognize the relevancy of their work to the everyday workplace and appreciate the value of the project. Students also find the professionals' evaluation of their projects motivating because students want to feel accomplished by making a difference or contribution to the profession and the outside-of-school world and by making an impact on the professionals.

Because PBL is centered around an artifact, the development of the artifacts needs to incorporate content-based national, state, and local standards and relevant, everyday, and workplace skills such as the SCANS (2000). Because PBL promotes interdisciplinary projects, teachers from various disciplines can work collaboratively to decide on an artifact that addresses various content standards. At the onset of PBL, teachers need to identify relevant standards and incorporate them in their evaluation process, both formative and summative, so that they can track student learning as students work on their projects. An artifact that is interesting for students, but one that does not address learning objectives would do little for student improvement and should be adamantly avoided in PBL. As teachers develop the idea of an artifact, preferably with the relevant professionals in the area of this end product, they should involve students so that students can understand what they are expected to learn and what skills they need to improve.

Another reason for involving students in the choice of the artifact is artifacts need to be both relevant to students and should strike their interest. Teachers would not want to make the students to work on a project that has no interest to them. The more students are excited about their artifact, the more likely it is that they will work towards developing a competent end product and be involved in the problem-solving situations they encounter during the project. Therefore, as teachers decide on an artifact, they should get the students' ideas and make a shared decision.

The artifacts can differ substantively regarding the knowledge and skills as well as the time and resources they require. For example, at the kindergarten level, PBL can incorporate role-playing activities where the end product for each student could be a different professional role they are interested in. On the other hand, a high school using PBL might require a building project where students are expected to design and construct a prototype of a building, taking into consideration virtually every aspect that architects in real-life deals do, such as the materials, cost, or sustainable design. Teachers need to carefully consider student characteristics such as their knowledge and skills when they decide on an artifact. Time and resources are two main constraints to classroom PBL implementation. Thus artifacts must be doable, given time limits and available resources. After specifying the artifact that fits the curriculum schedule, teachers can help students to manage their time by determining a timeline for the project (The George Lucas Educational Foundation, n.d.). In the timeline, the time periods that will be allotted for different phases of PBL can be identified. Although the timeline can be adjusted depending on the progress of the projects, it provides teachers and students with a schedule to follow. Regarding resources, administrators need to help teachers in terms of identifying and accessing currently available resources at school or provide them with necessary resources that the school does not possess. Teachers can also work in collaboration with their community to have access to supplies that are not readily available at their schools.

Although the development of an artifact and incorporating the learning objectives into the PBL environment require effort and time, the learning outcomes are prolific. Artifacts in PBL allow students to apply their knowledge, thereby making the knowledge long-lasting. Also, as the following proverb instructs, Tell me, and I will forget. Show me, and I may remember. Involve me, and I will understand. Thus PBL reinforces understanding more than memorizing and relying on formulas and procedures.

THE ROLE OF OUTCOMES

Well-defined student outcomes in PBL are multifaceted. In a PBL environment, student expectations include content-based learning objectives and skills that are essential in the workplace and in everyday life, such as those identified in SCAN reports. The outcomes that are expected in PBL should be established at the onset with the involvement of students. When students are involved in the process of setting benchmarks for learning objectives and expected skills, they think about their learning and reflect upon it as they go through the PBL, thereby improving their metacognitive skills (Barron et al., 1998).

Centered around a culminating project, the ultimate goal of PBL is to achieve effective and sustained content learning and to improve understanding through applying knowledge. Because one of PBL's tenets is the application of learned content, teachers can include working definitions of the learning objectives that specify what the applied outcomes of the learning are, which can be reflected in the development of the artifact. Another important aspect of student learning in PBL is, because of the interdisciplinary nature of PBL, students are expected to relate their knowledge in different subject areas. Teachers from various disciplines addressed within the project can specify interdisciplinary outcomes and make sure that every other content-area teacher understands these expectations. The evaluation of these interdisciplinary objectives may require teachers to have some level of knowledge in all the disciplines relevant to the project.

In addition to curriculum-based learning goals, PBL emphasizes the development of skills that are needed in professional life (Solomon, 2003). As students work in groups towards a shared goal, they improve their collaborative working skills. The necessity of conveying their perspectives and sometimes supporting their views against others' in the group helps students to strengthen their communication and negotiation skills. Also, as students present their projects to the class throughout the PBL activity at various intervals, they develop fundamental presentation skills.

One important outcome of PBL is due to its student-directed learning approach, it helps students to become effective lifelong learners, which is an essential skill in the age of ever-growing knowledge (Hmelo-Silver, 2004). As students work on the projects, they need to gather, analyze, and interpret data, benefiting their inquiry and research skills. PBL environments also support students' problem-solving abilities as students are involved in ill-defined problem situations (Tretten & Zachariou, 1995).

Another aspect of PBL outcomes is the emotional and motivational development of students (Yetkiner et al., 2007). The self-directed and collaborative learning approach of PBL motivates students to learn and improve their confidence as they seek answers to their questions. PBL also provides students a learning environment different than traditional classroom instruction in that it is authentic, relevant to the outside world, and engaging. This learning environment that simulates the real world has been found to motivate students and improve their attitudes towards learning (Bartscher, Gould, & Nutter, 1995).

The various essential student outcomes of PBL require multiple assessment models (Yetkiner et al., 2007). The effectiveness of PBL should be evaluated to determine if the benchmark knowledge and skills have been gained using formative and summative assessments throughout the learning process. The authentic assessment model used in PBL allows the evaluation of these various student expectations. One distinctive characteristic of authentic assessment is that it can evaluate not only content knowledge and understanding but also "the development of real world skills" (San Mateo County Office of Education, n.d.). Teachers can adapt different, authentic assessment strategies such as group presentations, self-reflections, and performance assessment to evaluate diverse student outcomes. Through the utilization of self- and peer-assessments in PBL, students are also encouraged to develop evaluation skills and reflect on their learning and thus improve their metacognition.

For example, the PBL activity on Non-Newtonian Fluid Mechanics (see Appendix) clearly demonstrates the connection between standards and expected knowledge skills, and the evaluation of these learning objectives must be planned through the design of various assessments. In the Non-Newtonian Fluid Mechanics PBL, students are engaged in several activities that foster the integration of standards across several disciplines. For instance, the students learn about the percent of water and viscosity of the silly putty (addresses the state science standard to investigate and identify properties of fluids, including viscosity), apply science process skills (addresses the state standard to collect and organize data, make and interpret scatterplots, and model, predict, and make decisions and critical judgments), and interpret graphical representations of the nonlinear response to stress of the substance (addresses state math standards to identify and use functions, including nonliner). Additionally, students will be able to build the applied knowledge necessary to understand functions and dependent and independent variables and develop tables and graphs. This PBL activity and the expected outcomes require interdisciplinary learning and standards, particularly in the areas of physics, chemistry, engineering, and mathematics, in addition to process standards such as problem solving, reasoning, and proof. Incorporating cross-curricular standards provides the potential to scaffold learning and build on learning across classes throughout the school day. Additionally, an ill-defined task can be modified easily by slightly changing the well-defined outcome. Imagine for a moment giving students the task to design a substance that could measure the volume of an irregular, three-dimensional shape (addresses volume standards).

By considering the standards as driving the well-defined outcome of the PBL design, it is easy to address key standards and to align assessment techniques to achieve maximal benefits. Because standards are paramount, knowing what students should be able to do allows the teacher to make prudent choices about what concepts and skills the student will need prior to engaging a particular aspect of the PBL. The use of PBL does not preclude direct instruction in small chunks; in fact, direct instruction is important because PBL should be an application of what students learn. Therefore, it is important for the teacher to explain graphing, describe the difference between linear and non-linear relationships, and provide examples of equations that produce each. The difference is that in the PBL environment, the direct instruction follows the student experience rather than preceding or supplanting the student experience. Students will then be able to maximize their experiences with the PBL. This puts the teacher in the position to make thoughtful and practical decisions about the development of instruction and the integration of assessment. When considering the assessments, teachers can use be a mix of assessments such as high-stakes type assessments and authentic assessments.

REFERENCES

Barron, B. J. S., Schwartz, D. L., Vye, N. J., Moore, A., Petrosino, A., Zech, L., et al. (1998). Doing with understanding: Lessons from research on problem- and project-based learning. *The Journal of the Learning Sciences, 7*, 271–311.

Bartscher, K., Gould, B., & Nutter, S. (1995). *Increasing student motivation through project based learning.* Master's Research Project, Saint Xavier University & IRI/Skylight. (ERIC Document Reproduction Service No. ED392549)

Beyer, B. K. (1995). *Critical thinking.* Bloomington, IN: Phi Delta Kappa Educational Foundation.

Blumenfeld, P., Soloway, E., Marx, R., Krajcik, J., Guzdial, M., & Palincsar, A. (1991). Motivating project-based learning: Sustaining the doing, supporting the learning. *Educational Psychologist, 26*, 369–398.

Gallagher, S., Stepien, W., Sher, B., & Workman, D. (1995). Implementing problem-based learning in science classrooms. *School Science and Mathematics, 95*, 136–146.

Greenwald, N. (2001). *Problem-based learning in science: Ill-defined problems are the right kind!* Retrieved June 1, 2008, from http://www.cct.umb.edu/pblscience.html

Hmelo-Silver, C. E. (2004). Problem-based learning: What and how do students learn? *Educational Psychological Review, 16*, 235–266.

National Council of Teachers of Mathematics. (2000). *Principles and standards for school mathematics.* Reston, VA: Author.

San Mateo County Office of Education. (n.d.). *Assessing student work with project-based learning.* Retrieved June 1, 2008, from http://pblmm.k12.ca.us/PBLGuide/AssessPBL.html

Secretary's commission on achieving necessary skills. (2000). *What work requires of schools: A SCANS report for America 2000.* Washington, DC: U.S. Department of Labor.

Solomon, G. (2003). *Project-based learning: A primer.* Retrieved June 5, 2008, from http://www.techlearning.com/db_area/archives/TL/2003/01/project.php

The George Lucas Educational Foundation. (n.d.). *How does project-based learning work?* Retrieved June 1, 2008, from http://www.edutopia.org/teaching-module-pbl-how

Tretten, R., & Zachariou, P. (1995). *Learning about project-based learning: Self-assessment preliminary report of results.* San Rafael, CA: The Autodesk Foundation.

U.S. Department of Defense Domestic Dependent Elementary and Secondary Schools. (n.d.). *A standards-based education system.* Retrieved January 3, 2008, from http://www.am.dodea.edu/ddessasc/aboutddess/standards/standardsbased.html

Yetkiner, Z. E., Anderoglu, H., & Capraro, R. M. (2007). *Research summary: Project-based learning in middle grades mathematics.* Retrieved June 1, 2008, from http://www.nmsa.org/Research/Research Summaries/ProjectBasedLearninginMath/tabid/1570/Default.aspx

Z. Ebrar Yetkiner
Department of Teaching, Learning and Culture,
Texas A&M University

Robert M. Capraro
Department of Teaching, Learning and Culture,
Texas A&M University

MARY MARGARET CAPRARO

8. INTERDISCIPLINARY STEM PROJECT-BASED LEARNING

INTRODUCTION

Project-Based Learning (PBL) is a "model for classroom activity that shifts away from the classroom practices of short, isolated, teacher-centered lessons and instead emphasizes learning activities that are long-term, interdisciplinary, student-centered, and integrated with real-world issues and practices" (Holbrook, 2007, Internet). "Additionally, PBL has been described as an "identification of suitable projects and integration into a curricular unit..." (Powers & DeWaters, 2004, p. 2).

As can be see from the above statements and the previous chapters, PBL previously defined as ill-defined tasks with well-defined outcomes, contain the integration of multidisciplinary subjects as an essential component for the most effective implementation of interdisciplinary PBLs.

CHAPTER OUTCOMES

When you complete this chapter you should be able to:
- determine how interdisciplinary PBLs help to develop conceptual understanding in students
- reflect if you are ready to plan an interdisciplinary PBL
- select the best environment for planning a PBL with the help of small learning communities and partners
- be aware of the advantages and limitations of interdisciplinary PBLs·
- When you complete this chapter you should be able to:
- decide if community partners can help you plan an interdisciplinary PBL
- be ready to begin planning an interdisciplinary PBL by using a concept map

If learning is relegated to only small components of information, the lowest level of learning generally occurs. Students learn only to pass a test or quiz at the end of a teacher-designed unit of instruction. This low level of learning is usually referred to as *procedural knowledge*. In comparison, learning that is long-lasting and requires high levels of cognition is referred to as *conceptual knowledge*. When students are engaged in PBL activities, a conceptual development of knowledge is sought. Research shows that conceptual knowledge results when disciplines are integrated and learners are involved in socially-interactive learning (Cobb & Bowers, 1999). This social learning can occur during cooperative learning, peer tutoring, and PBL. PBL activities are perfect matches for developing these

R.M. Capraro and S.W. Slough (eds.), Project-Based Learning: An Integrated Science, Technology, Engineering, and Mathematics (STEM) Approach, 91–101.

essential components of conceptual knowledge because they should be both interdisciplinary and social in nature. Thus, PBL facilitates integration of the content of different subjects, which naturally fits the science, technology, engineering, and mathematics (STEM) foci of this book. "PBL also provides opportunities for interdisciplinary learning. Students apply and integrate the content of different subject areas at authentic moments in the production process, instead of in isolation or in an artificial setting" (Holbrook, 2007). Too often school experiences are disjointed. Teachers need to continue to bring these experiences together to help make learning make sense to students.

SO WHAT DOES AN INTERDISCIPLINARY APPROACH TO TEACHING LOOK LIKE?

There are important and integral similarities and differences among traditional and PBL classrooms. Table 1 will be used as an advanced organizer for this chapter, providing a comparison of the two types of classrooms.

Table 1. Comparison Between Traditional and PBL Classrooms

Traditional Classrooms	PBL Classrooms
Defined task	Ill-defined task
Loosely-defined outcomes	Well-defined outcomes
Individual learning	Cooperative, group learning
T is the giver of knowledge	T is the facilitator of knowledge
Objective driven	Standards driven
Single subject/topic	Multidisciplinary
Textbook driven	Problem driven
Teaching based on covering skills	Teaching based on learning and curriculum needs
Success based on grades	Success based on performance
Individual activities with teacher-directed challenges	Cooperative activities with self-directed challenges
Focused on segmented coverage	Focused on culminating performance
Dependent problem solving	Independent problem solving
Narrow curriculum	Comprehensive curriculum
Tests and quizzes to assess knowledge acquisition	Culminating artifacts/experience at the end of the problem to determine knowledge gained

The definition of interdisciplinary is the mindful involvement and integration of several academic disciplines and methods to study a central problem or project (Jacobs, 1989). Put another way, ". . . interdisciplinary refers to the explicit recognition and connection of content and instruction from more than one subject or academic discipline in a teaching and/or learning experience (Taylor, Carpenter, Ballengee-Morris, & Sessions, 2006, p. 7). The terms multidisciplinary and interdisciplinary have in the past been and still are frequently used interchangeably. Multidisciplinary lessons focus on one problem from several disciplines, but there is no direct attempt to integrate the disciplines (Meeth, 1978). In contrast, interdisciplinary teaching truly melds disciplines together based on the needs and interests of the learner, thus some curriculum experts call it interdisciplinary learning. One approach is not considered better than another; the approach should be tailored to the topic under study and the student population. PBL is naturally tied toward writing and public speaking because students often communicate their finding to their classmates and beyond. These same PBLs are also naturally tied to the social sciences and government because the issues and problems that are investigated are real and are directly applicable. Because the focus of this book is on STEM PBLs that are relevant, conceptually oriented, and centered around experiences that integrate STEM, the rest of this chapter will concentrate on moving towards the creation of interdisciplinary PBLs. However, teachers must always keep in mind the readiness of their students—in order to benefit from interdisciplinary studies, students must have a solid foundation in the various disciplines that are being bridged (Jacobs & Borland, 1986).

Working towards this interdisciplinary approach requires the teacher to act as a facilitator. Additionally, teachers no longer find themselves working alone behind closed doors. Schools are focusing attention on the need for various teachers and school educators to work together effectively for the benefit of the students. In schools that are working toward establishing an interdisciplinary approach, teachers explicitly attempt to make connections between two or more sets of subject area knowledge. Additionally, teachers in these schools plan together. In some schools, this planning takes place before or after regular school hours. In other schools, the administrators or department heads might develop a schedule whereby teachers can plan either in small groups, among or across grade groups, or among or across subject areas depending upon the master schedule of the school. This type of scheduling requires coordination and cooperation on the part of all the stakeholders. During this planning, an interrelatedness of knowledge must be present between and among teachers. Subject-area boundaries would be difficult to distinguish if a school was truly striving to work towards this interdisciplinary approach. When teachers plan interdisciplinary PBLs together, topics or projects should necessitate understanding from various subject-area teachers. Thus, requiring the integration of subject-area curricula while striving towards planning learning experiences helps to develop conceptual knowledge in students.

FOSTERING UNDERSTANDING THROUGH PBL

PBL encourages students to become independent problem-solvers. While actively involved in projects, students are sometimes in cooperative learning groups working on meaningful activities that generally motivate students while appealing to their individual interests. As teachers carefully plan these projects, a natural interconnectedness of topics is supported that introduces curriculum more comprehensively. This comprehensiveness and connectedness fosters student understanding and motivation.

Of course, total integration of all subject areas with the implementation of every PBL is not possible or even desirable. Successful PBLs are not always inter-disciplinary and integrated. Potential integration is constrained by teachers and students who are not ready for these differing expectations of an interdisciplinary PBL, a lack of common, prior, student knowledge, ineffective collegial planning, and/or non-optimal scheduling. Various levels of integration are possible, as can be seen in Table 2 in the next section.

CONTINUUM OF PBL CURRICULUM INTEGRATION

So exactly what does this continuum look like in a school? Teachers are typically dispersed across all levels of the continuum. Table 2 below illustrates this moving continuum. If teachers truly want to develop an interdisciplinary classroom, they need to determine what it will take to progress through increasingly-integrated levels. In level one, all understanding is rigorously constrained to that which is explicitly defined within a single subject area. No intrusion of other subjects is encouraged. In levels two and three, there is an understanding from various subject areas that are connected or related together, however, topics are still treated as disconnected and discrete subjects. Teachers may plan together but each carries out lessons in their discrete subject areas during their own time blocks. Teachers may do some extensions to other subjects. In level four there is complete integration of subject areas to the degree that subject-area boundaries are no longer recognizable.

As the table is examined, one can locate the characteristics that more specifically define each of these levels. More specifically, one can determine what type of planning, topics, and learning environments would be typical of teachers and schools at each level. One can also locate the role of the teacher and student at each of these levels.

Table 2. Continuum of PBL Integration

Level	Planning	Standards Topic	Learning Environment	Role of the Teacher	Role of the Student
1 Individual classroom	Individual / Daily/ Weekly	Single Subject	Focus on Learning Objectives/ Single Classroom	Generally, Giver of all Knowledge	Generally, Works Individually/ Receiver of Knowledge
2 Themed Unit	Grade Level/ Subject Area/ Weekly	Theme/Unit/ No Attempt to Integrate	Generally Single Classroom Instruction	Knowledge Giver/ Sharer	Individually/ Small Group/ Receiver of Knowledge
3 Multi-disciplinary	Grade Level/ Subject Area/ Small Learning Communities (SLC)	Two or More Subjects, Some Attempt to Integrate	Focus on Student Achievement	Shared Learning/ Facilitator	Shared Learner/ Knowledge Gatherer
4 Total Integration/ Inter-disciplinary	Small Learning Communities	Seamless Integration Within and Between Disciplines	Focus on Acquisition of Knowledge	One of Many Facilitators of PBL	Knowledge Gatherer/ Work in Small Groups/ PBL in SLC

WORKING IN INTERDISCIPLINARY PLANNING TEAMS

Administrators need to arrange scheduling so that teachers have an opportunity to meet collaboratively in small teams of four to six members to engage in professional learning communities that are designed to improve student learning. These teams should meet regularly before, during, and after the school day. This time, protected by administrators, needs to be used to focus on improving teaching and student learning. For school-wide implementation of interdisciplinary PBLs, teachers within a school should be organized into one of these small teams. They can be comprised of teachers teaching the same subject to a similar group of students, but usually they are interdisciplinary in nature. The process connects the school's student data and the teachers' knowledge and experience to research and best practices. This process has been shown to increase student achievement (Anfara, Andrews, Hough, Mertens, Mizelle, & White, 2003; Sweetland & Hoy, 2000). Effective teams work professionally and collaboratively while they display a strong sense of community, are proactive rather than reactive, and have an intense commitment to student achievement. Additionally, these teams are focused on students and work closely with parents.

ESSENTIAL COMPONENTS FOR FORMING INTERDISCIPLINARY TEAMS

Common planning times, whether they occur before, during, or after the school day, promote team planning by teachers. This planning should encompass a sustained period of time with the same group of teachers over the year. These interdisciplinary teams of teachers are most effective when they have some control over establishing and maintaining student schedules. Working and planning in close surroundings, such as one wing of a building, helps promote the forming of these interdisciplinary teams. These teams should ideally consist of a limited number of teachers, somewhere between three and five, and a small student population of between 100-150 students.

These small teams could be the building blocks for Smaller Learning Communities (SLCs) as described by Cotton (2004). As teachers feel more comfortable planning and working collegially in these small teams, they can move into SLCs, which are interdisciplinary. A SLC may contain one or more teams but never more than a few hundred students. Each interdisciplinary team of teachers shares students in common and organizes instruction to gain more instructional time with fewer students. It becomes easier to move on the continuum from level one to level four, but change takes times, and so generally teachers move from one level to the next rather slowly. Chapter 9 discusses how one teacher worked in a SLC.

INTERDISCIPLINARY AND MULTIDISCIPLINARY PLANNING FOR A PBL: ALWAYS PLAN WITH THE END IN MIND

Planning necessitates identifying what learning objectives need to be covered in each of the subject areas by first determining the well-defined outcomes. Thus, teachers must determine if their students have achieved these outcomes. Authentic assessments with interdisciplinary rubrics can assist in this process as will be illustrated in the Chapter 13. Always plan with the end in mind. Teachers should always think first about what they want their students to know at the end of the PBL. Additionally, teachers must ensure that students at the culmination of the PBL can demonstrate this learned knowledge to their peers and their teacher using newly-created artifacts through culminating experiences shown in the Chapter 13. Using an interdisciplinary concept map can provide a picture for all the teachers in the SCLs, enabling them to visualize what skills need to be covered throughout the implementation of the PBL. This simple visual representation (see Figure 1) allows teachers to start to imagine all the possibilities for an integrated interdisciplinary approach. The concept map below is simplistic but can be developed to include all the state standards involved in a rocketry PBL.

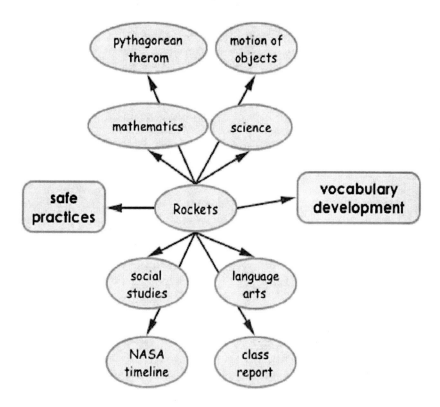

Figure 1. Interdisciplinary rocketry PBL concept map.

Planning together is not always easy. The sections below examine some of the issues that can arise when teachers attempt to plan together. If teachers are aware of these problems, they can be avoided. Another alternative is for teachers to plan ahead and work around the problems.

What are some of the issues that can arise when trying to plan together?

Some of the ingredients that might inhibit a school from putting together successful interdisciplinary teams are logistics, personalities, teacher roles, and student reactions. Logistics here refers to organizing and putting people together. At times this can be problematic. Differing personalities sometimes cause barriers to form rather than working partnerships. The first step will be to break down the barriers so all stakeholders can develop mutual understanding. The central focus always needs to be on what all stakeholders can do to improve the achievement of students. Teachers' roles and the attitudes can be in conflict when goals are not clear. Sometimes student reactions can be negative when teachers first begin to integrate subject areas; students may not understand and may question the process. Thus, teachers need to plan slowly and involve students whenever it is possible. Training in interdisciplinary teamwork is required if team members are to function effectively together. Teams work best when their roles are clear. Feedback from an experienced leader can be helpful in this process. Also, another resource to assist with planning is to involve outside businesses and community agencies as partners.

WORKING WITH BUSINESSES, COMMUNITY AGENCIES AS PARTNERS

Using these types of partners can be a mutually supportive arrangement between a school and a business, government agency, or community organization in which the parties commit to specific activities intended to benefit students, improve student achievement, and help accomplish school goals (Kanter, 1999). A school may initiate a partnership by recruiting a partner. Many high schools are moving towards forming academies around a subject-area theme to prepare students to enter the workforce. Involving partners from businesses and outside community agencies can strengthen these academies and the interdisciplinary PBLs that students engage in planned by the teacher. The points below can enable a school to decide if a partnership will be an asset in planning and assisting in implementing an interdisciplinary PBLs:

Excellent partnerships are: (1) designed to improve student achievement and are an integral part of the school planning, (2) committed to improving the quality of public education in order to prepare all students to live and work in the 21st century, (3) guided by written, realistic action plans that include planning, goal setting, communication, recognition, and evaluation, (4) able to demonstrate progress toward priority goals; thus, they should be able to assist in planning and contributing to activities that will strengthen the educational value to students, and (5) evaluative of their success primarily on the basis of improvements in student achievement rather than on programmatic success with their own structure (Broward County Public Schools, 2006).

A well-run partnership initiative results in a winning relationship for schools, for businesses, and for the community. The breadth of imagination is the only barrier to opportunities that can be afforded through these partnerships. Partners can help to develop a mock business in the school or classroom, serve as guest speakers, facilitate field trips to their business sites; students can also shadow partners in the workplace. Bank of America and Pizza Hut have helped schools set up restaurants and banks. Science museums, technology companies, work force organizations, and the arboretum could also serve as potential STEM partners. Partners can come to schools and guide students in setting up xeriscape gardens or recycling centers. Motorola has assisted with a robotics program. These are just some of the opportunities in which partners can provide support in this enhancement of the education of students (Broward County Public Schools, 2006).

Partnerships' benefits to schools and students include but are not limited to: (1) providing teachers with ideas for novel strategies for teaching, (2) providing additional human and financial benefits to schools, (3) reinforcing a school's goal that education is important for life, (4) supporting efforts to improve student achievement, (5) delivering a combined message that the community cares about students' academic success, (6) providing opportunities for greater career awareness, (7) increasing student self-esteem, and (8) enhancing learning opportunities in non-traditional settings.

ADVANTAGES AND LIMITATIONS OF INTERDISCIPLINARY PBLS

The advantages of using an integrated interdisciplinary PBL curriculum, according to Hall (1995), include:
- Elimination of fragmented curriculum – instead of the traditional curriculum that has been highly fragmented, integrated PBLs make sense. Learning is more natural and encourages students to bridge their understandings.
- Developmentally appropriate – with interdisciplinary PBLs, the curriculum changes depending upon the needs of the students. Students become active and engaged.
- Flexible curriculum – teachers can meet their curriculum mandates while leading students into their own explorations.
- Meets needs of diverse learners – students meet their needs by being empowered with the responsibility for their own learning while working in a variety of environments (Low & Shironaka, 1996).

Like any other instructional approach, interdisciplinary PBLs have some limitations as well (Coate & White, 1996). Some of these limitations include:
- Time constraints – not all educators think there is adequate time to plan and implement interdisciplinary PBLs.
- Difficulties in planning and implementation – making time for common planning for teachers from different disciplines can be difficult without administrative support.
- No textbook or classroom routine – students will be moving around and in various locations rather than one assigned desk. Not everyone is comfortable with the idea of not following a textbook that contains a set curriculum with questions at the end of the chapter. PBLs must be designed along with appropriate assessment strategies (Kain, 1996).
- Student prior knowledge – the student population in one classroom may possess different prior knowledge than the students in another classroom. Some teachers may lack the imagination to determine students' prior knowledge when working with so many skills, plus allow students to work at their own pace within their own levels.

– Student reactions – such as "why are we doing math in science?" These types of reactions can be eliminated if the PBLs are well planned and teachers work collegially to implement interdisciplinary PBLs.

EXAMPLES OF INTERDISCIPLINARY PBLS

Schoole (2004) developed a PBL called a "Chilling Project." Schoole describes a successful collaboration between a mathematics and technology teacher to develop an interdisciplinary PBL on mathematics, science, and technology where students were to build an ice container (ill-defined task). The teachers put together their classes once a week. Students worked as teams using their ideas about three-dimensional figures and technology in the design of the project. Additionally, the teachers collaborated together in this realistic project. At the conclusion of the project, students' designs were evaluated based on guidelines that were developed at the start of the project. This interdisciplinary project allowed students to reflect on how to improve their project.

In the next example, eighth-grade mathematics, language art, social studies, and science teachers developed a matrix of activities dealing with landforms. The central theme was mathematics. Included was a lesson plan, activities, and assessment strategies. The authors deduced that their method was a fairly easy way to integrate multiple disciplines (Horton, Hedetniemi, Wiegert, & Wagner, 2006).

This last article describes an integrated technology and mathematics lesson based on state standards (well-defined outcomes). The writers describe a hands-on activity using the design and construction of stair systems that link theory to practice. Mathematics and technology are integrated. A standards-based lesson plan is provided, focusing on standards for mathematics and technological literacy. At the culmination of the project, students were assessed on their stair designs, educational visions, pictorial representations of the project, and written papers describing the total project. The provided lesson plan includes the standards, objectives for students, activity procedure, and evaluation guidelines (Merrill & Comerford, 2004).

As demonstrated in this chapter, the interdisciplinary approach to PBL is much easier with a support system. Working together and planning with colleagues, whether in a small group or an official, professional SLC, can make the work of planning an interdisciplinary PBL easier to accomplish. As was shown, school environments where time is provided are more conducive to this collegial planning. Working with others, including the outside community and partners, brings in another set of unique advantages and opportunities. Teachers should always keep in mind that there are advantages and limitations to every new approach and innovation. Understanding the multiple perspectives of integrating interdisciplinary PBLs can be complex, therefore, it is important to be aware of the impact this process has on various school site personnel.

REFERENCES

Anfara, V. A., Andrews, P. G., Hough, D. L., Mertens, S. B., Mizelle, N. B., & White, G. P. (2003). *Research and resources in support of This We Believe*. Westerville, OH: Middle School Association.

Broward County Public Schools. (2006). *Partners in education: A handbook for school partnerships – Business, community, and schools working together*. Ft. Lauderdale, FL: Partners in Education.

Coate, J., & White, N. (1996). History/English core. *Social Studies Review, 34*(3), 1215.

Cobb, P., & Bowers, J. (1999). Cognitive and situated learning perspective in theory and practice. *Educational Researcher, 28*(2), 4–15.

Cotton, K. (2004). *New small learning communities: Findings from recent literature*. Reston, VA: National Association of Secondary School Principals.

Hall, A. (1995). Using social studies as a basis for interdisciplinary teaching. *State of Reading, 2*(1), 23–28.

Holbrook, J. (2007). *Project-based learning with multimedia*. Retrieved June 30, 2007, from http://pblmm.k12.ca.us/PBLGuide/WhyPBL.html

Horton, R. M., Hedetniemi, T., Wiegert, E., & Wagner, J. R. (2006). Integrating curriculum through themes. *Mathematics Teaching in the Middle School, 11*, 408–414.

Jacobs, H. H. (Ed). (1989). *Interdisciplinary curriculum. Design and implementation*. Alexandria, VA: ASCD.

Jacobs, H. H., & Borland, J. H. (1986). The interdisciplinary concept model. Design and implementation. *Gifted Child Quarterly, 30*, 159–163.

Kain, D. L. (1996). Recipes or dialogue? A middle school team conceptualizes curricular integration. *Journal of Curriculum and Supervision, 11*, 163–187.

Kanter, R. M. (1999). From spare change to real world change. The social sector as beta site for business innovation. *Harvard Business Review, 77*(3), 122–132, 210.

Low, J. M., & Shironaka, W. (1996). Letting go- allowing first graders to become autonomous learners. *Young Children, 51*, 21–115.

Meeth, L. R. (1978). Interdisciplinary studies: Integration of knowledge and experience. *Change, 10*, 6–9.

Merrill, C., & Comerford, M. (2004). Technology and mathematics standards: An integrated approach. *Technology Teacher, 64*(2), 8–12.

Powers, S. E., & DeWaters, J. (2004, November). Creating project-based experiences for university-K-12 partnerships. In *Proceedings of the frontiers in education conference*, Savannah, GA.

Schooler, S. R. (2004). A "chilling project integrating mathematics, science, and technology. *Mathematics Teaching in the Middle School, 10*, 116–121.

Sweetland, S. R., & Hoy, W. K. (2000). School characteristics and educational outcomes: Toward an organization model of student achievement in middle schools. *Educational Administration Quarterly, 36*, 703–729.

Taylor, P., Carpenter, B., Ballengee, C., & Sessions, B. (2006). *Interdisciplinary approaches to teaching art in high school*. Reston, VA: National Art Education.

Mary Margaret Capraro
Department of Teaching, Learning and Culture,
Texas A&M University

GERRI M. MAXWELL

9. ONE VETERAN EDUCATOR'S EXPERIENCE WITH PROFESSIONAL LEARNING COMMUNITIES

INTRODUCTION

In addition to the theoretical and practical information concerning the implementation of Project-Based Learning (PBL) in the classroom, this chapter provides evidence from the field supporting successful implementation of PBL and real-life connections to the process of implementing within a professional learning community (PLC).

CHAPTER OUTCOMES

When you complete this chapter you should better understand:
- that implementing PLCs is in itself an ill-defined process
- the considerations necessary for implementation of PLCs
- that you too can implement change through establishing PLCs
  When you complete this chapter you should be able to:
- use PLCs in support of implementation of PBL

OVERVIEW OF PLCS

Prelude

Professional Learning Community. Well, it sounds so professional. Maybe even sterile. Neat and tidy. In fact, building a PLC is far from that. It's messy work, and it's tough work. It is however, work that needs to be done, and whether you coin the current buzzword *PLC* (Hord, 1997) for the activities going on now or use some other term like *academic teaming* (Clark & Clark, 1994), many of the processes in developing PLCs are very similar to those networking leadership activities described in previous decades (Scribner, Sawyer, Watson, & Myers, 2007). These frameworks agree that creating a PLC is about creating cohesiveness, collaborating over a sense of purpose, focusing the direction of a group of learners, and facilitating the success of those learners. Those learners can be educators, students, groups of educators and students, business people, or other stakeholders.

After having worked on an academic team in the 1990s, I realized that even though I feel like a bit of a foreigner as a reading specialist on a university based Science, Technology, Engineering, and Mathematics (STEM) project. The

R.M. Capraro and S.W. Slough (eds.), Project-Based Learning: An Integrated Science, Technology, Engineering, and Mathematics (STEM) Approach, 103–115.

experience I had as a teacher-leader on a sixth-grade academic team (focused on interdisciplinary and hands-on instruction) was pertinent to the task of working with high-needs schools in large urban districts. Specifically, there is a need to build PLCs in order to build new instructional models. Once the logistics, such as common planning times, have been made part of the school day to facilitate and sustain PLCs, the groundwork will have been laid for successful implementation of PBL or for that matter, any other successful, school reform-effort.

A number of researchers support the need for PLCs. Senge (1990) says in the *Fifth Discipline*, "The organization that will truly excel in the future will be the organizations that discover how to tap into people's commitment and capacity to learn at all levels in an organization" (p.4). Advocates for school improvement have recommended that effective schools should also operate as strong PLCs (Cochran-Smith & Lytle, 1999; Giles & Hargreaves, 2006; Louis & Kruse, 1995; McLaughlin & Talbert, 2001; Scribner, Cockrell, Cockrell, & Valentine, 1999). Considering my experience with an interdisciplinary academic team, I was benefiting from my prior experiences in the current PBL STEM work.

I share my insights that building a PLC does not happen overnight or in a couple of workshops, based on my eight years of experience leading a middle school academic team. Building a PLC is a never-ending change process (Eeek! Change, the feared word). Because the participants in a PLC are constantly learning, they themselves are changing. Thus, the interactions between participants and decisions made by the learners as a PLC constantly have this ebb and flow of change and redirection and refinement of purpose. This constant change makes for very tough work, especially early on. Fortunately, though, research on teaming such as Tuckman's (1965) well-known evolution of groups (forming, storming, norming, performing) can facilitate PLC development by addressing the inherent landmines as professionals learn to deal with each other under new conditions. The reality is that PLC frameworks that are initiated have some real challenges ahead, and if the members of the learning community are not nurtured or the have the necessary drive to elevate their work to a higher plane, no PLC will emerge. Many have tried. Many have failed, but for those who endure, the rewards are great. Success will come.

Student success at the middle school where I worked was formally recognized when our campus was named a Texas Successful School. Then, that campus was crowned six years later (with many of the teaching staff from the three sixth-grade academic teams still in place as a PLC) a National Blue Ribbon campus.

Being honored as this exemplar is attributable to a number of factors, including a low teacher/administrator turnover for a couple of decades. The teachers and administrators on this campus and the PLC of this student-centered campus began in the academic-team learning framework and continued to build on lessons learned to create what has been cited as one of the best public schools in the nation. With confidence, I share my experiences on this academic team to inform the current work and research in the area of PLCs.

Experience is a Great Teacher

Between 1992 and 2000, I was the academic team leader of a sixth-grade interdisciplinary team (one of three academic teams at grade six) in a public, middle school in Texas. The group of teachers I led over this eight-year period totalled 11 different teachers. Most of the teachers on the team were veteran teachers. At that time, I was one of the least experienced teachers in the group. I am not certain why my principal continued to ask me to lead the team because truly, I learned more from my veteran teacher-colleagues than I ever did in college coursework, and I had been teaching for about ten years at the time.

Efforts to improve instruction over this eight-year period were generally two-fold. First, the academic team was motivated to succeed and intrigued by the current "teaming" philosophy we heard about at various middle school conferences. The content sounded interesting and academically made a lot of sense based on the research we had been exposed to and sought out. We worked to integrate our instruction thematically, trying to build in curricular connections across the content areas for our students. We attended various interdisciplinary curriculum trainings including the Roger Taylor Model (Drake, 1998), along with other instructional-strategy trainings such as cooperative learning and the New Jersey Writing Project (Alloway, 1979). We were determined to take this smorgasbord of professional development we had received and make sense of it. This determination was facilitated by working among a group of colleagues that all cared considerably about impacting student success.

During this eight-year period, with the demographics of this district changing as well as pressures from increased state accountability, our school like many others at the time needed reform to meet these increasing challenges. The principal for whom I worked was "ahead of his time" and understood many of the premises of initiating a PLC, which was at that time referred to in school leadership literature as "academic teaming." This principal had served a tour in Vietnam, and he understood the importance of teamwork, communication, and distributing leadership. Researchers like Scheurich and Skrla (2003) suggest that, "all school staff can and should consider themselves simultaneously both a leader and a follower" (p. 100). This was our principal's philosophy at the time. He sent us to middle school conference after conference to learn more about academic teaming. We did school visits. We researched the concept. I was asked on behalf of our campus site-based team to present a proposal to our school board to provide additional funding to support an academic-teaming framework. Apparently, we were convincing enough to have the school board agree to provide an additional $30,000 – $90,000 in funding as we phased in this academic-teaming framework one grade level at a time over a three-year period.

Although I do not recall feeling that we were a school in crisis at the time, in retrospect, we were indeed just that. The demographics of this growing, what some would consider "rural" school district were changing as was the nature of school accountability in Texas. Student achievement for our African American students was low. As I recall, nine percent of our African American students were succeeding on all state standardized tests at our grade level. At that time in Texas, we were in the final stages of the TEAMS (Texas Educational Assessment of Minimum Skills) test and beginning stages of the TAAS (Texas Academic Assessment of Skills) test. The campus itself had a grade six through eight configuration, and student disciplinary referrals were high. The building in which we were housed was built to support a student population of 700, and we had 1100 students on campus, so we were pretty overcrowded. I even recall parents of students coming to the campus to have premeditated altercations among themselves. Although I didn't realize it at the time, our principal was under fire about the safety of students on the campus. The teachers at the campus, myself included, attended a school board meeting in support of our principal as he had been asked to address the school board about the safety of students on our campus. Indeed we were a campus with incredible challenges facing us. It was time for a new direction, and academic teaming was selected by the campus improvement team as the framework to facilitate this change.

FIRST STEPS

Actually, in retrospect, the principal of our campus already had laid the groundwork for a move to academic teams by creating a positive climate among the teachers on the campus with his charismatic leadership style. For some time, our district had been involved in the Effective Schools framework (Lezotte, 1991), and as a campus, the principal and the teachers had worked on school climate. As the site-based leadership team, which the principal ensured met on a regular basis, convened multiple times to consider a shift to academic teaming, we addressed a number of logistical, personnel, and curricular issues.

The initial logistics in creating and situating academic teams on this overcrowded campus included several strategies. These strategies included attention to: (1) the physical location of the teams, (2) selection of the teaching team members, and (3) class scheduling to create an additional conference period for common planning time for the academic teams.

Physical Location of the Teams

One of the first steps the site-based team determined was necessary was to locate the team classrooms of core academic teachers in proximity with one another. This proximity assisted in communication among the core teachers and confined student traffic for large blocks of the day, which somewhat alleviated the overcrowding. This proximity was necessary as the concept of teaming itself implies a distribution of leadership. For Scribner, Sawyer, Watson, and Myers (2007), "because teacher teams meet face to face, the primary medium of interaction for this social distribution of leadership is conversation" (p. 73). Thus, to facilitate conversation between the team teachers, classrooms were located near one another. Also, in considering a location for these teams, other logistical matters such as restroom and water fountain access were attended to so that traffic patterns of the students and teams were directed to specific locations for use of these facilities.

By strategically placing these groups of classrooms, locating them as schools within a school or *houses*, as in current smaller learning community terminology (Cotton, 2001), even within only a single grade level in the first year of academic-teaming implementation on the campus, there was an immediate impact on discipline on campus. Students at once had both the freedom of interaction with a confined group of students and separation from interaction with other students. This was helpful in alleviating some of the familial and other rivalries among students on the campus as well as allowing this group of five teachers to share a common group of students and bond almost as a family. This arrangement also allowed teachers greater control over students between passing periods, decreased the amount of student traffic in an overcrowded building in specific areas at specific times, and allowed for better timing of the traffic flow in the common hallways.

As the months and years passes, the proximity of these teams truly helped each academic team develop an identity as a school within a school. Each team had a "mascot" and team name and planned both academic and fun academic team activities together, thus instilling a true sense of community among the team of students and teachers and collaboration and a professional learning climate among the teachers on the team.

Collaboration was not confined to the individual teams as the proximity of each team to another academic team in a grade level allowed for some collaboration across teams, as well. Activities such as turning the entire hallway into the Nile River during the Egypt unit or creating a castle entrance to the hallway when studying Medieval Times created a real sense of identity and teamwork among not only the teams individually but across the grade level. Everyone felt a part of something very special on this campus. As teachers, a number of us had students and parents tell us years after having left our team that the sixth-grade year had been an important one in their education in great part because of the sense of belonging this teaming created for students, teachers, and parents alike.

Selection of the Teaching Team Members

A second strategy attended to primarily by the principal was selection of team members for each team. Although he made these team assignments based primarily on his knowledge of the personalities of the teachers involved, he annually communicated with team leaders and team members about the team makeup. For the first couple of years, the primary focus of these teams was related to quite honestly getting the campus under control and learning to work together. Although our principal may have been operating on a hunch at the time, leadership research since then has found that the rapidly changing environments in which self-managed teams work, as a result of group interaction, yields effective problem solving (Sawyer, 2003; Schien, 1992). Fortunately (or unfortunately), state accountability was in its early stages, and so in some respects, we had the luxury of some time to build these teams, these PLCs. Although I wasn't as familiar with the makeup of the personalities on the other academic teams, I could see that the principal was making decisions about the skill sets of the various persons on each team and also about the leadership for each team. Certainly, each team had a teacher for each of five content areas: English, reading, math, science, and social studies, but the principal also gave some consideration to which math teacher, which science teacher, and so on, would work best on each team. Additionally, teacher certification in some cases impacted the population of students served. For example, there was an increasing number of English as a Second Language (ESL) students, so students on my team were 15% non-English speakers. Other teams had teachers with special education experience, and so as we implemented first the concept of "mainstreaming" and then "inclusion" (which were phrases coined to described having special education students served among the regular student population), a team with teachers with that expertise served those students.

In some cases, it took a while for teacher teams to "gel." Also, some teams "got" the concept of academic teaming better than others. The principal took it all in stride, and we all learned from one another how to make this structure of working on a teamwork for our students and work for us. We did make it work. Academic teaming and the relationships we formed with each other professionally and with our students in this predecessor of PLCs facilitated our work.

Class Scheduling for Common Conference Periods

Key to our success in implementing academic teams was the common conference period we shared daily. This was a 45-minute planning time, in addition to our personal conference periods, that allowed all five content area teachers on our team to meet together daily. There were three sixth-grade academic teams on the campus, so I am certain that scheduling was a considerable challenge for the campus counselor. In reality, due to various electives being scheduled during a particular period, a specific band instrument practicing during a specific band period, and so on, our academic teams either had band students, choir students, ESL students, and so on based on what other periods in the schedule were "locked in" due to these elective periods. What did facilitate scheduling was the extra teaching position added at the grade level to allow for three "pure" academic teams that could share the same, approximately-135 students. We had tried academic teams for one year without a common conference period until the benefits were recognized and the school board approved the cost of this additional teaching position to create flexibility in scheduling. Once we had this common conference period, we were able to do so much more in the way of creating essentially the "school within a school" concept.

NEXT STEPS

Once these initial logistics were in place, our team then focused on refining what we did during common planning times including: (1) establishing some norms for daily meetings, which often included processes and strategies for dealing with student discipline, and ultimately, (2) working to improve instruction and curriculum once these other logistics and processes were fairly established.

Establishing Norms for Daily Meetings

In establishing norms for our daily meetings, our site-based teams had the advantage of having done a number of school site-visits where academic teams were already functioning. We had also attended a number of sessions at the Texas Middle School Conference over a couple of years prior to implementing academic teams on our campus. So, we already had some collective ideas about the time management of a common conference period.

One of the key logistical strategies was to implement a daily agenda. As the academic team leader, I was responsible for the daily agenda. At first, as I recall, the agenda was self-setting. That is, there was so much to consider, we seldom lacked discussion topics, but rather prioritization of topics was usually the concern. School research on teams indicates that:

> Teams are often not hierarchically structured; rather, group meetings are free flowing—akin to a brainstorming session, in which the loose structure enables creative solutions to emerge. A teacher team might be particularly effective at solving a difficult problem that does not have an obvious solution. Before this form of group creativity can emerge, the team itself must be organized in a distributed fashion, allowing all members to contribute, in meetings that do not have rigidly structured agendas. (Scribner et al., 2007)

Along with trying to get our academic team up and running, we were essentially running a school within a school and so sometimes the agenda changed at a moment's notice, depending on which parent had called, which students had fought, which teaching team member had a personal crisis, etc. As the team leader, it was my job to keep our team on task, but also be willing to be flexible according to whatever each day brought. Sawyer (2003) found that teacher teams often do not have set agendas but rather the emergent process of group interaction provides necessary creative solutions. I found this to be true on our team. If you have lived and worked in a middle school, you know that no two days are ever the same or very predictable and in retrospect, our agendas were pretty fluid.

Setting Team Meeting Topics

In this section, I share the various topics we tackled during team meetings as part of our ongoing, somewhat-flexible agenda. These include: (1) setting goals, (2) dealing with discipline, (3) dealing with interpersonal issues among the members of the team, or (4) planning curriculum.

Setting goals

In prioritizing our path as a team, we focused on goal setting. We were learning on our feet how to run an academic team, run a school within a school, teach class, and grade papers. It was pretty wild and crazy for a while!

As an academic team, we all had the philosophy that motivation of students was a primary goal. In fact, the students sort of decided this for us! We had some real challenges among our student population. So, realizing our challenges and wanting to incorporate what we had been learning about trying to integrate instruction between our content areas, we decided to chart out a yearly thematic plan for instruction and incorporate student-incentive activities correlated to these various themes. Once we had done this annual planning, the theme of the six weeks was often the impetus for activities on our agenda. We tried to incorporate all team activities around the instructional theme, whether it was the theme of time or one of the various historical periods of time within that overarching theme. Each six weeks, we established a student-behavior incentive and we correlated that incentive to the theme. One that comes immediately to mind is our Egypt theme. Students could earn Papyrus Points daily based on individual criteria each teacher on the team set. Students who earned enough Papyrus Points would be able to participate in the culminating activity for the unit that was in this case Egypt Day. (I will talk more about Egypt Day when I discuss curriculum later in this chapter).

Dealing with discipline

In addition to the daily agenda addressing the planning and logistics for our student motivational incentives, we often had a specific student in for a conference with the team of teachers regarding some student disciplinary issue. This was a very effective first step in dealing with student discipline. Often between the motivational activities we planned and the team teachers working together in these student/team conferences, we were able to redirect student behavior very effectively. Eventually, there were years with virtually no student discipline referrals. By contrast, we had more than our share of student behavior challenges during the first six weeks. Eventually, students figured out that this year was going to be different and maybe even fun!

Resolving personnel issues on the team

Sometimes the daily agenda was about resolving conflicts among the team members. Yes, this was just part of the process – the messy but often necessary part of creating a team. Some years there were no personnel issues on the team. Other years, as teachers occasionally moved or changed campuses, our team membership changed. In some years, a couple of team members had to agree to disagree and separate their personal differences from professional goals for students on the team. And to their credit, they were able to do so. This often required some legwork in the background by our principal or me, but we knew it was necessary work, and so we kept trying. Often, recognizing the strengths of each team member and distributing leadership of the team in various team tasks assisted the collaboration among team members.

Developing curriculum

In the early years, as I mentioned previously, as we met in these common planning times, we laid out a yearly plan of themes that we decided to try to incorporate. We selected an overarching theme under which we could incorporate as many content areas as possible in trying to make connections for our students. We decided as a team (and a grade level) to write a semester-long, thematic unit focused on time. So, as the reading teacher in the group (and in collaboration with the two reading teachers from the other academic teams), I selected a novel, *The Phantom Tollbooth*, which was focused around a fantasy journey into another place and time. Within this overarching unit, we charted out with the social studies teacher the required state curriculum that covered ancient times including studies of Greece, Rome, and Egypt, and so we also incorporated the study of mythology and a unit on Egypt and King Tutankamen. Within these contents, we aligned the state curriculum to ensure objectives were taught and covered in sync across content areas as much as possible, and we created matrices to accomplish these curricular connections as teaching guide charts. In teaching the concept of time, science teachers were able to integrate their content by integrating the timeline of the earth and tectonic plate movement as related to the changing topography of the earth itself. The math teacher was able to integrate some content on time as well; however, the math class was probably the most difficult to integrate into our thematic units from the math teacher's perspective, but the approach of the team was to support math as much as possible in our own content areas. In reading, we attempted to integrate the use of charts and graphs as much as possible, as did the social studies and science teachers.

Within these thematic units we created, various teachers attempted to integrate hands-on and problem-solving learning as much as possible. Some examples of these included a culminating activity to our Egypt unit where students used Papyrus Points to participate in the various activities of the day. One of these activities included creation of an archaeological dig grid using popsicle sticks, string, and mathematical measurement. Another project-based, problem-based, thematically-oriented activity included a space theme. In reading class, we read an account of Apollo 13, and students had to problem solve and create their own hands-on replica of the duct tape/box filters that had ultimately saved the lives of the astronauts. When we studied the Titanic, students created cause-effect board games based on the various events of the Titanic tragedy.

Our team (and our grade level composed of three academic teams) was also among the first to integrate technology into instruction. Our students researched inventors and created Hyperstudio presentations with the results of their work. (Our campus had five COWs —Computers on Wheels – huge, lethargic things I crowded into my classroom to do the Hyperstudio presentations. The kids loved this!) We used Accelerated-Reader, individualized testing on three computers in my classroom (Apple IIe's – remember those?) as one "work station" in our daily classrooms to assess student understanding of reading. So, in thinking about integrating hands-on, PBL and technology into public school classrooms as part of this STEM initiative I am involved in eight to ten years later, I certainly have a sense of deja vu.

Impact of State Accountability on our Curriculum Efforts

About midway through this eight-year period, due in great part to increasing demands for student achievement as dictated by the Texas accountability system, our academic team piloted a modified block schedule and worked among ourselves to reschedule our students in order to facilitate this extended class time for both instructional (primarily math) and logistical purposes. Also, we continued to attempt to refine student traffic issues on the overcrowded campus, and by staggering our schedule against that of other teams and grade levels, we were able to do restroom breaks when the halls were empty, which further assisted the overcrowding. It was very common for ideas such as this modified block scheduling to come out of our academic team conversations as we continually worked to improve instruction for our students.

As state accountability demands continued to increase and the concept of integrating curriculum was fairly well-established on our team, our team efforts morphed in a couple of other ways. First, the reading teachers met across teams (thus creating another team/PLC) to write daily and weekly assessment questions in the same format as the current state-standardized test. This strategy was labor intensive, but by working as a "team," we divided the work and shared our products with one another, which facilitated student success. Additionally, we increasingly made more straightforward efforts particularly to support student achievement in math on our team. The benefit of these common planning times facilitated us weekly reviewing student data on math tests and creating strategies or extended periods of time to either pull students not needing as much intervention support from the math teacher for other enrichment while providing her with a reduced teacher/pupil ratio or additional time to tutor students who needed extra assistance.

Another example of collaboration around a particular curriculum or instructional need on our team might have been choosing to focus on a specific math objective, which we all would attempt to support in our own content area. Sometimes, I would take time out of my reading class to do a math warm-up (mini-lesson) on a specific math skill, and sometimes the reading curriculum lent itself to incorporating math skills, such as when studying graphs and charts. Other times, an item on the academic team agenda might be students who were not doing enough independent reading. We used Accelerated Reader (Paul, VanderZee, Rue, & Swanson, 1996), which is a computerized, individual book-assessment. Students were required to earn a specific number of minimum points each six weeks. So, sometimes we would strategize how to get students to accomplish this. Sometimes strategies included restructuring the partnering of students from neighboring team-teacher-classrooms with other students for oral partner reading in the hall during the daily common study hall time after lunch.

PUTTING IT ALL TOGETHER

The PBL book would be incomplete without addressing the importance of forming groups of teachers committed to school change. That key piece means understanding the school contexts to facilitate change and establishing a PLC that has norms for behavior and specifics for teacher learning and accountability.

You might ask, how do you start building a PLC? Well, the first thing is that ultimately, it is important to understand that there is no one right way to do this. Also, there is no neat and easy way to do this. In fact, I would say that the stronger the personalities of the people involved in creating the PLC, the messier the process is going to be and the greater the struggle, but the emergent end result will be an exceptionally strong organization with people who are committed not only to the fidelity of their content work but also to each other in the organization. By being committed to each other, they are committed professionally and even personally to the success of every aspect of every person in the PLC.

When I worked as a teacher leader on an academic team, I was a babe leading veteran teachers to in some respects change what they were doing, but they taught me more about teaching than I ever learned in coursework. I think realization of the benefits we all bring to an academic team or PLC is the first step. Be kind to one another. View each other as an undeniable and equal team member who brings invaluable contributions to the team. Look beyond your differences and revel in your shared vision.

CONCLUSION

I hope this account from a veteran educator who worked in an emerging PLC for the implementation of an interdisciplinary PBL has been helpful. In addition to common planning times in schools as a necessary component of establishing a PLC, the landscape of how educators and all of us communicate and develop community has drastically changed during the past five to ten years. In the next chapter, the importance of technologies in facilitating will provide insights about other areas around which PLCs can be helpful to facilitate instructional change.

REFERENCES

Alloway, E. (1979). *New Jersey writing project*. Published by a consortium project of Rutgers University, the Educational Testing Service, and nineteen New Jersey public school districts.
Clark, S., & Clark, D. (1994). *Restructuring the middle level school*. New York: SUNY.
Cochran-Smith, M., & Lytle, S. (1999). Teacher learning communities. *Review of Research in Education, 24*, 24–32.
Cotton, K. (2001). *New small learning communities: Findings from recent literature*. Portland, OR: Northwest Regional Educational Laboratory.

Drake, S. (1998). *Creating integrated curriculum: proven ways to increase student learning.* Thousand Oaks, CA: Corwin Press.

Giles, C., & Hargreaves, A. (2006). The sustainability of innovative schools as learning organizations and professional learning communities during standardized reform. *Educational Administration Quarterly, 42*(1), 124–156.

Hord, S. (1997). *Professional learning communities: Communities of continuous inquiry and improvement.* Austin, TX: Southwest Educational Development Lab.

Juster, N. (1961). *The phantom tollbooth.* USA: Random House.

Leithwood, K., & Louis, K. S. (Eds.). (1998). *Organizational learning in schools.* Downington, PA: Swets & Zeitlinger.

Lezotte, L. S. (1991). *Correlates of effective schools: The first and second generations.* Okemos, MI: Effective Schools Products, Ltd.

Louis, K., & Kruse, S. (1995). *Professionalism and community: Perspectives on reforming urban schools.* Thousand Oaks, CA: Corwin Press.

McLaughlin, M., & Talbert, J. (2001). *Professional communities and the work of high school teaching.* Chicago: University Press.

Paul, T., VanderZee, D., Rue, T., & Swanson, S. (1996, October). *Impact of the accelerated reader technology-based literacy program on overall academic achievement and school attendance.* Paper presented at the National Reading Research Center Conference "Literacy and Technology for the 21st Century", Atlanta, GA.

Sawyer, R. (2003). *Group creativity: Music, theater, collaboration.* Mahwah, NJ: Erlbaum.

Schein, E. (1992). *Organizational culture and leadership.* San Francisco: Jossey-Bass.

Scheurich, J., & Skrla, L. (2003). *Leadership for equity and excellence.* Thousand Oaks, CA: Corwin.

Scribner, J., Cockrell, K., Cockrell, D., & Valentine, J. (1999). Creating professional communities in schools through organizational learning: An evaluation of a school improvement process. *Educational Administration Quarterly, 35*(1), 130–160.

Scribner, J., Sawyer, R., Watson, S., & Myers, V. (2007). Teacher teams and distributed leadership: A study of group discourse and collaboration. *Educational Administration Quarterly, 43*(1), 67–100.

Senge, P. (1990). *The fifth discipline: The art and practice of the learning organization.* New York: Doubleday.

Tuckman, B. (1965). Developmental sequence in small groups. *Psychological Bulletin, 63,* 384–399.

Gerri M. Maxwell
Assistant Superintendent,
Sommerville ISD

LAUREN CIFUENTES AND SERKAN ÖZEL

10. USING TECHNOLOGY TO SUPPORT STEM PROJECT-BASED LEARNING

INTRODUCTION

The goal of this chapter is for teachers to (1) learn how to use technological tools to develop and assess Science, Technology, Engineering, and Mathematics (STEM) Project-Based Learning (PBL) and (2) support students in using technology as they conduct PBL. Best teaching practices support students as they apply technology while actively participating in and manipulating STEM content. Using technology, students can intentionally direct and regulate their own learning to attain their learning goals. In addition, technology can facilitate student work in more authentic contexts than traditional classrooms afford by providing connections to complex, real-life experiences and problems. Students can apply telecommunications technology to articulate and reflect upon their activities so that their understanding can grow. Perhaps most importantly, technology provides tools for cooperative, collaborative, and conversational activity that supports social construction of meaning (Jonassen, Howland, Marra, & Crismond, 2008). Meaningful and productive uses of technology in classrooms support students as they engage in active knowledge construction, collaboration, conversation among other students and with instructors, reflection, and articulation through writing, speaking, and visualization.

CHAPTER OUTCOMES

When you complete this chapter you should better understand:
- how to address desired outcomes
- how to support PBL by using technology
- When you complete this chapter you and your students should be able to use technology to:
- address desired outcomes, assess both processes and outcomes, and give and receive feedback during PBL
- support PBL by providing direction, guidance, and structure
- make STEM relevant
- help students collaborate with each other, make thinking visible, and conduct minds-on activities and research
- promote transfer, autonomy, and lifelong learning

R.M. Capraro and S. W. Slough (eds.), Project-Based Learning: An Integrated Science, Technology, Engineering, and Mathematics (STEM) Approach, 117–133.

Let's Begin with a Scenario

Students enter a classroom that has six workstation areas. Each takes a seat at a workstation area that is grouped for cooperative learning among five or fewer students. At each workstation, activities have statements of goals and objectives and have directions for students to follow as they work on a project. The content of the six lessons is functions in Algebra I, and each lesson relates to a project, called Functions at Home, in which students learn about using technology to explore algebraic functions in a home environment. Each lesson is designed to support students as they work to meet standards. For this chapter, the Texas Essential Knowledge and Skills (TEKS) is used; however, by simply substituting state or local standards, each example should be similar. For convenience and ease of comparison, the complete standards can be located at http://www.tea.state.tx.us/teks/.

At a workstation named *Redesign your Home*, students study vocabulary used to describe functions and identify household situations in which functions are applied, such as painting, carpeting, wallpapering, and shopping for exhaust fans. Students quiz each other on the definition of terms using either computer-based flash cards and crossword puzzles or teacher-generated, paper-based flash cards and crossword puzzles (depending on number of computers available). The teacher can create flash cards and crossword puzzles using online resources such as Discovery Education's Puzzlemaker, Crossword Puzzle Games, Flash Card Machine, and Flash Card Maker (see Figure 1). This workstation addresses foundations for functions (TEKS 111.32 b.A.1).

At another workstation named *Home Improvement*, students study relations, functions, and domain and range concepts by applying them to home improvements such as working on floor plans, deciding the amount of paint needed, and choosing a fan for the bathroom. They follow instructions on a video disc that guides them through the application of functions to home improvements. This workstation addresses foundational concepts for high school mathematics, function concepts, underlying mathematical processes (TEKS 111.32. Algebra I [a.1] [a.3] [a.6]), foundations for functions (TEKS 111.32. Algebra I [b.1.A] [b.1.D] [b.1.E]), and linear functions (TEKS 111.32. Algebra I [b.5.A] [b.5.C]).

At a third workstation named *Measure Twice, Cut Once*, students study data collection and interpretation and different measurement systems. They apply an Internet-enabled computer, preferably equipped with a webcam and microphone, to communicate with international buddies to share and discuss their data. The international connection allows them to learn that measurement is an invention and methods vary across cultures. This workstation addresses foundations for functions (TEKS 111.32. Algebra I [b.1.A] [b.1.B] [b.1.C] [b.1.D] [b.1.E]), properties and attributes of functions (TEKS 111.32. Algebra [b.2.B] [b.2.D]), the power of symbols to represent situations (TEKS 111.32. Algebra [b.3.A] [b.3.B]), linear functions (TEKS 111.32. Algebra [b.5.B] [b.5.C]), and the slope and intercepts of the graphs (TEKS 111.32. Algebra [b.6.B] [b.6.F]).

At a fourth workstation named *Functional Fish Pond*, students study data collection, table creation, and linear functions. They collect data and use an excel spreadsheet to record that data, create tables, sketch graphs, and then create a Power Point presentation to show their findings to the class. This workstation addresses foundational concepts for high school mathematics, function concepts, underlying mathematical processes (TEKS 111.32. Algebra I [a.1] [a.3] [a.6]), foundations for functions (TEKS 111.32. Algebra [b.1.A] [b.1.D] [b.1.E]), and linear functions (TEKS 111.32 [b.5.A] [b.5.C]).

At a fifth workstation named *Come in, the Water is Fine*, students study positive and negative slope and the concept of rate of change. They identify ways of saving water in the home in which functions might be applied. They employ a scientific calculator to enter data and sketch graphs and then discuss findings in a word-processed document. This workstation addresses function concepts, the relationship between equations and inequalities, algebraic thinking, underlying mathematical processes (TEKS 111.32. Algebra I [a.3] [a.4] [a.5] [a.6]), foundations for functions (TEKS 111.32. Algebra [b.1.A] [b.1.B] [b.1.C] [b.1.D] [b.1.E]), properties and attributes of functions (TEKS 111.32. Algebra [b.2.B] [b.2.D]), the power of symbols to represent situations (TEKS 111.32. Algebra [b.3.A] [b.3.B]), linear functions (TEKS 111.32. Algebra [b.5.B] [b.5.C]), the slope and intercepts of graphs (TEKS 111.32. Algebra [b.6.A] [b.6.B] [b.6.E] [b.6.F]), and the formulation of equations and inequalities (TEKS 111.32. Algebra [b.7.A] [b.7.B] [b.7.C]).

At a sixth workstation named *The Doghouse*, students study quadratic and step functions as well as linear functions and explore the relationship between perimeter and area by designing a doghouse. They use a scientific calculator to enter data and sketch graphs and discuss findings in a word-processed document complete with multiple representations of data. This workstation addresses function concepts, the relationship between equations and inequalities, algebraic thinking, underlying mathematical processes (TEKS 111.32. Algebra I [a.3] [a.4] [a.5] [a.6]), foundations for functions (TEKS 111.32. Algebra [b.1.A] [b.1.B] [b.1.D] [b.1.E]), properties and attributes of functions (TEKS 111.32. Algebra [b.2.B] [b.2.D]), the power of symbols to represent situations (TEKS 111.32. Algebra [b.3.A] [b.3.B]), linear functions (TEKS 111.32. Algebra [b.5.B] [b.5.C]), and formulation of equations and inequalities (TEKS 111.32. Algebra [b.7.C]).

In all of these activities, students apply functions, connect the rate of change to positive and negative slopes, convert metric units to and from standard units, or derive a "solution" of a function. They apply technology and learn by doing as they conduct the work of algebraic functions. Each student rotates through the workstations until they have completed all five of the activities; the five activities combined compose a home maintenance plan. During their work on the home maintenance project, students are actively engaged in inquiry, research, and/or design, and they have collaboratively produced meaningful products for assessment by the teacher.

Of course, prior to the students' arrival, the teacher designed the classroom environment by developing lessons, collecting necessary materials, and distributing activities and materials across workstations. He or she also designed rubrics describing how students will be assessed so that both the teacher and the students have clarity regarding expectations and so that the teacher has a tool for providing feedback to each student. As students work, the teacher addresses students' questions regarding both content and structure of the activities. The teacher also intervenes when he or she sees that the students are acting upon a misconception. The teacher provides guidance where it is needed and offers expert suggestions. After students hand in their projects, the teacher uses the rubrics to give them feedback and to generate scores for the grade book.

- Discovery Education's Puzzle Maker - http://puzzlemaker.school.discovery.com/
- Crossword Puzzle Games - http://www.crosswordpuzzlegames.com/create.html
- Flash Card Machine - http://www.flashcardmachine.com/
- Flash Card Maker - http://www.kitzkikz.com/flashcards

Figure 1. Helpful websites for creating materials for students.

Technology Integration in Curriculum

The five-phase Technology Integration Planning (TIP) Model (Roblyer, 2006) provides teachers with an approach for effectively integrating technology into teaching to specifically address standards and the needs of their students (see Figure 2). To help adopt and align objectives and assessments, teachers need to ask the following questions in phase one: "What exactly do I want students to learn and how will I know students have learned?" In the second phase teachers need to ask, "Why should I use a technology-based method?" to determine the relative advantage of integrating technology. In phase three teachers ask, "What teaching strategies and activities will work best?" In phase four teachers ask, "Is adequate hardware, software, and technical support available?" And in phase five they ask, "What worked well, and what could be improved?" For more information about Roblyer's TIP model, see Prentice Hall's Roblyer Gateway site (http://www.prenhall.com/roblyer).

Roblyer (2006) summarizes how to know when technology has been appropriately integrated in instruction with the following criteria: (1) an outside observer sees the technology activity as a seamless part of the lesson, (2) the reason for using the technology is obvious to you, the students, and others, (3) the students are focusing on learning, not on the technology, (4) you can describe how technology is helping a particular student, (5) you would have difficulty accomplishing lesson objectives if the technology were not there, (6) you can explain easily and concisely what the technology is supposed to contribute, and (7) all students are participating with the technology and benefiting from it. When all of the above criteria are met, teachers can have full confidence that technology is being effectively applied in their classroom.

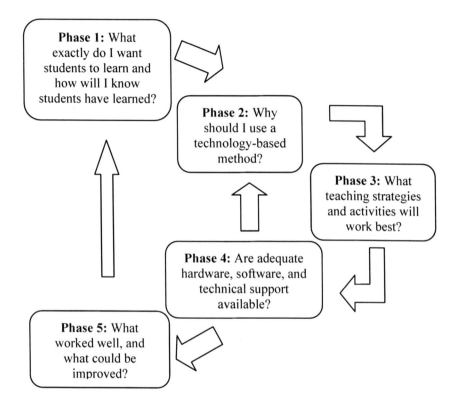

Figure 2. Five-phase technology integration model.

Teachers and Students Using Technology to Address Desired Outcomes, Assess Processes and Outcomes, and Give and Receive Feedback during PBL

The National Council of Teachers of Mathematics' Principles and Standards, the National Research Council's National Science Education Standards, and the International Society of Technology in Education's National Educational Technology Standards for both teachers and students all stress that technology is essential in teaching and learning in today's world. PBL, which calls for students to participate in lengthy, rich, and authentic tasks, can help them meet many standards simultaneously. Today's technology can be used by students to work effectively and creatively in science and mathematics when developing projects and solving problems, and students can participate in PBL collaboratively with diverse and even geographically dispersed groups.

With the vast array of possible technology applications comes the expectation that when teachers and students use technology in classrooms, learning takes place. However, to be effective, technology integration should be a response to a need for supporting student achievement of standards in the curriculum. The edutopia website provides teachers with a variety of suggestions for using PBL to boost student achievement (http://www.edutopia.org/projectbasedlearning).

Technology can be used by teachers to improve their teaching and the instruction they deliver and can expand and enrich learning opportunities for students so that they reach the highest standards of achievement. The way to assure that this happens in classrooms is to focus on desired student performances described by standards and align technology use with those performances. The technological capability applied by students during learning should align with both the objective and the assessment, (e.g., see Table 1).

Table 1. An Example of Technological Capability Aligned with Objective and Assessment

Objective	Assessment	Technological Capability
Replicate, display, and interpret temperature data in an experiment in pairs without assistance.	A rubric with points assigned to the quality of each step done in the experiment, graphs and spreadsheets produced, written summaries, and group work.	Collect, analyze, display, and interpret data using a calculator-based laboratory.

Just as scientists and mathematicians use technology every day as they conduct tasks, students need to know how to use technology to perform scientific and mathematical processes. There are two major categories of technology that empower students to collaboratively and cumulatively learn from instructors, experts, and peers in ways that they could not before. The first category is "applications" and includes multimedia tools (e.g., Audacity, QuickTime, Adobe Premiere, and Final Cut Pro), spreadsheets (e.g., Microsoft Excel and OpenOffice Calc), data analysis software (e.g., SPSS and SAS), telecommunication tools (e.g., iVisit, Adobe Connect, and WebEx) and graphics software (e.g., Macromedia Fireworks and Adobe Photoshop). These tools can be used by students as they create products. In addition, spreadsheets and gradebooks can be used by teachers to facilitate student assessment and feedback to students.

The second category is "web-based technologies," environments where students contribute to knowledge bases. Such technologies include blogging, wikis, image galleries, and webcasts. Blogs (e.g., http://www.weblogs.com) are websites that are publicly shared and are similar to a personal journal where entries are written in chronological order. Wikis (e.g., http://wikipedia.com) are collaborative websites where students can both contribute entries and edit others' entries. Image galleries (e.g., http://flickr.com) are sites that allow users to post and comment on photos and graphic image productions in public galleries much like photo albums.

Webcasts (e.g., United Nations Webcast at http://www.un.org/webcast/) are the streaming of a media file over the Internet for public listening and/or viewing and commenting. This technology can be used for providing peer and instructor feedback to students regarding their written and multimedia productions as they work on projects.

Such technology supports higher-order learning, and often, when it is thoughtfully applied, it empowers students to achieve objectives that they could not achieve without technical tools. With the help of technology, students can confidently embark on projects requiring them to investigate, experiment, write, model scientific and mathematical phenomena, collaborate, express, design, and visualize.

Sample web pages with PBL designed to address the curriculum include the Jason Project, Journey North, ePals Classroom Exchange, and The Global Grocery List Project. One website that provides educators with information about how to effectively integrate technology is the Education with New Technology website, which provides resources, interactive tools, and pictures of practices that support the integration of technology in curriculum and instruction (see Figure 3).

Just as instructional strategies should align with desired standards to be met by students, assessment strategies should align with standards addressed by PBL. For instance, after students have participated in PBL, teachers can hold them accountable for more than factual and conceptual knowledge. In fact, after participating in PBL, students might be assessed on their abilities to discriminate relevant from irrelevant information, create or produce a product, critically evaluate a similar project, or solve problems in the domain explored during the PBL experience.

Teachers can use technology for assessing student processes as they participate in PBL and on the products of a PBL activity. That is, teachers can enter student assessments on a hand-held computer customized for specific tasks as students progress trough the PBL. Knowing that they are being assessed as they proceed with their projects will encourage most students to work effectively within their groups. Depending on students' need for structure, teachers might assess them on a daily, weekly, or project-wide basis. Criteria might include staying with the group, sharing ideas, listening to others' ideas, and contributing to specific project-development steps. Once students have completed their projects, the teacher might choose to assess products of the group as a whole or as individuals, regarding student contributions to the products. Frequent assessment means that students receive frequent feedback and can adjust their processes and products accordingly.

During PBL, students could be required to reflect upon and document each learning activity in reflective journals. In addition, they can produce digital artifacts and organize them coherently in e-portfolios to represent work that addresses specific learning outcomes or standards. Student portfolios are "a collection of students' work products over time, arranged so that they and others can see how their skills have developed and progressed" (Roblyer, 2006, p. 27). For a teacher to grade individual artifacts in a portfolio, criteria for judging content should be specified by the teacher in advance.

- Prentice Hall's Roblyer Gateway - http://www.prenhall.com/roblyer
- The International Society of Technology in Education -
  http://www.iste.org
- Edutopia - http://www.edutopia.org/projectbasedlearning
- The Jason Project - http://www.jason.org/
- Journey North - http://www.learner.org/jnorth/
- ePals Classroom Exchange - http://www.epals.com/
- The Global Grocery List Project - http://landmark-project.com/ggl/
- Education with New Technology - http://learnweb.harvard.edu/ent
- Learning Point at the North Central Regional Educational Laboratory -
  http://www.ncrel.org/tech/
  http://www.ncrel.org/sdrs/areas/issues/educatrs/leadrshp/le700.htm
- Internet4Classrooms -
  http://www.internet4classrooms.com/integ_tech_lessons.htm
- Recipes4Success -
  http://myt4l.com/index.php?v=pl&page_ac=view&type=tools

Figure 3. Helpful websites for using technology to address desired outcomes.

During PBL, a meaningful way of specifying criteria for judging the quality of processes and products is through a rubric, "a tool represented as a set of scales used for assessing a complex performance," (Jonassen et al., 2008). When well designed, rubrics function in multiple ways for teachers and their students. First, they clarify expectations and provide an anticipatory set. Second, they structure an activity and guide students. Third, they provide for self-assessment and feedback. Selecting from a bank of existing rubrics or designing a rubric and then giving the rubric to students as they begin a project clarifies for both the teacher and student the goals and objectives of a project. Several rubric banks and tools for creating rubrics are available for teachers online (see Figure 4).

- Discovery School's Assessment and Rubric Information -
  http://school.discoveryeducation.com/schrockguide/assess.html
- Rubrics.com - http://www.rubrics.com
- Rubistar - http://rubistar.4teachers.org
- Rubric Machine - http://landmark-project.com/rubric_builder/

Figure 4. Helpful websites for creating rubrics.

Teachers and Students Using Technology to Provide Direction, Guidance, and Structure for PBL

As suggested above, rubrics selected from a rubric bank or created using a rubric development tool provide students with guidance and structure during PBL. They provide: (1) direction by clarifying expectations regarding the tasks, (2) guidance by describing the quality of elements of products and outline the stepwise processes so students can avoid being overwhelmed by the scale of a project, and (3) structure by describing standards for quality collaborative activity, the products and describes how points will be allocated for meeting deadlines.

In addition to using rubrics, successful teachers provide guidance by identifying conceptual misconceptions and providing scaffolds for learning. Students' misconceptions are best addressed by repeated manipulation of examples and non-examples that clearly illustrate distinguishing attributes of concepts (Cifuentes, McKintosh, & Douglas, 1997). Such illustrations can be generated by teachers and even by students using graphics software that typically come with computers (Cifuentes & Hsieh, 2001).

Scaffolds are controlled instruction for "the task[s] that are initially beyond the learner's capacity, thus permitting him to concentrate upon and complete only those elements that are within his range of competence" (Wood, Bruner, & Ross, 1976, p. 90). Tutorials and visualizations that scaffold complex concept acquisition are available on thousands of topics and can be accessed by learners on an as-needed, individualized basis if teachers point their students in the right direction. Information technology enables all learners, regardless of location and socioeconomic status, to access resources, information, experts, mentors, and peers. Technology enables teachers to address misconceptions and provide scaffolds for students with diverse learning styles, abilities, and interests by providing them with multiple modes of representation of content including audio or visual presentations; text-based materials; kinesthetic, hands-on materials; and music (see Figure 5).

- Merit Software - http://www.meritsoftware.com/
- Wolfram Demonstration Projects - http://www.demonstrations.wolfram.com/
- Web Lessons - http://www.weblessons.com/
- Vmath Live - http://www.vmathlive.com/
- Plato Learning - http://www.plato.com/
- Texas Instruments - http://www.ti.com/

Figure 5. Helpful websites for providing guidance and structure for PBL.

Teachers and Students Using Technology to Make STEM Relevant During PBL

"Why do we have to do this project?" is just an example of the questions teachers may face in a classroom where students participate in PBL. What this question suggests is that students think the topic they are studying is not relevant to them, and therefore, they are not motivated to work on the project. The Attention, Relevance, Confidence, and Satisfaction (ARCS) model was developed by Keller (1987) as a system for addressing student motivation by delivering instruction that appeals to the learner. The model represents "the principles for (1) gaining and then maintaining learner attention through instruction that is (2) perceived by the learners to be relevant for their personal needs and goals, (3) at the appropriate level of difficulty so that learners are confident they can succeed if they try, and (4) perceived by learners as satisfying in terms of rewards for their investments" (Dick, Carey, & Carey, 2005, p. 353).

Technology can be applied to address ARCS during PBL. To gain students' attention, teachers need to identify their students' interests. Once they know their students, at the beginning of instruction they can use attention getters such as short movie clips, stories, or current events related to the project. For example, teachers can search online video databases such as Discovery Education Streaming and ReefVid to identify video clips that might trigger interest in their students (Cifuentes & Dylak, 2007). Once attention is gained, a teacher must sustain the attention during PBL by guiding students through projects that are perceived by them to be relevant. Teachers can build blogs or discussion boards where students reflect upon project activities by answering questions such as, "Why is this project important? How might you use what you are learning in the future? Or, what aspects of the project interest you most?" Online resources such as Multimedia Educational Resource for Learning and Online Teaching (MERLOT at http://www.merlot.org) or National Library of Virtual Manipulatives (NLVM at http://nlvm.usu.edu) provide tools that have a history of successfully motivating students (see Figure 6).

Confidence comes from building a level of expectation for success (Dick et al., 2005) and students who expect to succeed are more motivated than under-confident and over-confident learners. Thus, teachers' knowing the entry skill level for each student is important so that they can assign students projects on which they can succeed. Frequent assessment using rubrics and quizzes helps teachers provide different levels of instruction on an individualized basis. The feedback from those assessments gives students both confidence during PBL that they can master the objectives and satisfaction after PBL that they have met the challenge and are learning.

Students gain satisfaction both by learning, which is intrinsically motivating, and through extrinsic reinforcements. Teachers can use, for example, free time, grading, some form of recognition, applause, or a certificate as an extrinsic reinforcement. Because students experience success in PBL at their own level and are challenged to learn, they tend to experience more confidence and satisfaction than they do in more traditional drill and practice activities (Starkman, 2007).

- Discovery Education Streaming -
  http://streaming.discoveryeducation.com
- ReefVid - http://www.reefvid.org
- Multimedia Educational Resource for Learning and Online Teaching
  (MERLOT) – http://www.merlot.org
- National Library of Virtual Manipulatives (NLVM) - http://nlvm.usu.edu
- Apangea Learning - http://www.apangea.com/

Figure 6. Helpful websites for creating relevant materials for students.

Teachers and Students Using Technology to Learn Collaboratively, Make Thinking Visible, and Conduct Minds-On Activities

When students are learning collaboratively and making their thinking visible, they provide evidence that their minds are on topic. Taking full advantage of technology tools that support collaborative and cooperative construction of knowledge among students honors and nurtures the diverse intelligences manifested within teachers' classrooms (Gardner, 1999). Cooperative, collaborative learning involves "students working together in a small enough group that everyone can participate on a collective task that has been clearly assigned" (Cohen et al., 1994). During such group work, students complete tasks without the direct or immediate input from the teacher. Rather, students make their own decisions in consultation with the teacher serving as a facilitator or coach.

Emergent read/write web (Web 2.0) technology such as wikis, weblogs, Real Simple Syndication, webcasts, and interactive photo/video galleries such as *YouTube* (http://www.youtube.com) empower users to actively contribute to the content of the Internet and broadly share learning with each other. Web 2.0 technology allows learners to add or edit content on a web page with little or no knowledge of html coding. Students can contribute ideas to a global conversation and archive that contribution for future audiences (Cifuentes & Dylak, 2007). For instance, see Apple's Educator Advantage website for ideas for how iPods can be used by students for mathematics and science learning (http://www.apple.com/education/educatoradvantage/).

By 2003, 44% of adult Internet users had participated in the interactive capabilities of the Internet by posting in at least one Web 2.0 environment (Lenhart, Fallows, & Horrigan, 2004), and, as many know, youths are blogging and vlogging as much as youth of earlier generations watched television or played video games. Internet 2.0 technology affords collaborative construction of content from diverse sources with students serving as contributors, editors of others' contributions, and consumers. When an educational goal involves evaluating, gathering, managing, and disseminating information, Web 2.0 technology is an excellent media. All of the tasks described above can be accomplished collaboratively, efficiently, and democratically with read/write web technology and can affect a broad audience.

Telecommunications tools, including Web 2.0 technology, allow students to "telecollaborate" (Harris, 1998) or accomplish curriculum-related goals in groups of two or more. A discussion of types of telecollaborative activities are described at Virtual Architecture's website (http://virtual-architecture.wm.edu/). Harris categorizes telecollaborative activities that support curricular goals as (1) interpersonal exchange, (2) information collection and analysis, or (3) problem solving.

With today's technology, students can learn from the perspectives of students and experts around the world. Pairs or groups of students can participate in interpersonal exchange using email, conferencing software, real-time audio or video conferencing, collaborative documents, or webcasts. Students might be each others' keypals simply for purposes of negotiating meaning about scientific and mathematical concepts, or they might serve as mentors or mentees to each other. Experts can serve as guest speakers in classrooms without ever leaving their homes or workplaces. A projection system allows an entire classroom to meet with an expert via desktop videoconferencing systems such as MicroSoft's NetMeeting, Adobe Connect, Centra, or Breeze.

Several websites support partnerships with global classrooms for shared investigation of phenomena among global citizens. For instance, the iEARN project (http://iearn.org) provides resources teachers need to connect their students in the United States with classrooms in countries around the world. A teacher's manual of suggested activities and methods is at http://iearn.org/teachersguide.pdf. In addition, the GlobalSchoolNet.org website provides multiple links to teacher and student resources, student competitions, a registry of global projects to join, and hundreds of other helpful tools to support exchange among students.

During information exchange, virtual field trips, database creation, pooled data-analysis, and electronic publishing activities, students are able to collect, compile, and compare information from different sources and therefore gain a broad view on a science or mathematics topic. For instance, the largest, most sustainable, and most successful project of its kind, Global Learning and Observations to Benefit the Environment (http://www.globe.gov), is a worldwide, hands-on, primary and secondary school-based, science and education program that supports and encourages students, teachers, and scientists to collaborate on inquiry-based investigations of the environment and the Earth system.

As students conduct PBL, they can collaboratively problem solve by sharing and compiling results of information searches, they can respond to each others' questions and misconceptions by providing each other with peer feedback online, or they can synthesize or add to each others' work in databases or online collaborative documents facilitated by software such as Google Docs, which allows them to together contribute to and edit a document from different desktops (see Figure 7).

Visual thinking. Current educational reform efforts seek to improve student understanding of STEM by promoting lifelong learning such that knowledge can be integrated across topics in school and applied to real-world problems (Linn, 2000). On the other hand, in schooling, the processes of thinking are often invisible to both the students and the teacher. Cognitive apprenticeship, which is a model of instruction that goes back to traditional apprenticeship but incorporates elements of schooling (Collins, Brown, & Newman, 1989), can be used as a model of instruction that works to make thinking visible (Collins, Brown, & Hollum, 1991). Each project that students participate in can be thought of as a brief, cognitive apprenticeship. In the traditional notion of apprenticeship, the process of carrying out a task to be learned is usually easily observable. Thus, in cognitive apprenticeship, one needs to deliberately bring the thinking to the surface, in other words, to make it visible to make learning happen (Collins et al., 1991).

Researchers in both education and science agree that visualization facilitates scientific and mathematical thinking (Hsieh & Cifuentes, 2006). Clark states that "visualization has been the cornerstone of scientific progress throughout history. Much of modern physics is the result of the superior abstract visualization abilities of a few brilliant men.... Virtually all comprehension in science, technology, and even art calls on our ability to visualize" (as cited in Earnshaw & Wiseman, 1992, p. v). In fact, the ability to visualize is almost synonymous with understanding. The expression "I see" is often used to mean "I understand."

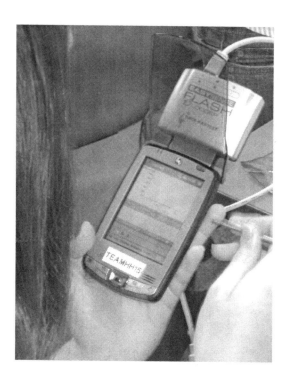

- Apple's Educator Advantage website -
  http://www.apple.com/education/educatoradvantage/
- Virtual Architecture's website - http://virtual-architecture.wm.edu/
- iEARN project - http://www.iearn.org/projects/
- iEARN project - A Teacher's Guide to a Global Classroom -
  http://iearn.org/teachersguide.pdf
- GlobalSchoolNet.org - http://www.gsn.org/
- Global Learning and Observations to Benefit the Environment
  (GLOBE) - http://www.globe.gov/
- Google Docs - http://docs.google.com
- Marcos' Seaworld of Facts - http://itc.blogs.com/marcos/
- Manila Website and Weblog Publishing System -
  http://manila.userland.com/
- Pre-Cal 40S - http://pc40s.blogspot.com/
- EduBlog Insights - http://anne.teachesme.com/
- Bloglines - Most Popular Blogs -
  http://www.bloglines.com/topblogs
- Blogger - http://www.blogger.com/
- Wikipedia - http://en.wikipedia.org/wiki/Weblog
- Pbwiki - http://pbwiki.com/education.wiki
- Flickr - http://www.flickr.com/
- TeacherTube - Teach the World - http://www.teachertube.com/
- Jamendo - Open Your Ears - http://www.jamendo.com/en/
- Stumble Video - http://video.stumbleupon.com/
- MediaFire - Free File Hosting Made Simple -
  http://www.mediafire.com/
- Veoh - Online Video Guide -
  http://www.veoh.com/browse/videos.html?category=Education
- Digital Ethnography -
  http://mediatedcultures.net/ksudigg/?page_id=2
- SC Education Program Wiki - http://sc07.sc-
  education.org/wiki/index.php/Main_Page

Figure 7. Helpful websites for creating collaborative learning environment for students.

An almost infinite array of tools provide teachers with existing visual representations that will help them illustrate concepts they want their students to understand. For instance, Discovery Education Streaming (http://streaming. discoveryeducation.com) contains a database of searchable video clips that teachers can show their students when delivering a lesson; clipart galleries such as

Classroom Clipart website (http://classroomclipart.com) contain images that can be incorporated into instruction; and websites such as National Geographic's Education website (http://www.nationalgeographic.com/education) contain illustrations embedded in thousands of lesson plans (see Figure 8). In addition, teachers can generate their own instructional graphics using paint and draw packages such as PhotoShop, Flash, and Illustrator. Instruction in how to create graphics for learning and performance are at Lohr's (2008) Visual Literacy website (http://www.coe. unco.edu/LindaLohr).

In addition to teacher-presented visuals that help students understand concepts with fundamental understandings, opportunities for students to generate visuals provide active engagement with content, practice with feedback, revision, and reflection. Rather than simply receiving content from a teacher, students can create visuals as they build understanding in the context of mentoring from their teacher who helps them find connections among concepts. Connections that are obvious to a scientist or teacher may be far from obvious to a pupil. Concept-mapping tools such as Inspiration and MicroSoft Visio can facilitate this process (Hsieh & Cifuentes, 2003, 2006; Kwon & Cifuentes, 2007).

Collins et al. (1991) proposed that students "make thinking visible" by generating textual representations, diagrams or illustrations, and models and simulations. Textual representations describe in words various aspects of a phenomenon, diagrams or illustrations represent static features of a phenomenon, and models and simulations attempt to show the casual mechanisms as well as dynamic and temporal features of a phenomenon. Each type of knowledge representation supports different information-processing affordances for learners (Cifuentes & Hsieh, 2003a, 2003b).

- Discovery Education Streaming -
  http://streaming.discoveryeducation.com
- Classroom Clipart Web site - http://classroomclipart.com
- National Geographic Education -
  http://www.nationalgeographic.com/education/
- Linda Lohr's Visual Literacy Web site -
  http://www.coe.unco.edu/LindaLohr

Figure 8. Helpful websites for visual thinking.

Teachers and Students Using Technology to Promote Transfer, Autonomy, and Lifelong Learning from PBL

One of the beauties of PBL is that students work on complex tasks that actively engage them cognitively. Making sure that skills and understanding gained from a PBL experience are retained for accountability testing and application during later life are important concerns. "This can best be done by setting some variety of new tasks for the learner—tasks that require the application of what has been learned in situations that differ substantially from those used for the learning itself" (Gagne, Wager, Golas, & Keller, 2005). Variety and novelty of new projects that require students to apply their new skills and understanding repeatedly will assure that students transfer their learning to new contexts, are able to work autonomously, and pursue lifelong learning.

One of the complexities of PBL is that, because students tend to take different paths to fulfill the requirement of a project, each student learns slightly different skills. Therefore, the authors recommend that teachers keep a digitized record of skills learned by each learner during any given PBL and systematically readdress those skills in subsequent PBLs. A record of student competencies will help teachers fill gaps in each student's understanding, reinforce skill learning, and provide appropriate, individualized guidance and scaffolding.

Conclusion

In this chapter, by way of example, some technology tools have been presented that can be used by teachers to develop and assess PBL and support students as they embark on the complex tasks of PBL. Thousands of tools not mentioned in this chapter are available to teachers to support students' PBL. Those tools can be applied to clarify expectations, provide for frequent assessment and feedback, direct and guide students, provide structure, provide relevance, support collaboration and visible thinking, and promote transfer to other contexts for any given PBL. The classroom environment described at the beginning of the chapter was meant to provide an illustration of how technology can be used to support active, engaged learning in relevant problem solving. The authors hope that teachers can use this chapter to envision students conducting PBL in their own classrooms and that Roblyer's TIP Model will systematize the technology integration process to assure that technology is being used to facilitate rigorous student activities and not simply for its own sake. When teachers apply technology appropriately in classrooms, students are empowered to work autonomously and become lifelong learners.

REFERENCES

Cifuentes, L., & Dylak, S. (2007). Trigger visuals for cross-cultural online learning. *The International Journal of Continuing Engineering Education and Lifelong Learning, 17*(2–3), 121–137.

Cifuentes, L., & Hsieh, Y. C. (2001). Computer graphics for student engagement in science learning. *TechTrends, 45*(5), 21–23.

Cifuentes, L., & Hsieh, Y. C. (2003a). Visualization for construction of meaning during study time: A qualitative analysis. *International Journal of Instructional Media, 30*, 407–417.

Cifuentes, L., & Hsieh, Y. C. (2003b). Visualization for construction of meaning during study time: A quantitative analysis. *International Journal of Instructional Media, 30*, 263–273.

Cifuentes, L., McKintosh, K., & Douglas, J. (1997). What's wrong with this picture? Creating nonexamples in Adobe Pphotoshop. *Learning and Leading With Technology, 25*(2), 58–61.

Cohen, E. G., Lotan, R. A., Whitcomb, J. A., Balderrama, M. V., Cossey, R., & Swanson, P. E. (1994). Complex instruction: Higher-order thinking in heterogeneous classrooms. In S. Sharan (Ed.), *Handbook of cooperative learning methods* (pp. 82–96). Westport, CT: Greenwood Press.

Collins, A., Brown, J. S., & Hollum, A. (1991). Cognitive apprenticeship: Making thinking visible. *American Educator, 6*(11), 38–49.

Collins, A., Brown, J. S., & Newman, S. E. (1989). Cognitive apprenticeship: Teaching the craft of reading, writing and mathematics. In L. B. Resnick (Ed.), *Knowing, learning, and instruction: Essay in honor of Robert Glaser* (pp. 453–494). Hillsdale, NJ: Erlbaum.

Dick, W., Carey, L., & Carey, J. O. (2005). *The systematic design of instruction* (6th ed.). New York: Addison-Wesley.

Earnshaw, R. A., & Wiseman, N. (1992). *An introductory guide to scientific visualization.* New York: Springer-Verlag.

Gagne, R. M., Wager, W. W., Golas, K. C., & Keller, J. M. (2005). *Principles of instructional design.* (3rd ed.). Belmont, CA: Wadsworth.

Gardner, H. E. (1999). Multiple approaches to understanding. In C. M. Reigeluth (Ed.), *Instructional-design theories and models* (pp. 69–89). Mahwah, NJ: Erlbaum.

Harris, J. (1998). Curriculum-based telecollaboration. *Learning and Leading with Technology, 26*(1), 6–15.

Hsieh, Y. C., & Cifuentes, L. (2003). A cross-cultural study of the effect of student-generated visualization on middle-school science concept learning. *Educational Technology Research and Development, 51*(3), 90–95.

Hsieh, Y. C., & Cifuentes, L. (2006). Student-generated visualization as a study strategy for science concept learning. *Educational Technology and Society, 9*(3), 137–148.

Jonassen, D. H., Howland, J., Marra, R. M., & Crismond, D. (2008). *Meaningful learning with technology.*((3rd. ed.). Columbus, OH: Prentice Hall.

Keller, J. M. (1987). Strategies for stimulating the motivation to learn. *Performance and Instruction, 26*(8), 1–7.

Kwon, S. Y., & Cifuentes, L. (2007). Using computers to individually-generate vs. collaboratively generate concept maps. *Journal of Educational Technology and Society, 10,* 269–280.

Lenhart, A., Fallows, D., & Horrigan, J. (2004). *Content creation online: 44% of US internet users have contributed their thoughts and their files to the online world.* Pew Internet & American Life Project.

Linn, M. C. (2000). Designing the knowledge integration environment. *International Journal of Science Education, 22,* 781–796.

Lohr, L. (2008). *Creating graphics for learning and performance: Lessons in visual literacy* (2nd ed.). Upper Saddle River, NJ: Prentice Hall.

Roblyer, M. D. (2006). *Integrating educational technology into teaching* (4th ed.). Upper Saddle River, NJ: Pearson/Merrill Prentice Hall.

Starkman, N. (2007). Problem solvers. *THE Journal, 34*(10), 35–42.

Wood, D. J., Bruner, J. S., & Ross, G. (1976). The role of tutoring in problem solving. *Journal of Child Psychology and Psychiatry, 17,* 89–100.

Lauren Cifuentes
Department of Education Psychology, Educational Technology,
Texas A&M University

Serkan Özel
Department of Education Psychology, Educational Technology,
Texas A&M University

DENNISE A. SOARES AND KIMBERLY J. VANNEST

11. STEM PROJECT-BASED LEARNING AND TEACHING FOR EXCEPTIONAL AND DIVERSE LEARNERS

INTRODUCTION

Today's classroom is a heterogeneous grouping of students with diverse backgrounds and languages and with disabilities or special challenges in learning and behavior. This chapter is about how to reach these students through the use of Science, Technology, Engineering, and Mathematics (STEM) Project-Based Learning (PBL). Although the strategies and issues presented here are "best practice" for the instruction and management of students with enriched backgrounds, extensive vocabularies, and strong self-advocacy and self-management skills, these types of students may learn well without them. However, students with diverse or disabling conditions require these strategies for successful participation and learning. Students who are diverse, disabled, or not among this population will benefit from a learning environment where these practices are used skillfully. This chapter begins with a section on the characteristics and learning considerations for exceptional and diverse learners, followed by a section on the key elements of STEM PBL for diverse learners, and concluded with a section on how these elements can address learner characteristics to improve student participation and performance.

CHAPTER OUTCOMES

When you complete this chapter you should better understand:
- the characteristics and issues of diverse learners
- the essential elements of STEM PBL for diverse learners
- strategies to facilitate STEM PBL with learners who are diverse or disabled
  When you complete this chapter you should be able to:
- design STEM PBL to include exceptional and diverse learners
- modify STEM PBL to include exceptional and diverse learners

WHO ARE EXCEPTIONAL AND DIVERSE LEARNERS?

There is increasing interest in schooling and educating students effectively and efficiently so children ultimately take productive roles in society after schooling is over. This effort includes all students: disabled, nondisabled, culturally diverse, linguistically diverse, migrant, and native (Gonzalez, Yaw key, Minaya-Rowe, 2006;

R.M. Caparo and S. W. Slough (eds.), Project-Based Learning: An Integrated Science, Technology, Engineering, and Mathematics (STEM) Approach, 135–158.

No Child Left Behind, 2001; *Individuals with Disabilities Education* Act, 1997). Students from culturally and/or linguistically diverse backgrounds, as well as those who learn in atypical ways, bring diverse perspectives, skills, and experiences to the educational process, and this diversity enriches education but can challenge singular methods of instruction. Educators and educational systems have evolved to understand and better address the changing student population in public schools and communities.

A variety of terms are used to describe or characterize children for purposes of providing services, organizing instruction, and understanding learner characteristics. Although there are many children with diverse and/or disabled characteristics, each is individual and should first be recognized as such. However, terms help to identify and define the "types" of student groups, which will be discussed in this chapter. For our purposes of this chapter, students will be discussed and described by the terms English Language Learners (ELLs), children with Learning Disabilities (LD), and children with Emotional and Behavioral Disorders (EBD).

CHARACTERISTICS OF STUDENTS WHO ARE ENGLISH LANGUAGE LEARNERS

Definition

ELLs are students whose first language is not English and who need language assistance to participate fully in the regular curriculum. ELL students are also called Limited English Proficient (LEP) students, Second Language Learners, and sometimes Culturally and Linguistically Diverse (CLD).

Prevalence in Classrooms

The ELL student population continues to grow more rapidly than the student population as a whole. According to the National Center for Educational Statistics (U.S. Department of Education, 2006) the general population has grown 9% from

1993 to 2003, while the ELL population has grown 65% in that same time. The ELL student population now comprises 10% of all students (National Clearinghouse for English Language Acquisition and Language Instruction, 2006).

Characteristics

ELL students face the challenging task of mastering a new language while also learning subject-area content, and they are unlikely to have English-language assistance at home for academics or language acquisition. Although there have been signs of progress, including higher reading and mathematics scores for ELL students (Perie, Moran, & Lutkus, 2005), more improvement is needed. ELLs receive lower grades, are judged by their teachers to have lower academic abilities, and score below their classmates on standardized tests of reading and mathematics (Moss & Puma, 1995).

Special Considerations with ELL

Culture. Cultural differences can be a source of misunderstanding for teachers and their ELLs. People of all cultures express themselves both verbally and non-verbally. Non-verbal cues in one culture may represent something entirely different in another. For example, in Western cultures, when a student smiles at the teacher, it often indicates understanding. However, in many Asian cultures, smiling often camouflages confusion or frustration.

It is easy to forget that not all students share the same background knowledge or experiences. Analogies are often used to help students understand new concepts. Teachers of ELLs must be careful to consider whether their ELL students share the background knowledge to benefit from analogies. Analogies often refer to shared histories or cultural experiences. For example, comparing something to a common American childhood experience such as summer camp or Little League may not resonate with an ELL.

Educational experiences. New knowledge is built on the basis of what is already known by an individual. Schema is the connecting of meaning by cognitively attaching words on the page to related background knowledge. Often, school texts assume a common experience that, in fact, is not shared by all students; ELLs may not fully understand these texts and consequently, will be less likely to remember the content material. Students whose background experience is limited or different will often need additional explanation and examples to draw the connection between new material and their existing knowledge bases. However, these experiences may be tempered by their immigration status. The immigration status may also impact a learner's ability to participate in class projects that involve extended periods of time when their family travels with the parent's work group Students may not have access to resources outside of the classroom to complete assignments that involve home-school partnerships or negotiating the community. Both students and parents may have missed formal educational opportunities if immigration involved refugee status, long migration periods, war in homeland countries, extreme family hardship, or separation of parents and children. Tenuous legal status in the U.S. can lead to compromised learning and diminished benefit from PBL. Therefore, it is important to understand that students with high mobility may not benefit as much as those who have sustained PBL experiences.

CHARACTERISTICS OF STUDENTS WHO HAVE LEARNING DISABILITIES

Definition

The legal term schools use to classify a range of students for a service provision under federal mandate is learning disabled. A learning disability is identified by a discrepancy in intelligence scores and performance or as a failure to respond to effective instruction and repeated intervention. An LD is commonly demonstrated as a deficit in one or more of the following skill areas: language, reading, writing, listening, speaking, reasoning, and mathematics. The most commonly used definition first appeared in Public Law 94-142, the Education for All Handicapped Children Act (Federal Register, 1977). It was also a part of Public Law 101-476, the 1990 Individuals with Disabilities Education Act (IDEA) and is also a component of the 1997 Amendments to IDEA, Public Law 105-17. It reads as follows: The term "specific learning disability" means those children who have a disorder in one or more of the basic psychological process involved in understanding or using language, spoken or written, which disorder may manifest itself in imperfect ability to listen, think, speak, read, write, spell or perform mathematical computations.

Prevalence in Classrooms

In the United States, as many as 1 out of every 5 people have a LD. Almost 3 million children (ages 6-21) have some form of a LD and receive special education in school. In fact, over half of all children who receive special education have a LD (Twenty-Fourth Annual Report to Congress, U.S. Department of Education, 2002).

Characteristics

Students with LDs usually demonstrate needs in a variety of areas, such as performing consistently, following and understanding directions, reading, comprehending, writing, organizing and sequencing thoughts, retaining information, following more than one-step instructions or directions, interacting with peers appropriately, and self-esteem and confidence.

Special Considerations

Many LDs are not always "identified" formally, and some students may struggle with issues that remain unidentified. Students with slower mental processing but strong adaptive skills may avoid classification but still struggle with academic tasks and school performance demands. Government and institutional guidelines for identification also vary, and the term and definition itself is under scrutiny from the field. Regardless of identification or "status," students who struggle will benefit from best practice instruction. Teachers should be aware of that they may need to adjust the learning tasks, the deliverables, or the assessment for identified students. However, it is probably more important for teachers to remember that far more students go unidentified, yet they, too, would benefit from some form of accommodation that provides for modified expectations.

CHARACTERISTICS OF STUDENTS WHO HAVE EMOTIONAL AND BEHAVIORAL DISORDERS

Definition

The term EBD reflects a large, heterogeneous group of students who have emotional and or behavioral disabilities that interfere with school and learning. The federal definition of EBD includes the demonstration of severe social, emotional, or behavioral functioning that is significantly different from generally accepted, age appropriate ethnic or cultural norms, and these differences must appear for extended periods of time across a variety of settings. These social, emotional, or behavioral functions include social relationships, personal adjustment, classroom adjustment, self-care, and vocational skills. (Code of Federal Regulation, Title 34, Section 300.7(b)(9)).

Prevalence in Classrooms

The Methodology for Epidemiology of Mental Disorders in Children and Adolescents study estimated that almost 21% of U.S. children ages 9-17 had a diagnosable mental or addictive disorder associated with at least minimum impairment (Shaffer et al., 1996). In the 2000-2001 school years, 4.1% of pre-schoolers ages 3-5 and 8.2% of children and youth were provided special education and related services in public schools under the eligibility of Emotional and Behavioral Disabilities (Twenty-Fourth Annual Report to Congress, U.S. Department of Education, 2002). Boys outnumber girls somewhere between 2 to 1 and 10 to 1. Costello, Messer, Bird, Cohen, and Reinherz (1998) found "there were no clear ethnic differences" (p. 411), and poverty doubled the risk of severe emotional disturbance (SED). One in four children with identified with SED has received mental health care (Costello et al.)

Characteristics

By definition, students with EBD have many characteristics that interfere with school learning. Not surprisingly, many students with emotional disturbance experience poor academic performance. They fail more courses, earn lower grade point averages, miss more days of school, and are retained more than students with other disabilities

(Kauffman, 2001; Nelson & Rutherford, 1990; Nelson Rutherford, Center, & Walker, 1991). Fifty-five percent leave school before graduating (U.S. Department of Education, 2002). Within three years of leaving school, more than 50% of EBD students have had at least one arrest (Wagner, 1989), a stunning figure that is even more disturbing when one considers that experts in law enforcement estimate that there is, on average, only one arrest for every 10 "arrestable" offences committed (Merrell & Walker, 2004).

Special Considerations

Many children who do not have emotional disturbances may display some of these same behaviors at various times during their development. However, when children have an emotional disturbance, these behaviors continue over long periods of time, and their reaction to relatively small events is unexpected. Their behavior thus signals that they are not coping with their environment or peers. Students who are depressed due to the death of a parent are not EBD students, although they certainly are in need of special considerations. A student who is depressed and aggressive given no precursor needs a different level of intervention and has a different trajectory for recovery. Although PBL may help to ease students into social environments and create a bridge for mainstream learning, the teacher must be cognizant of the work that must be done to help prepare EBD students to work with peers and to help prepare those peers to work with EBD students.

For EBD students, additional services beyond strong academic programs are needed, but those special services should not supplant rigorous academic instruction. Students with EBD should not be removed from academic instruction and essential content to receive counseling or behavioral supports; instead, ideally, the PBL enviornment will support the student and provide opportunity for additional services concurrently with academics rather than present an "either or" scenario where struggling students fall farther behind academically.

Students with EBD may lack the social or parental support to accomplish aspects of projects that require sustained resources, access to community, or innovative approaches to problem solving. Sometimes students with inadequate coping skills or a history of trauma and neglect are members of a family system struggling with the same issues but without the mental health or behavioral support to assist them in developing coping mechanisms. Therefore, it is probably insufficient to expect the family alone to provide the necessary external supports to ensure that EBD students are successful with PBL. The teacher can make PBL accommodations for EBD students that do not compromise the academic rigor but do not rely on environments external to the school. For example, the teacher may choose to provide more structure by substituting early morning, late afternoon, or targeted assistance during school, especially during the PBL process.

KEY ELEMENTS OF STEM PROJECT-BASED LEARNING

PBL is an approach for classroom instruction that utilizes learning activities that are child-centered, have well-defined outcomes, are long-term in nature, and include interdisciplinary missions. In this section, the key elements of PBL and articulated examples for how these elements facilitate improved learning opportunities for diverse and disabled students are identified.

The context for where PBL typically takes place is a heterogeneous classroom. Webster's *Collegiate Dictionary* defines *heterogeneous* as "consisting of dissimilar ingredients or constituents: mixed" (Merriam Webster, n.d.). Rarely are students grouped by perceived ability-level or in heterogeneous learning environments. More than likely, students with different maturity levels, development levels, language, and disabilities are in the same classroom, which can add pressure to a stressed system or single instructor. Effective, efficient opportunities for learning content across disciplines in a way that is meaningful and allows individual strengths to be utilized and demonstrated are needed.

Students need to be able to successfully interact with an increasingly heterogeneous society. Because heterogeneous classrooms are a mix of various abilities and traits, students will have opportunities to work with others of various languages and intellectual, emotional, and physical development. These skills and experiences can generalize beyond individual projects. Heterogeneity allows students to socialize with, model, and adjust to a variety of peer influences (Spear, 1992).

Settings for PBL vary, but the nature of the task has child centeredness, extended time, well-defined outcomes, and an interdisciplinary mission as essential elements. PBL is child centered and as such reflects the experience and values of individual students while accomplishing the goals and objectives of the instructional leader. Extended time allows for deeper exploration and more opportunity for engagement. Well-defined outcomes make expectations explicit and provide structure to encourage student participation. The interdisciplinary mission allows for repeated exposure to content, explicit connections when necessary, and opportunities to generalize skills to deepen understanding.

Child Centered

Definition. A child-centered learning environment is structured to facilitate independence, self-direction, and autonomy. Child-centered learning encourages critical thinking and problem solving. PBL is an instructional method centered on the learner. Instead of a lesson plan that directs learner activity specifically towards learning outcomes or objectives, it specifies the learning with myriad activities and options intrinsic in an ill-defined task. The child or learner (rather than the instructor) directs his or her activities towards that end.

Relevance and significance. PBL allows in-depth investigation of a topic worth learning more about (Harris & Katz, 2001). Through the building of artifacts, learners represent and demonstrate what they learned (Harel & Papert, 1991; Kafai & Resnick,

1996). Potentially, learners demonstrate more autonomy and self-determination over how they learn and sometimes what specifically they learn. This is theorized to maintain interest and motivate learners to take more responsibility for their learning (Tassinari, 1996; Wolk, 1994; Worthy, 2000) and be more actively engaged. More independence allows learners to "shape their projects to fit their own interests and abilities" (Moursund, 1998, p. 4) or to accommodate their difference or disability.

Extended Period of Time

Definition. Extended period of time (EPT) is a characteristic of PBL and identifies a task or assignment, objective or outcome that requires multiple, distributed efforts to complete. Extended time might also be conceptualized as an extended task. A project as part of its nature has multiple components, each requiring time to complete, and all of which lead to the well-defined outcome. Some call this problem-based learning; however, it is essential to conceptualize PBL as being composed of many problems that need to be solved to successfully complete the project. For more information, see the Introduction to Chapter 1 and Chapter 5, Etiology of STEM PBL.

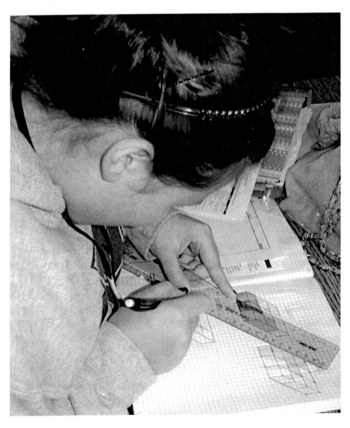

Example of Child Centeredness and PBL: How child centeredness is illustrated in PBL is demonstrated in this science example. Students independently or in groups organize by interest and are asked to develop "science for mankind" projects. Students use their interests, expertise, strengths, and experiences to first identify and then solve a community problem. One student from Tijuana who crosses the border to attend school in San Diego may observe that trash blows both directions across the border and that neither town wants to "pick it up," in his words, because no one feels like it is theirs. Other students join this "team" to brainstorm solutions and decide to write an ad campaign called "Wind and waste have no borders" *"El viento y el desecho no tienen las fronteras"* and to write letters to city leaders to add more trash cans along the pedestrian walks and within a one-mile radius. They also determine to sponsor a weekend for trash pick up once a year and find adult service groups to help make tortillas and face-paint children. T-shirts with the slogan in English and Spanish are designed and sold, and the classroom donates the money to fund more trashcans and a billboard on both sides of the border.

A teacher's role and responsibility is to create a "concept"-rich classroom— providing materials, tools, opportunities, and guidance, encouraging children to make choices and to interact with the environment and other children. Students learn to gain and demonstrate knowledge and skills through meaningful experiences. Play and experimentation are valued as contexts in which learning takes place. The elements that make child centeredness successful with students who are diverse or disabled are (1) Creating an environment that is risk tolerant and safe for "un-success," (2) maintaining active engagement, (3) scaffolding for success, and (4) encouraging self-reliance, problem solving, and critical thinking.

Figure 1. Example of child centered PBL.

Relevance and significance. Learning is related to time on task or engaged time. The time special learners spend learning, leading, thinking, directing, responding, planning, and executing is time well spent. This is opposed to discrete tasks, where there is no explicit connection to the next task or the one that preceded it. Extended time to complete a project facilitates understanding and application of knowledge and skills in meaningful ways. Extended time projects teach students the same content typically taught through lecture and discussion but add the components of relevancy and extended engagement to the learning task. PBL teachers find that they assign considerably less "busy work," spending less time generating these

Example of PBL that demonstrates extended time. Traditional research papers quickly come to mind, but school publications in all their variations are also examples of extended time projects. Yearbooks, school papers, newsletters, campus blogs, or calendars are some of the variants. Consider a science class newsletter; this could be as relevant for a high school freshman as a fourth-grader. Emma and Jack are creative storytellers, Fisher and Dalton are strong spellers, Lo Lo, Bart, and Mike like to know everybody's business and frequently sneak food from the cafeteria. Barry is an organizer whereas Ally and Ben are more socially- than academically-minded. The teacher, Mr. Agerwal, decides to start an ongoing, science class newsletter. Students are assigned roles based on teacher-observed interest. With an organizational chart established, this assignment takes place every Friday. Science facts and new science spelling words are incorporated, some students collect and/or write fiction, others edit, a student with significant disabilities contributes jokes of the month whereas others distribute papers, some students are responsible for counting and tallying words and space, some are responsible for "management and organization," other students keep track of science experiments, and one or two do interviews with science-related people in a "guess who" section that is a favorite of students. Weekly tasks relate to monthly publishing, ongoing features are carried forward, and certain students develop strengths in writing up the news whereas others learn to motivate their peers.

The extended time and ongoing nature of the science newsletter allows students to mentally remain on task even when not specifically engaged in writing assignments; as students go about their day on campus they think of new story ideas or ways to make the newsletter better. Some jobs might be rotated based on interest and skill or as a reward for contribution. On the board there is a list of story ideas and the enduring brainstorming keeps kids involved and interested. Ben decides to add cartoon humor when he notices a Sunday paper at home. Ally wants to add "dress for weather" tips for each month as a regular feature. Barry decides to explore the business aspect and develops a business plan that includes expenses and income based on paying students for stories and charging parents a quarter for the newsletter. Bart adds recipes from the cook at school, and Fisher loves being asked how to spell science words. Mr. Anderson, a mathematics teacher, even has a regular section on "solving the latest math jumble." State standards in science, mathematics, spelling, reading, social studies, writing, and problem solving are addressed each week in the curriculum and revisited recursively as the class publishes one newsletter each month for the academic year.

Figure 2. Example of PBL that demonstrates extended time.

tasks, managing behavior, and evaluating the "busy work." However, there is a time trade-off with PBL because projects require time to plan, but teachers have more time to work with students once a project is under way, and assessment is an integral component of this time spent with students.

The elements that make extended time especially beneficial for students who are diverse or disabled are the repeated opportunities to engage the material, the explicit connections, and the increased time on task.

Scaffolding

Diverse learners usually have difficulty working independently and require extensive guidance at first. "Scaffolding" refers to the personal guidance, assistance, and support that a teacher, peer, or task provides to a learner. One way to scaffold instruction for diverse learners is to differentiate learning tasks and materials and provide a variety of verbal and academic supports from both the teacher and more-proficient peers, so that students are able to meaningfully engage in content-area learning and acquire the necessary language and academic skills necessary for independent learning.

- Successful scaffolding includes a variety of components:
- First, teachers must provide continuity in the classroom. In this way, teachers present tasks that are repeated throughout instructional sequences with variations that are interconnected to each other and the curriculum.
- Secondly, teachers must also provide support from context. Students should be encouraged to explore topics in a risk-free learning environment and be provided with a variety of ways to meet learning goals and objectives.
- Finally, teachers must create learning contexts where learners increase their autonomy as their skills and confidence increase.
- Continuity of tasks will facilitate learners in being able to take over portions of the task and become independent learners.

Well-Defined Outcome

Perhaps the most challenging element in PBL, but key for diverse learners, is the idea of a well-defined outcome. "Without a destination, any road will take you there," is a good adage for the use of PBL without well-defined outcomes. Well-defined outcomes ensure two things: explicit expectations for the student and an appropriate outcome for measurement and evaluation. Learning is ultimately a change in behavior for students who say, "I know that" but cannot demonstrate how they know it, which is an unfortunate position. Demonstration of knowledge and skills is ultimately what teachers must rely on until new technology for measuring what students know is available.

Definition. Well defined is not the same as predetermined. A well-defined outcome is a clear articulation of purpose and expectation. For example, a teacher may assign an artistic representation of the voyage of the pilgrims that includes three factual depictions and one illustration of causation. But it does not predetermine that the project must show a model ship or Plymouth Rock or reflect oppression or religious freedom. The desired outcome is selected first, and the curriculum is created to support the intended outcome, in this case, facts about the voyage and an understanding about causation.

Relevance and significance. Investment in long-term substantive learning is prompted by relevant tasks that are meaningful to students and not because they need to learn them for a test. Engaging in the activity will help students learn and provide opportunity for them to be stimulated, demonstrate skills, and experience successes. Clearly-defined outcomes reflect the notion that having outcomes articulated is not stifling but supportive. Well-defined outcomes produce structure, goals, and mutual understanding about purpose while affording individuality in the selection of the path to the destination. This concept promotes three basic premises: (1) All students can learn and succeed, but not all in the same time or in the same way, (2) successful learning promotes even more successful learning, and (3) schools (and teachers) control many of the conditions that determine whether or not students are successful at school learning.

Well-Defined Outcomes. There are three levels of defining outcomes: (1) global outcome descriptor, (2) outcome with required components, and (3) outcome valuations in fair and credible ways.

Figure 3. Example that demonstrates well-defined outcomes.

Table 1. Examples of Levels of Defined Outcomes

Global Outcome Descriptor	Outcome with Required Components	Outcome, Components, and Valuation
Produce a slide show of native plants	Produce a slide show of native plants	Produce a slide show of native plants
	Show 5 plants in one genus	Show 5 plants in one genus (25 pts, 5 each)
	Use text from 2 sources	Use text from 2 sources (20 pts, 10 each)
	Use photos from surrounding flora	Use photos from surrounding flora (25 pts, 5 each, bonus for more plant examples, additional sources, creativity (up to 5 pts)

Well-defined outcomes allow diverse and disabled learners to have appropriate levels of scaffolding, make choices about task relevance, and better understand teacher expectations for performance.

Interdisciplinary

There is also an interdisciplinary aspect of PBL. The interdisciplinary nature of PBL allows diverse students to learn horizontally across curriculum rather than only vertically. Interdisciplinary projects also allow for instructional collaboration, cross pollination of ideas, and the repetition of concepts in new and different applications to understand the relevance and facilitate fluency, mastery, and generalization of skills.

Definition. Interdisciplinary teaching involves a conscious effort to apply knowledge, principles, and/or values to more than one academic discipline simultaneously. The disciplines may be related through a central theme, issue, problem, process, topic, or experience (Jacobs, 1989). The organizational structure of interdisciplinary/ cross-curricular teaching is often referred to as a theme, thematic unit, unit, or project, which is a framework with goals/outcomes that specify what students are expected to learn as a result of the experiences and lessons that are a part of the unit. In general, PBL is thematic in nature and nearly impossible to consolidate into single subject areas.

Relevance and significance.   Although students are learning the basic information in core subject areas, they are not learning to apply their knowledge for effective thinking and reasoning (Applebee, Langer, & Mullis, 1989). Interdisciplinary/ cross-curricular teaching provides a method by which students can use knowledge learned in one context as a knowledge base in other contexts in and out of school (Collins, Brown, & Newman, 1989). Clarity on the relationship of content to standards provides opportunities to articulate relevance in instruction and assignments. In this way, teachers better ensure that the students learn a concept necessary for a project. Teachers working together can develop ways to tie projects in with their curriculum goals (Bottoms & Webb, 1998).

Example of the interdisciplinary nature of problem-based learning. Juniors at Theoretical High School take two standard electives each fall, *Home Economics* and *Intro to Business*. These two class teachers, one in a high school Home Economics department and the other in the Business department, develop a joint class project where students will operate a student store selling baked goods and sandwiches. Students rotate tasks of manager, sales, accounting, distribution, and maintenance while in the business class, and these same students use the budgets and funds to plan menus, purchase ingredients, and produce the food items for sale. Back in the business class, different mathematics applications are used to count money, deposit money, and develop staff schedules. Students have to plan meet payroll when "pay" is earned and profits are distributed. The class sells stock to teachers and charges extra for premium delivery service. Adding menu items is determined based on sales; decision-making, based on data, is an outcome for both the home economics course and the business class.

Teachers dedicate some days a month for "block" classes that run back to back so students can work in groups. As the semester progresses, the speech class has students become involved in "arbitration" and disputes about pay and management style. The science teacher uses the opportunity to collect bacteria samples from old chicken salad, and students see and participate in interdisciplinary learning opportunities.

Figure 4. Example of the interdisciplinary nature of problem-based learning.

Many of the important concepts, strategies, and skills taught in the language arts are "portable" (Perkins, 1986). They transfer readily to other content areas. The concept of perseverance or conflict of ideas, for example, may be found in literature and science, mathematics, geography, history, vocational arts, and fine arts. Strategies for monitoring comprehension can be directed to reading material in any content area. Critical thinking can be applied in any discipline. Cause-and-effect relationships exist in literature, science, and social studies. Interdisciplinary/cross-curricular teaching supports and promotes this transfer by providing different applications and practice opportunities that are relevant and more naturally occurring. It is this interdependency of the learning that maximizes learning for the diverse student and these experiences that will reinforce their learning and compensate for deficits in the home environment.

Implementation of STEM PBL offers teachers a useful, logical, and flexible way to organize for interdisciplinary teaching over a block of time (Tchudi, 1991). Throughout the project, teachers are able to integrate content-area study and engage students in meaningful and functional learning activities (Tompkins & Hoskisson, 1991). Interdisciplinary units should comprise the types of activities that promote and support the active construction of meaning for students (Pappas, Kiefer, & Levstik, 1990). These include opportunities for students to work independently or cooperatively to solve "real world" problems (Ward, 1988); opportunities to read and respond to authentic literature; discussions with peers and the teacher about what has been read or heard; teacher-led lessons for the whole class or small groups that focus on a needed concept, strategy, or skill; and self-selected student activities such as books to be read or activities to be done.

With PBL, students synthesize and collaborate on their learning in response to the project question(s) by examining evidence or previous knowledge from multiple disciplines.

COMMON FEATURES AND CHALLENGES FOR DIVERSE LEARNERS

For teachers, success in the classroom is not just a matter of knowing the subject; it is a matter of knowing the students. Having a working knowledge of the characteristics of development and differences or disabilities of students is critical to the success of the teaching and learning experience. Each key element and common feature of PBL has its own challenges for diverse learners.

In this chapter the characteristics of diverse learners were identified and next some key elements of PBL were articulated with examples for heterogeneous classrooms. These two things, characteristics of learners and elements of PBL, can work together in powerful ways to address the needs of diverse and disabled learners and assist in ensuring the successful participation and performance of all students.

Certain characteristics of students who are diverse or disabled pose particular challenges for the classroom and learning. This section will articulate some of the most common characteristics in students that create challenges for instructors.

Language and Cultural Differences

Differences and disabilities in language knowledge and skills can make traditional lecture inaccessible for the students. Heterogeneous learning environments provide opportunities to close the learning gap when peers are engaged in peer-tutoring in small, cooperative grouping. Working on group projects in heterogeneous learning environments provides an opportunity for both ELLs and native English-speaking students to be immersed further in a topic by taking more time to comprehend a topic through peer explanation and recursive activities. Extended time to engage when language may interfere with understanding provides more opportunity for learning. Child centeredness can facilitate all students' interest and motivate engagement and can take advantage of cultural capital. The interdisciplinary nature of PBL provides repeated opportunity to engage with the vocabulary and concepts in new and different contexts.

Further, instructors can accommodate the lack of background knowledge often faced by ELLs by creating opportunities for experience and language acquisition to provide more background knowledge through active participation and physical experience rather than lecture or text. PBL offers an alternative method for demonstrating knowledge and skill by including assignments that use model presentation, visual presentation, graphs, maps, and pictures.

Reading Complications

Many diverse, disabled learners read below their age or grade level, making text inaccessible as a method of learning. PBL can enhance students' ability to access content through the introduction of a variety of "scaffolding" techniques (learning aids, models, training strategies). Teachers can provide schematic maps, visual aids, charts, and graphs; they can simplify text, pre-teach key vocabulary, and provide audio supplements. Other strategies to teach students include the skill of breaking down tasks, creating models, content mapping, highlighting, and looking for cues in text. Teachers in class can use prompting and coaching to teach strategies for thinking and problem solving.

Deficits in Processing Speed

Slower-than-typical processing can occur as a disability or due to second language learning conditions. Teachers can address the variation in the speed with which students perform cognitive activities by utilizing the extended time of PBLs, and they can modify their instruction to include writing down the well-defined outcomes, adjusting the pace of instruction, and providing more time for asking and answering questions.

Motivation

Students with disabling or diverse backgrounds may find much of what is done in school to be irrelevant, or students may have experienced lack of success to the extent that they are no longer willing to try, risk, or engage. The use of PBLs can address this in several ways. The child-centered nature of the task addresses relevancy and interest to propel motivation. The extended for learning time and interdisciplinary nature of PBL may provide a context for students to risk participation and pull from a content knowledge strength to assist in the learning of skills in other content areas. Well-defined outcomes can provide safe and structured environments where students understand clear expectations and are willing to engage. PBL can feel more palatable and be motivating for students as the pace, topic, and level of difficulty can be individualized with projects broken into smaller, manageable assignments with extended periods of time for completion. Lack of motivation in diverse learners is an issue. Students tend to "check out" when they don't understand the task at hand. PBL can be created around themes that students help choose. Students who are exposed to pro-social peers and might find high-interest, child-centered projects motivating, thus increasing attendance. Important problem-solving and social skills are taught and modeled throughout the process. Projects with depth, duration, and complexity challenge students and motivate them towards the construction of knowledge. They will acquire problem-solving, communication, collaboration, planning, and self-evaluation skills.

Off Task

Off-task behavior is a term used to describe occasions when a child is engaging in behavior that is not related to the activity set by the teacher. Students are off task for a variety of reasons for students to escape the task, or because of attention issues, a learner becomes distracted and is attending to other things in the environment. Some strategies that increase on-task behavior include the use of self-monitoring, the tangible rewarding of on-task behavior, and prompting students with visual or physical cues to return to the task. For off-task behavior that is escape driven, students may need breaks contingent on task engagement. Using PBL can engage these learners in an activity that may be more rewarding by identifying parts of the project that the child is responsible for and able to complete. This can increase confidence though successful engagement.

Impulsivity

Some children have difficulty staying with the task at hand. Their verbalizations seem irrelevant and their performance indicates that they are not thinking reflectively about what they are doing. PBL can assist by giving a rubric of project expectations, which helps students set long-range goals but subdivides the goals into realistic parts. Using PBL tends to work from well-defined outcomes and allows teachers to probe impulsive students about irrelevant responses for possible connections to the questions. Therefore, when introducing a new project, the teacher can begin by having the all children generate questions about it before providing them with much information, allowing students to tap into previous knowledge and background and creating a stronger connection to PBL for the impulsive child who might have difficulty remaining focused.

Lack of Organization

Diverse and disabled learners, in particular, can demonstrate difficulty in organization. This is evidenced both in work completion and in memory (storage and retrieval). Organizing an extend-time project will require scaffolding and task simplification with additional teacher monitoring for these students. Time management may also be an issue and will interfere with task completion or organizing and managing the smaller steps needed to accomplish larger projects. Students may miss "team meetings" or forget where their materials are, who is in their group, or the purpose of the assignment. Learning new knowledge, skills, abilities, or attitudes and applying them to subject matter is particularly challenging with organizational deficits.

Teachers can facilitate organization through memory cues, ignoring repeated forgetfulness, increasing visual reminders, or teaching self-cuing skills. Teachers can use a variety of techniques to make the teaching comprehensible, including scaffolding and a variety of graphic organizers to draw on background knowledge. Teachers can also make sure the students have weekly or monthly assignment sheets and a list of materials needed to complete project components.

BENEFITS OF PBL AND ACADEMIC SUCCESS FOR DIVERSE LEARNERS

The essence of PBL lies in the engaging experiences that involve learners in complex, real-world projects through which they develop and apply skills and knowledge. Table 2 provides an outline of common features and how to set up a project for learners of all skill levels using best instructional practices.

Table 2.Common Features of Project-Based Learning (Grant, 2002)

Features	Description
Introduction	Use an introduction that includes "The Big Ideas" or anchor for the project. This often contributes to motivating learners, provides focus, and increases performance.
Task	The task, guiding question or driving question explicates what will be accomplished and embeds the content to be studied. The tasks should be engaging, challenging, and doable. This allows the learner to choose, plan, and design based on previous knowledge, background, and skills on how to obtain new knowledge. Students need frequent opportunities to respond and variations in how to respond.
Investigation	The process and investigation include scaffolding the steps necessary to complete the task and reinforcing participation at each step, including answering the guiding question. The process should include activities that require higher-level and critical thinking skills, such as analysis, synthesis, and evaluation of information. Students at a variety of cognitive and language levels may need alternative methods to demonstrate comprehension and performance at appropriate levels.
Resources	Resources provide data to be used and can include hypertext links, computers, scientific probes, compasses, CD-ROMs, eyewitnesses, and so on. Resources should be provided in an environment that students can access. Internet access is not available to all students, neither are computers for typing, materials for projects, or adult help in problem solving.
Scaffolding	Guidance and scaffolding are needed at different levels for different students and may include organization, social, planning, resource help, student-teacher interactions, practice worksheets, peer counseling, guiding questions, job aides, and project templates.

Collaborations	Many projects include groups or teams, especially when resources are limited, but cooperative learning may also employ rounds of peer reviews or group brainstorming sessions.
Reflection	The superior examples of PBL offer an opportunity for closure, debriefing, assessment, or reflection. These may include relevant in-class discussions, journal entries, follow-up questions about what students have learned, or even an assessment over learning.

Introduction for Special Learners

The most essential aspect of planning a project begins with the introduction. Although there is great variation in motivational levels from learner to learner, the importance of high motivation for diverse learners is clear. Start with the big ideas or anchors, which will provide the conceptual focus and activate prior knowledge.

In addition to activating prior knowledge and generating interest, teachers need to prepare students conceptually for big ideas and concepts. Teachers must seek concrete ways (e.g., visuals, objects, and metaphors) to represent the concepts and big ideas their students do not already know. Because many students do not learn best through tasks requiring literacy or numerical representation, both the experiential and conceptual introduction should incorporate diverse modalities and precede grade-appropriate literacy or abstract mathematical tasks. The goal is for students to understand key concepts and big ideas prior to reading about them or solving abstract problems.

Task

It is imperative that educators identify and teach the big ideas. These key principles and generalizations (statements of the relationships among important concepts) point the direction for all instruction. Once the essence of instruction or steps is clearly stated, teachers can more readily identify critical concepts to be taught and develop lessons that have a strong conceptual focus. When identifying lesson objectives, the content objectives state what students will do to demonstrate understanding of the big ideas. Related language objectives reflect how students will access and express the big ideas and key concepts. Once the instructional essence has been stated as big ideas, teachers need to create an experiential base for instruction. It is important to first build on prior knowledge and to create common experiences that generate emotional responses. The purpose of these activities is to provide relevant experiences, generate curiosity, and motivate diverse learners.

Investigation

During the investigation phase of the project, students task analyze in order to complete the steps necessary to finish the project. Teachers must seek every opportunity to promote higher-order thinking. Students who think analytically and creatively and who develop strategies for learning always seem "head and shoulders" above the rest. Teachers need to provide mental challenges and specifically teach the strategies that enable all students to effectively develop the thought processes and procedures for meeting their thinking goals.

There are multiple ways to promote higher-order thinking, but the procedures used should be related to the big ideas being taught. For example, students can engage in activities that enable them to construct meaning and discover those important ideas for themselves. Graphic organizers are particularly valuable for helping students process the tasks and organize related details. To that end, educators choose organizers that match the thinking required for understanding the big ideas being taught. In a lesson, teachers need to also include clear expectations that are related to the project's well-defined outcomes. Teachers need to define how students demonstrate their use of the strategies or knowledge taught. For further ideas consider the chapter on assessment.

Resources

Too often, instructional decisions are based on the materials available, rather than insightfully selecting materials that are the most appropriate for the educational goals of the population being taught. Educational materials take a lot of work and often need to be cut, shaped, strengthened, and polished. It is rarely possible to purchase a program that would be an exact match for the curriculum in any discipline. Resources to consider:

- Graphic Organizers as the visuals, manipulatives, and other materials needed to preview the concepts in concrete ways
- Text-like materials and trade books
- Multiculturalism that includes: choice of themes and topics of investigation, multicultural literature, texts that incorporate diverse perspectives, materials designed to reduce bias and promote cultural sensitivity, authentic sources, the Internet, personal interviews, and so forth
- The many resources generated by the students themselves that can be used for multiple educational purposes
- The materials that reflect the interests and experiential backgrounds of the students, and
- Materials that match the range of students in the class (e.g., materials with different reading levels) as well as materials for any specialized needs, such as, materials in the native language or materials for the blind
- The Internet brings many resources from around the world into the classroom. In addition, students generally move beyond the classroom as they use parents, community members, businesses, and organizations as educational resources.

Collaborations

Collaboration of student groups provides diverse learners with essential opportunities to use language in meaningful, purposeful, and interesting ways, build self-esteem

and self-confidence, and develop academic, communication, and social skills. The students are responsible for one another's learning as well as their own, which requires group interdependence, motivation, persistence, and flexibility (Abrami, 1995). Collaboration methods to consider for PBL:
– Classroom arrangement.
– Teachers organize groups in a variety of ways including mixed academic achievement, interest, language, project, language, and friendship.
– Small group work is structured to so that students need to be concerned about the learning of all group members as well as themselves. Groups are expected to help and encourage their members to master academic content.
– Each student in the group is individually accountable for his or her learning.

If collaborative-skill instruction occurs regularly, teachers can consistently process how effectively groups work and learn together.

Reflection

Reflection and assessment are an integral, ongoing part of instruction and become more visible in the upper grades. Although reflection and assessment generally come last in the PBL phase, they are considered at each phase of planning. Assessment enables teachers to meaningfully report learning, provide feedback, determine needs, and improve instruction. Different methods for reflection include:
– Journaling, interest inventories, and classroom observations, which can demonstrate what students know, what they can do, and how they feel.
– Self-assessment and peer assessment.
– Assessment of the classroom climate for learning.
– Verbal presentations about their feelings, insights, and opinions about the tasks, learning context, or learning environment.
– Examining their motives either through discussion, in writing, or some other creative outlet for either on- or off-task behaviors.

SUMMARY

A STEM PBL is an extended inquiry into various aspects of a real-world topic that is of interest to students and judged worthy by teachers. Because of its real-world appeal, students are motivated to investigate, record, and report their findings. The hallmark of project learning is greater independence of inquiry and "ownership" of the work on the part of students. When contrasted with more formal instruction, it allows students a greater degree of choice and capitalizes on internal motivation. When students participate in experiences, they see the value of what they are learning and become more actively engaged (Resnick, 1987).

As with any teaching method, STEM PBL can be used effectively or ineffectively. At its best, STEM PBL can help teachers create a high-performing classroom in which the teacher and students form a powerful learning community focused on achievement, self-mastery, and contribution to the community. It allows the teacher to focus on central ideas and salient issues in the curriculum, create engaging and challenging activities in the classroom, and support self-directed learning among students. It assists in overcoming the dichotomy between knowledge and thinking while supporting students in learning and practicing skills in problem solving, communication, and self-management. Most of all, PBL can create positive communication and collaborative relationships among diverse groups of students.

REFERENCES

Abrami, P. C. (1995). *Classroom connections: Understanding and using cooperative learning.* Toronto: Harcourt Brace.

Applebee, A. N., Langer, J. A., & Mullis, I. V. (1989). *Crossroads in American education: A summary of findings.* Princeton, NJ: Educational Testing Service.

Bottoms, G., & Webb, L. D. (1998). *Connecting the curriculum to "real life." Breaking ranks: Making it happen.* Reston, VA: National Association of Secondary School Principals.

Collins, A., Brown, J. S., & Newman, S. E. (1989). Cognitive apprenticeship: Teaching the crafts of reading, writing, and mathematics. In L. Resnick (Ed.), *Knowledge, learning and instruction: Essays in honor of Robert Glaser* (pp. 453–494). Hillsdale, NJ: Erlbaum.

Costello, E. J., Messer, S. C., Bird, B. H. R., Cohen, P., & Reinherz, H. Z. (1998). Prevalence of Sserious Eemotional Ddisturbance: A Rre-Aanalysis of Ccommunity Sstudies. *Journal of Child and Family Studies, 7*, 411–432.

Education for All Handicapped Children Act of 1975, Pub. L. No. 94–142.

Federal Register. (1977). Procedures for evaluating specific learning disability. December 29, *42*(250), pp. 65082– 65085.

Gonzalez, V., Yawkey, T. D., & Minaya-Rowe, L. (2006). *English -as-second language teaching and learning: Pre-K-12 classroom perspectives for students' academic achievement and development.* New York: Pearson Education.

Grant, M. (2002). Getting a grip on project-based learning: Theory, cases, and recommendations. *Meridian: A Middle School Computer Technologies Journal, 5*, 1.

Harris, J. H., & Katz, L. G. (2001). *Young investigators: The project approach in the early years.* New York: Teacher's College Press.

Harel, I., & Papert, S. (Eds.). (1991). *Constructionism.* Norwood, NJ.

Individuals with Disabilities Education Act Amendments of 1997, 20 U.S.C. section 1400 et seq.

Individuals With Disabilities Education Act of 1997, Pub. L. No. 105–17 [Amending 20 U.S.C. § 1400 et seq.].

Jacobs, H. H. (1989). The growing need for interdisciplinary curriculum content. In H. H. Jacobs (Ed.), *Interdisciplinary curriculum: Design and implementation* (pp. 1–11). Alexandria, VA: ASCD.

Kafai, Y., & Resnick, M. (Eds.). (1996). *Constructionism in practice: Designing, thinking and learning in a digital world.* Mahwah, NJ: Erlbaum.

Kauffman, J. M. (2001). *Characteristics of emotional and behavioral disorders* (7th ed.). Upper Saddle River, NJ: Prentice-Hall

Learning Disabilities Act. (1969–1970). Title VI, Pub. L. No. 91–230.

Merrell, K., & Walker, H. (2004). Deconstructing a definition: Social maladjustment versus emotional disturbance and moving the EBD field forward. *Psychology in the Schools, 41*, 899–910.

Merriam-Webster's collegiate dictionary (10th ed.). (1993). Springfield, MA: Merriam-Webster.

Moss, M., & Puma, M. (1995). *Prospects: The congressionally mandated study of educational growth and opportunity: Language minority and English language learners.* Washington, DC: U.S. Department of Education.

Moursund, D. (1998). Project-based learning in an information-technology environment. *Learning and Leading with Technology, 25*(8), 4.

National Clearinghouse for English Language Acquisition. (2006). *Resources about secondary English language learners.* Washington, DC: Author. Retrieved on April 20, 2008, from http://www.ncela.gwu.edu/resabout/ells/index.html

Nelson, C. M., & Rutherford, R. B. (1990). Troubled youth in the public schools: Emotionally disturbed or socially maladjusted? In P. E. Leone (Ed.), *Understanding troubled and troubling youth: Multidisciplinary perspectives,* (pp. 38–60). Newbury Park, CA: Sage.

Nelson, C. M., Rutherford, R. B., Center, D. B., & Walker, H. M. (1991). Do public schools have an obligation to serve troubled children and youth? *Exceptional Children, 57,* 406–415.

No Child Left Behind. (2001). *No child left behind.* Retrieved June 29, 2007, from http://www.ed.gov/nclb/landing.jhtml

Pappas, C. C., Kiefer, B. Z., & Levstik, L. S. (1990). *An integrated language perspective in the elementary school: Theory into action.* New York: Longman.

Perie, M., Moran, R., & Lutkus, A. D. (2005). *NAEP 2004 Trends in Aacademic Pprogress: Three Ddecades of Sstudent Pperformance in Rreading and Mmathematics* (NCES 2005–464). U.S. Department of Education, Institute of Education Sciences, National Center for Education Statistics. Washington, DC: Government Printing Office.

Perkins, D. N. (1986). *Knowledge by design.* Hillsdale, NJ: Erlbaum.

Resnick, L. (1987). Learning in school and out. *Educational Researcher, 16*(9), 13–20.

Shaffer, D., Fisher, P., Dulcan, M. K., Davies, M., Piacentini, J., Schwab-Stone, M. E., Lahey, B. B., Bourdon, K., Jensen, P. S., Bird, H. R., Canino, G., & Regier, D. Aet al. (1996). Methods for the epidemiology of child and adolescent mental disorders Sstudy. *Journal of the American Academy of Child and Adolescent Psychiatry, 35,* 865–877.

Spear, R. (1992). Appropriate grouping practices for middle level students. In J. Irvin (Ed.), *Transforming middle level education: Perspectives and possibilities.* Needham Heights, MA: Allyn and Bacon.

Tassinari, M. (1996). Hands-on projects take students beyond the book. *Social Studies Review, 34*(3), 16–20.

Tchudi, S. (1991). *Planning and assessing the curriculum in English language arts.* Alexandria, VA: ASCD.

Tompkins, G. E., & Hoskisson, K. (1991). *Language arts: Content and teaching strategies.* New York: Merrill.

U.S. Department of Education, National Center for Education Statistics. (2006). *Digest of education statistics.* (NCES 2006-030), Chap.ter 2). Washington, DC: aAuthor.

U.S. Department of Education, Office of Special Education and Rehabilitative Services (OSERS). (2002). *Twenty-fourth annual report to congress on the implementation of the individuals with disabilities education act.* Washington, DC: U.S. Department of Education.

Wagner, M. (1989, April). *The natural transition study: Results of a national longitudinal study of transition from school to work for students with disabilities.* Paper presented at the annual meeting of the Council for Exception Children, San Francisco.

Ward, G. (1988). *I''ve got a project on.......* New South Wales, Australia: Primary English Teaching.

Wolk, S. (1994). Project-based learning: Pursuits with a purpose. *Educational Leadership, 52*(3), 42–-45.

Worthy, J. (2000). Conducting research on topics of student interest. *Reading Teacher, 54,* 298–-299.

Perie, M., Moran, R., & Lutkus, A. D. (2005). *NAEP 2004 trends in academic progress: Three decades of student performance in reading and mathematics* (NCES 2005–464). U.S. Department of Education, Institute of Education Sciences, National Center for Education Statistics. Washington, DC: Government Printing Office.

Dennise Soares, M. Ed.
Department of Education Psychology, Special Education,
Texas A&M University

Kimberly Vannest, Ph.D.
Department of Education Psychology, Special Education,
Texas A&M University

JAMES R. MORGAN AND SCOTT W. SLOUGH

12. CLASSROOM MANAGEMENT CONSIDERATIONS: IMPLEMENTING STEM PROJECT-BASED LEARNING

INTRODUCING CLASSROOM MANAGEMENT

The issue of classroom management in a Science, Technology, Engineering and Mathematics (STEM) Project-Based Learning (PBL) classroom is really two distinct issues; the first issue is how to design a PBL activity to maximize learning and the positive behavior of the learner; the second issue lies in a variety of topics related to the management of a classroom with groups of students working together. There is a mistaken perspective that PBL simply involves creating an open-ended question and letting the students do all of the work, but this could not be further from the truth. Our definition of a *well-defined outcome* and an *ill-defined task* for PBL has profound implications for classroom management. Although it may sound oxymoronic, a well-designed, ill-defined task does more than promote student learning. It promotes student motivation and engagement and when paired with a well-defined outcome, eases teacher and student concerns related to classroom management. Students are still expected to be on-task; restrict conversations to planning, investigating, problem solving, and communicating results; work in groups and individually; and follow procedures and routines (Wong & Wong, 2004). This chapter first deals with the design of a PBL, as a good design will solve a great deal of the classroom management concerns for both the teacher and the students. Secondly, it will deal with the issue of managing students working in groups because the implementation of projects in a class works better when both teachers and students are comfortable with the dynamics of a cooperative learning environment.

CHAPTER OUTCOMES

When you complete this chapter you should better understand:
- the issues related to students working in groups or teams
- the dynamics of a cooperative learning environment
- the features of an effective project
    When you complete this chapter you should be able to:
- design ill-defined tasks that encourage student learning and minimize classroom management concerns
- form, develop, train, and manage student groups
- develop effective STEM Project-Based Learning activities

R. M. Caparo and S. W. Slough (eds.), Project-Based Learning: An Integrated Science, Technology, Engineering, and Mathematics (STEM) Approach, 159–170.

DESIGNING ILL-DEFINED TASKS TO PROMOTE LEARNING AND MANAGE BEHAVIOR

It is important to remember that the primary justification for PBL is that active engagement generally leads to improved learning outcomes (Hake 1988), which is fully supported by our definition of PBL as a *well-defined outcome* and an *ill-defined task*. Classroom management in a PBL environment is based on increasing active engagement and controlling the chaos. The first decision that promotes active engagement and control of chaos is the design the PBL itself. The well-defined outcome includes expectations for learning and behavior—even if the behavior expectations are not explicitly stated. The ill-defined task is included to increase student motivation and engagement. Boredom, repetition, confusion about expectations, and easily completed tasks are a teacher' enemy. It is a teacher's responsibility to set the tone that you expect students to learn and to behave during PBL, just like the rest of the year. You do not get a second chance to make a good first impression. Well-established procedures and routines that allow students to actively engage in the task are critical and must be designed with as much care as selecting the learning objective. Remember the focus in a PBL is on what the student knows and is able to do, not what the teacher covered. Therefore, instead of procedures that emphasize listening to the teacher and following predetermined steps to problem solve, procedures that emphasize student engagement, decision making, and problem solving need to be emphasized. Eventually, students internalize procedures into unprompted routines. For a full discussion of procedures and routines see Wong and Wong (2004).

Examples of some procedures for students to follow that are specific to PBL include:

- Check the board to see who is initiating project work today—the teacher or the students.
- Record **all** design ideas in your lab notebook/journal.
- Record **all** trials in your lab notebook/journal.
- Keep in mind how you are going to communicate your results to others.
- Keep in mind how you are going to answer your own questions.
- Work cooperatively, not competitively.
- All students are responsible for all phases of the project, regardless of their temporary roles within the group (see discussion on groups and roles below).

In addition to the PBL-specific routines that support increased student engagement, motivation, and problem solving, specific routines that deal with working in groups need to be developed as well. The scariest part of adopting an active, inquiry-based pedagogy for many teachers is the potential loss of control of individual students and control of the classroom. Consistent application of traditional and PBL-specific procedures will go a long way towards managing the behavior and learning of individual students and the class as a whole. Many teachers have been surprised by the increased attendance that accompanies team activities in class (students are sometimes willing to disappoint teachers but less willing to let down their classmates/ team). Many techniques are listed in the active-learning literature; all are simple, some are silly, but most require agreement in advance and practice to be effective. Some examples include:

- *Touchdown signal* – the teacher makes a touchdown signal. Students seeing the signal raise their hands in a touchdown signal; students seeing this signal raise their hands in a touchdown signal, and so on. It is surprising how quickly a classroom becomes quiet—students who don't see the signal notice that room is getting quiet and look up from their work. Of course, the students have to be informed that the signal means to (1) raise their hands, (2) stop talking, and (3) turn their attention toward the teacher.
- *Single raised hand* – this method works much the same as the touchdown signal except that the teacher raises only one hand.
- *Air horn, bell, or buzzer* – the signal is audible and (if neighbors are not nearby or if they are very understanding) can be either loud enough or at a frequency that will be noticed by even the most engaged students.
- *Blinking classroom lights* – this method is silent and very effective; however, it must be used with caution if students are up and moving around or if there are obstacles in the room.
- *Other* – many teachers have luck simply moving to the middle of the room and quietly giving verbal instructions; nearby students notice and become quiet; the teacher repeats the instructions; more students notice and become quiet, and the sound of silence propagates throughout the room.

All of these procedures work if explained in advance, consistently applied by the teacher, and complied with by the students. Usually, students recognize the advantages to active participation versus passive learning and are thus willing to learn new procedures and routines as they solve new problems in more authentic learning environments.

Beyond the development, implementation, and reinforcement of new procedures and routines, care must be taken to design projects that are in fact motivating and engaging to the students, not just the teacher. As such, projects that engage students in higher levels of learning through authentic tasks often result in the emergence of various learning outcomes in addition to the ones anticipated. Often, such projects include the characteristics of student-centered learning, students as teachers, teachers as coaches or facilitators, students working in groups, and performance-based assessment.

There are a variety of sources with lists of attributes of a good project. Although these lists are not the sole answer for designing good projects, they do provide a useful checklist. Outstanding projects commonly:

- Recognize students' drive to learn,
- Make project work central rather than peripheral,
- Lead students to in-depth exploration of important topics,
- Require the use of essential tools and skills, self-management of learning, and projects,
- Incorporate investigation, research, or reasoning,
- Include frequent feedback (opportunities to learn from experience),
- Include high expectations and performance-based assessments, and

– Encourage collaboration through small groups, student presentations, or peer and class evaluations of projects (Thomas, Mergendoller, & Michaelson, 1999).

This list provides a convenient checklist when developing a project, converting problems into projects, or converting learning objectives into projects. The following sections give tips on modifying other PBL activities; modifying other inquiry activities; and modifying more traditional lesson plans to a Project-Based Learning format.

Modifying other PBLs

A well-designed PBL will have a *well-defined outcome* and an *ill-defined task.* If one is lucky enough to inherit a well-designed PBL, then modification consists of assessing student prior knowledge and providing adequate resources, continuous individual and small group scaffolding, and the occasional whole-class discussion or direct instruction on an as-needed basis. Starting with a well-designed PBL is an excellent way to develop the procedures and routines you will implement in future PBLs.

Modifying Other Inquiry Activities

The first task in modifying an inquiry activity into a STEM PBL is to develop a *well-defined outcome.* This assures that the activity is aligned with the local, state, and national standards and communicates clear expectations for learning and behavior to the students. The second task is to check or modify the inquiry task to make sure that it meets the definition of *ill defined.* This ensures that the primary elements of the PBL in place, which will minimize off-task behavior.

Modifying Teacher-Centered Instruction

Modifying teacher-centered instruction requires the same emphasis on designing *well-defined outcomes* and *ill-defined tasks.* Good teacher-centered instruction should have easily modifiable learning objectives; the primary task at this point is to consider new behavioral objectives. Converting a teacher lecture or verification lab into an *ill-defined task* is quite another task. The first priority for creating *ill-defined tasks* is to find a problem that has multiple, reasonable solutions or multiple paths to a single solution.

The connection between the *well-defined outcome* and the *ill-defined task* is as important to student behavior as it is to student learning. The consistent application of these two elements is the first routine that teachers should establish for themselves as they design STEM PBL. As teachers and students become more comfortable with this new style of learning, most of the new procedures will become routine. Teachers have to learn to trust themselves enough not to provide all of the answers, and they have to learn to trust that the students will be able to get to the place teachers want them to be without a step-by-step procedure. Although it does not matter how they get there, ***it is essential that they do get there.***

Communication in STEM PBL

A final component of the design of the well-defined outcome that is essential to managing learning and behavior is the constant communication of learning and communication to learn. Students are communicating their conceptions, ideas, problems, and observations constantly within the PBL. The teacher must support the active learning represented by this communication process or it becomes chaotic. It is important to share or post intermediate and final results of a project. This can be done by having different teams share their work or by the teacher summarizing the different approaches used by different teams of students. Either way, it is important to connect the projects back to the learning objectives; often, students can solve a problem or submit a good project and not realize that they used algebra, geometry, trigonometry, physics, and/or English (even though all are present in their solution). It is up to the teacher to help them celebrate their accomplishment and build self-confidence in applying the concepts that they have mastered and will need to demonstrate on the test.

Mrs. Gonzalez's Ninth Grade Integrated Physics and Chemistry (IPC) Vignette

In a PBL on Non-Newtonian Fluids (see Appendix A) Mrs. Gonzalez introduces the following ill-defined task while playing with a large ball of silly putty at the front of the class (engagement 5E model):

> *What effect does %water have on the viscosity of silly putty . . . and how can the general forms of functions help us interpret this relationship?*

The students are then given time to explore how to make silly putty, what exactly is viscosity, how is it measured, what is the general form of a function, what do we have at the school that can be used to make silly putty and measure viscosity, and why is Mrs. G using math terms in a science class? The classroom becomes a blur of motion, and the noise level increases. As an experienced teacher, Mrs. Gonzalez seems to ignore the noise and student motion. But, closer inspection shows us that she is moving from group to group checking progress, providing suggestions—never "the answer"—and keeping students on-task. After the initial exploration phase (5E model), Mrs. G has the students share ideas with the whole class before full-scale testing occurs.
Day 2
Mrs. G is still working the room. Students have found various recipes for making silly putty, GAK, and a host of other substances on the Internet. Mrs. G has provided a limited set of materials, so the students are forced to chose the recipe that includes glue + borax + water = silly putty. After all of the groups have experimented with the mixture, Mrs. G again has a whole-class discussion to make sure that all of the students are on-task and to remind them how important taking good notes and multiple trials will be in the next phase of data collection.

Day 3
Students are wrapping up their explorations and beginning explanation (5E model). Mrs. G is focused today because she know how critical today's transition is . . . without good data, the students' explanations will be weak. She has really taken a risk by requiring that the students use functions to explain their science, but as she checks the students notes she only needs to make gentle reminders as the groups have all recorded good data. As the students begin to analyze data, questions about what type of graph to use and how many points it takes to make a graph and a variety of questions about functions start to permeate the room. After she conducts several small group interventions, Mrs. G decides to have a short, whole-class review on functions and graphing. She takes the time to find out where each group is at and facilitates an exchange that is largely student driven because she knows where the groups and individuals are in the process. The students return to their groups and work well to complete their analysis and start with their presentations.
Day 4
It is the fourth day in a multi-day PBL, and Mrs. G is rewarded by students coming into class and starting immediately on their projects. Most of the students are really focused on completing graphs and placing them in PowerPoint presentations. Mrs. G notices that although the students were able to collect good data and were able to determine the equation on their lines, they really hadn't focused on answering the question. From experience, she had expected this and had planned some extension activities (5E model) that would hopefully prompt the students to think beyond just the graph and to understand how the shape or form of the line was critical to differentiating between linear and non-linear flow. Examples of appropriate extensions include: what would the data for a Newtonian fluid look like? Or how do engineers take advantage of nonlinear flow?

Parts of this vignette are also shared in Chapter 3 to illustrate why PBL works.

The vignette above shares a brief introduction to how an experienced teacher and well-trained students are able to perform in a PBL environment. Not all procedures for active learning and student problem-solving are readily apparent, but they are present as students are comfortable with Mrs. G checking their work rather than giving them the answers. Students are able to transition from group work to full class discussions and direct teacher instruction without devolving into chaos. Students have taken good data and are planning their presentations. They even demonstrate a transition from a teacher-driven procedure to a student-driven routine by starting the fourth day without prompting from Mrs. G. Was this classroom quiet for the four days? Certainly not! Was this class engaged for the four days? Apparently yes! Did chaos ever rule this class during the four days? Probably not. Can regular classroom teachers and professors implement a few new procedures and routines to effectively manage student learning and behavior? Absolutely yes!

STUDENTS WORKING IN GROUPS

The purpose of cooperative learning is cooperating to learn, not learning to cooperate (Wong & Wong, 2004). There is a wealth of information on the issues related to effectively using student groups in a classroom. These issues range from maximizing student learning to balance individual and team activities to controlling the classroom. In addition to these issues, it is sometimes important to consider the difference between a student group and a team of students.

The distinction between student groups and student teams is largely one of longevity. Groups of students are often assigned on the fly for in-class cooperative activities and also can be used in PBL. Projects often take longer, so in Project-Based Learning it is important to deal with the interpersonal dynamics that may affect team performance such as:
- Training
- Roles
- Goals and rules
- Monitoring team progress
- Accountability
- Regaining order from chaos

Additional information, hints, and techniques can be borrowed from research on active learning, collaborative learning, and cooperative learning (Bonwell, & Eison, 1991; Johnson, Johnson, & Holubec, 1986; Johnson, Johnson, & Smith, 1991; Katzenbach & Smith, 1993; Seat & Lord, 1999).

Training

Although orientation to group work is a good idea in any cooperative learning environment, it is essential in PBL. Like anything else, teachers should train students as they would at the introduction of any new concept. Even those who have played successfully on a sports team will not naturally apply their experiences to a classroom environment. The process of teaming is not instinctive but can be learned.

Team training should include a picture of expectations: the forming, *norming, storming, and performing* team development cycle (Tuckman & Jensen, 1977); what makes a good team player (i.e., *expectations*); and how performance will be evaluated (teacher only, peer evaluation, or both). Training also should include tools such as how to set an agenda, how to run a meeting, verbal and non-verbal communication, and decision-making processes (consensus is much better for a team than voting—rarely do the students think past voting unless prompted to do so). When groups are expected to work outside of the school environment to complete a project, they need to develop additional procedures to follow. One example might be to include agendas with the following elements:

Agendas need to include a few essential items:
  – When and where will the meeting take place?
  – What is the purpose of the meeting?
  – What resources do we need?
  – Who will bring what to the meeting?
  – When will the meeting end? (Some of us have a life outside the team and need to be able to plan for living it.)

Figure 1. Essential items for agendas.

Roles

In a team environment, it is often desirable to have students take on a variety of different roles **and to rotate** these roles. Different roles are desirable because efficiency can be obtained through dividing the work and because it reduces the time when one or more team members are watching the others work and waiting for someone to tell them what to do. Rotating roles is desirable because some jobs are more/less desirable than others **and** because students often do not know which jobs they will be good at until they have a chance to experience the role (*and improve performance when they repeat the experience*). Although there are many possible roles, common roles include the following:
– Facilitator – preferable to leader – this person facilitates team meetings and discussions and makes sure everyone knows where meetings will occur, when they will start/end, what to bring, and so on.
– Recorder – this member keeps notes of action items (minutes of meetings are rarely necessary), that is, a list of who agreed to do what by when. This record needs to be shared with all members of the team to minimize any misunderstandings.
– Time keeper – this person is in charge of keeping track of the timeline (both for the project as a whole and for individual team meetings or activities), keeping the team on task, and reminding team members of when items are due and how much/little progress has been made towards completion of the deliverable.
– Gatekeeper/encourager – this person is responsible for making sure everyone has an opportunity to participate in team discussions and activities by noticing

that one member has not said anything and asking his/her opinion or gently reminding a vocal teammate that others may have something to share.

Roles can be combined, and additional team roles are possible. However, teams larger than three or four are generally less effective because of the decreased accountability and corresponding increased likelihood of someone disengaging or slacking off. Depending on the complexity of the project, teams of two are possible, but teams of three or four are generally ideal. It is important to note that these roles are **not** "for the duration of the project"; **roles should be rotated on a daily** (or at least weekly) **basis**. All students deserve the opportunity to practice each role multiple times—**this cannot be stressed too much**. Also, be certain that students do not see different roles as opportunities to not participate in the project.

Goals and Rules

It is important for project teams to establish goals and rules within the larger classroom-based procedures and routines. These could be viewed as shared norms for the team and should be available to each team member and to the teacher at all times. The goals should include the *teacher's goal* that all members of the team master the learning objectives included in the project as well as whatever goal the team wishes to set (*winning the competition, finishing ahead of schedule, everyone passes, etc.*). In addition to goals, the team needs to set rules; these are called ground rules, codes of cooperation, rules of engagement, and other things. Rules are simply an agreement among team members about expected behavior and agreed-upon penalties. Often rules include unrealistic promises such as *everyone will give 110% and put the team first above all things*. It is a good idea to have teams revisit and revise the rules on long projects. On shorter projects, classroom procedures and routines can suffice. **REMEMBER**: a good set of rules, which have been agreed to by all members of the team, goes a long way towards avoiding problems as the team struggles to approach the deadline.

Team Ground Rules
1. All meetings will begin and end on time
2. Sarcasm is left at the door
3. All members will participate in group decisions
4. Conflict will be managed and resolved before irritations become overwhelming
5. All debates are no-fault discussions
6. State the purpose of the meeting
7. Only one conversation at a time
8. No cheap shots or personal attacks

Figure 2. Team ground rules.

Some are not comfortable with the concept of **rules**; this easily is handled by using an *agreement to cooperate.*

Sample Agreement to Cooperate
- All members will attend meetings or notify the team by email or phone in advance of anticipated absences.
- All members will be fully engaged in team meetings and will not work on other assignments during meetings.
- All members will complete assigned tasks by agreed-upon deadlines.
- Major decisions will be subject to group discussion and consensus or majority vote.
- The roles of recorder, facilitator, and timekeeper will rotate on an agreed-upon timeframe (all members will take their turn—NO EXCEPTIONS).
- The team meetings will occur only at the regularly scheduled (weekly) time OR with at least a two-day notice.

Monitoring Team Progress

The primary job of the teacher/coach/facilitator is to monitor learning and behavior, not to solve all of the problems or transmit the knowledge. The teacher needs to balance student frustration and motivations. Give the students the answers and they will not try to solve the problem on their own; ignore legitimate questions and they will become so frustrated that they will quit. Although the students need to find their own way through the winding path of discovery, they must occasionally be guided gently down the proper path. Frequent questioning, whether formal or informal, is the best way to monitor progress. Sometimes the answers to these questions will lead to helping a team reengage. Other times, a question will help the team avoid a brick wall or discover that they learned something in this or another class that might be helpful. Answers also might allow the teacher to discover that the team is making progress (perhaps on an unexpected path). Communication and participation within the group is essential and must be monitored and supported by the teacher.

Accountability

The issue of accountability is both an issue of motivation and an issue of fairness. Students are more engaged if they have a clear understanding of expectations and know they will be held individually accountable. Students are more engaged if they know that the members of their team will be held accountable (even if only in part) for their individual failure. Everyone is less concerned with fairness if they know that at the *end of the day, week, project, or semester,* more credit will be received by those who deserve more credit, and less credit will be received by those deserving less.

Most accountability systems include both observations by the teachers and peer assessments of performance on the team (Felder & Brent, 2001; Kaufman, Felder, & Fuller, 2000). Peer evaluation aids the perception of fairness—those who work harder usually get more credit, **and** those who slack off get less credit. In addition, in most classes, the team component of the course grade is rarely the major factor. Those who depend mostly on teammates to carry the load do not typically achieve the learning objectives and therefore do not do well on the individual quizzes, tests, and exams. On the other hand, the fun factor associated with Project-Based Learning, combined with peer pressure to participate, results in fewer disengaged students, fewer students failing exams, and so on.

Possible alternative questions for a peer evaluation include questions about whether a teammate:
1. Contributes to group discussions
2. Welcomes comments from others
3. Listens even when he/she disagrees
4. Comes prepared to meetings

Figure 3. Possible alternative questions.

CONCLUDING THOUGHTS

Classroom management in a PBL environment is based on increasing active-engagement and controlling the chaos. The central components of our PBL definition, the *well-defined outcome* and the *ill-defined task,* help support proper management of learning and behavior. The thoughtful identification and implementation of appropriate procedures and routines are essential to the well-defined outcome and when paired with the motivating and engaging components of ill-defined tasks, provide a framework to actively engage and control. It also is important to realize that different methods can be used to satisfy the requirements of a project—**all can be correct approaches, and all are valuable learning opportunities!** Students can learn a great deal from each other, from the process of struggling to find the information needed to complete the project, and in applying the concepts they have learned in the class (and previous classes).

REFERENCES

Bonwell, C., & Eison, J. (1991). *Active learning: Creating excitement in the classroom*. Washington, D.C.: George Washington University. (ERIC Clearinghouse on Higher Education Service No. ED346082)

Felder, R. M., & Brent, R. (2001). Effective strategies for cooperative learning. *Journal of Cooperation and Collaboration in College Teaching, 10*(2), 69–75.

Hake, R. R. (1988). Interactive-engagement vs. traditional methods: A six-thousand-student survey of mechanics test data for introductory physics courses. *American Journal of Physics, 66*, 64–74.

Johnson, D. W., Johnson, R. T., & Holubec, E. J. (1986). *Circles of learning: Cooperation in the classroom*, (Revised ed.). Edina, MN: Interaction Book.

Johnson, D. W., Johnson, R. T., & Smith, K. (1991). *Active learning: Cooperation in the college classroom*. Edina, MN: Interaction Book.

Katzenbach, J. R., & Smith, D. K. (1993). *Wisdom of teams*. Boston: Harvard Business School Press.

Kaufman, D. B., Felder, R. M., & Fuller, H. (2000). Accounting for individual effort in cooperative learning teams. *Journal of Engineering Education, 89*(2), 133–140.

Seat, E., & Lord, S. (1999). Enabling effective engineering teams: A program for teaching interaction skills. *Journal of Engineering Education, 88*, 385–390.

Thomas, J. W., Mergendoller, J. R., & Michaelson, A. (1999). *Project-Bbased Llearning: A Hhandbook for Mmiddle and Hhigh Sschool Tteachers*. Novata, CA: Buck Institute for Education.

Tuckman, W., & Jensen, M. A. (1977). Stages of small-group development revisited. *Group and Organization Studies, 2*, 419–427.

Wong, H. K., & Wong, R. T. (2004). *How to be an effective teacher: The first days of school*. Mountain View, CA: Harry K. Wong Publications.

James R. Morgan
Zachry Department of Civil Engineering
Texas A&M University

Scott W. Slough
Department of Teaching, Learning, and Culture
Texas A&M University

ROBERT M. CAPRARO AND Z. EBRAR YETKINER

13. NEW VIEWS ON ASSESSMENT IN STEM PROJECT-BASED LEARNING

INTRODUCTION

Science, Technology, Engineering, and Mathematics (STEM) Project-Based Learning (PBL) integrates assessments across different aspects of learning experiences by shifting the focus from summative to formative assessments. Because of the nature of PBL, which is centered on developing real-world projects where students can apply their understandings of various concepts, authentic assessment underlies both formative and summative assessments. Rubrics are a central component of both formative and summative assessments, helping students to transition from authority-imposed regulation to self-regulation of their learning. As a consequence of PBL, projects are often executed in groups, so this environment lends itself to group assessment while holding individual accountability paramount.

CHAPTER OUTCOMES

When you complete this chapter you should better understand:
- the nature of PBL assessment
- various forms of PBL assessment
- complexities teachers face when assessing PBL
  When you complete this chapter you should be able to:
- develop an assessment plan that matches your learning outcomes for your PBL activity
- communicate clearly with administrators and parents about valuing student learning and not just evaluating it
- assess student learning in terms of academic progress instead of meeting some arbitrary decision points (e. g. 90, 80, 70, 60).

OVERVIEW OF ASSESSMENT

Role of Assessment

Assessment is an essential component in PBL. Fortunately, assessment is also an integral component that holds the project components together, maintains motivation (Brophy, 2004), and provides the teacher with useful information about each student's learning (Kulm, 1994). PBL requires a whole new view of assessment.

R. M. Capraro and S.W. Slough (eds.), Project-Based Learning: An Integrated Science, Technology, Engineering, and Mathematics (STEM) Approach, 171–186.

There is a shift from summative to formative assessment. When the focus is formative, (1) assessment is used to extinguish behaviors the teacher wants to diminish and foster behaviors the teacher wants to reinforce, (2) the score or grade has minimal impact on the summative or final grade the student will earn, and (3) students are keenly aware of what they need to do to earn full points. Summative assessments are planned concurrently with lesson development but can also be adapted or new ones created during lesson delivery. Summative assessments no longer are relegated to the last day of instruction but can occur in smaller increments throughout instruction. Most importantly, formative assessment is an accumulation of learning artifacts assembled by students with clear and explicit directions from teachers that align the expected learning outcomes to the project. When taken as a whole, the artifacts used for assessment are summaries of student knowledge or are knowledge products that depict a richer and more complete picture of what students know. The new view of assessment should not totally replace assessments that help students build proficiency with multiple-choice items. Success with multiple choice items will continue to be an important benchmark for teachers and indicators of teaching; not that authors agree, but currently this is the world in which we all work. However, this new view should be a means for helping students apply their knowledge, thereby owning the knowledge rather than spitting out formulas, as well as thinking and writing about what they learn. These skills lead students to be flexible with their knowledge (Boaler, 1998) and develop critical-reading skills in each content area necessary to ensure students have the ability to comprehend the reading presented in multiple-choice items on high-stakes state tests.

In typical practice, assessment is synonymous with grading and unfortunately, passing or failing. This approach leads students to strive to do well on tests in order to get a good grade rather than focus on learning objectives. For students, this approach also precludes the interpretation of assessment as a means of feedback towards the desired learning goals. A common belief about the role of the teacher is that teachers need to understand what students do not know so that they can adjust teaching content, teaching style, and the ways they assess student learning to improve student understanding. Therefore, for the purposes of this chapter and this book, assessment is inextricably interwoven with pedagogy. The major focus of this book has been on the practical integration of knowledge so that students can demonstrate what they have learned in meaningful ways to be academically successful. This chapter concentrates on determining what students can do and on facilitating them to do more than they thought they could. The emphasis will be in formative rather than summative assessments, but due to accountability, making connections to grading and evaluating knowledge products will be paramount.

Formative and Summative

Generally speaking, there are two broad categories of assessments: formative and summative. Formative assessments provide students with regular feedback to assist and manage their learning, whereas summative assessments primarily concentrate on evaluating the learning that has taken place following a predetermined

instructional period. Formative assessments can differ based on several aspects of the PBL environment:
– the setting (e.g., group or individual)
– the content
– outcome expectations
– allotted time frame
– the time students spend on the activity
– constraints in the design brief
– criteria

PBL assessment should evaluate both individual and group performance. It is important to match the formative assessment to the learning activity and the setting in which the learning took place. For instance, individualized formative assessment of a group activity is less productive than a more encompassing, group-based assessment of that learning. If students pursue learning individually, then group-based assessments may create dissonance with individualized learning and negatively impact student achievement. For group-based assessment, if group membership is heterogeneously assigned, less customization of the assessment is required, whereas when students are randomly- or self-assigned, the assessment needs to be modified for each group's personality and academic idiosyncrasies. The content is an essential variable that should be accommodated when considering the form of the assessment. One group where customization was important may only demonstrate one specific leaning goal of the PBL as compared to students who provide more comprehensive artifacts (see Figure 1).

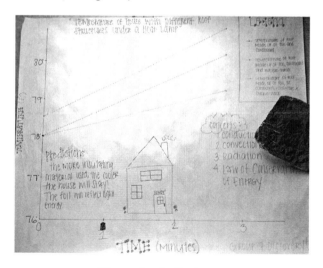

Picture kind of light

Possibly the most complicated form of formative and summative assessments is authentic assessment. Although there is no clearly agreed-upon definition of authentic assessment, the major focus is that the knowledge product is relevant to real-world applications and to the learner. Authentic assessment matches the content being learned and knowledge products with student interests guided by clearly defined outcomes. Examples of authentic assessment can include things as simple as students listing what they learned to get to some point in the project or might be as complicated as filing a report of their progress and the steps involved in solving the problem. Authentic assessment fits with various aspects of PBL to different degrees. For example, when assessment of procedural skills is the focus, authentic assessment is less suitable as compared to when the goal is to understand how students apply those procedural skills in context.

The Venn Diagram below (see Figure 1) helps distinguish between various summative and formative assessments, some of which are more closely aligned to the intent of PBL than those peripherally associated.

PBL   Traditional Instruction

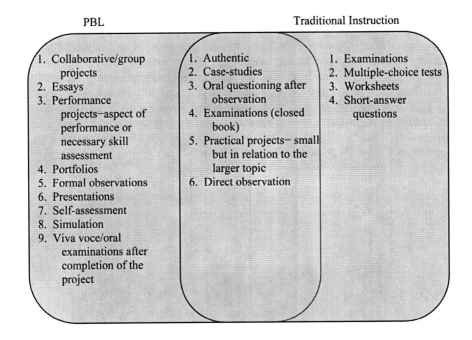

1. Collaborative/group projects
2. Essays
3. Performance projects–aspect of performance or necessary skill assessment
4. Portfolios
5. Formal observations
6. Presentations
7. Self-assessment
8. Simulation
9. Viva voce/oral examinations after completion of the project

1. Authentic
2. Case-studies
3. Oral questioning after observation
4. Examinations (closed book)
5. Practical projects– small but in relation to the larger topic
6. Direct observation

1. Examinations
2. Multiple-choice tests
3. Worksheets
4. Short-answer questions

Figure 1. Assessment comparison.

PBL ASSESSMENT

It is essential to integrate assessment and instruction in each PBL (Solomon, 2003). In the practical design of PBL, the standards are clearly delineated, and it is from this position that assessment and instruction are intertwined. When teachers are keenly aware of the standards, they base their student expectations on these standards and develop a PBL environment that addresses these expectations. It is not essential for the teacher to predetermine every aspect of the assessments to be used with the PBL at the onset. Different assessment models may be chosen sometime after the initial selection of standards and perhaps even during the actual PBL activity because assessments need to be aligned with the learning environment. For instance, teachers can adjust the assessment model based on the setting because the assessment of the same content or standard can differ depending on whether learning occurs in groups or individually. When students learn in group settings, it is important to respect the group intelligence and assess in group settings with individual accountability.

There are several strategies that accommodate group intelligence yet encourage individual accountability. Peer assessment is one of those strategies that can provide valuable insights to the teacher about individual contributions to group intelligence. Additionally, it is important to use individual assessments that mirror those of state assessments because students need to be able to demonstrate their learning on that format. It is on high-stakes assessments that schools, teachers, and students are measured. Any educational innovation that fails to provide measurable impact on high-stakes assessments is doomed. Therefore, it is paramount to achieve equilibrium between authentic assessments and high-stakes assessments when considering individual accountability. However, in a PBL environment where the instruction focuses on designing, constructing, and synthesizing, it is important that assessment is similarly focused and that sufficient weight is given to these concepts as opposed to the high-stakes variety. One way to reflect student accountability in authentic assessment is through the careful design and application of rubrics.

Development of Rubrics

Rubrics are one means for providing students with formative and summative feedback about their learning. Rubrics help teachers to evaluate student learning efficiently (Andrade, 2000), and they provide guidance for students throughout the self- and peer-assessment processes (Andrade, n.d.). The specific and clear criteria identified in rubrics are particularly helpful for those professionals who are not teachers and thus not familiar with assessing student performance as they evaluate projects. A well-designed rubric contains components that reflect the specifics of the standards and conceptual generalities of an activity as well as intangible aspects like those reflected in the Secretary's Commission on Achieving Necessary Skills Report (2000). Various attainment degrees of the learning goals are specified in the rubrics (Andrade, n.d.). Rubrics should also provide sufficient information to help students understand what they know and do not know and some guidance about what they need to learn (Zimmaro, 2004).

The rubric's scale can be closely related to the grading system or be one that obfuscates the relation between the scale score and the A to F grade equivalency. For example, a rubric can either be interpreted by point value and the points converted to a percentage score, or the six-point mastery rubric can be interpreted directly from A+ to F. Contrarily, a rubric can be based on a three- or four-point scale that does not align well with the conventionally-based A to F grading scale.

An even number of ratings (such as four or six) precludes a midpoint decision on the part of the rater. This is often considered desirable. What is most important when designing a rubric is to assign more weight to the critical and important aspects of the task while placing less emphasis on things tangential to the clearly-defined outcomes.

SAMPLE GENERIC RUBRIC

1. Rating	2. Brief Description
1 - Nascent	Student displays preliminary knowledge and skills related to the learning task.
2 - Constrained	Student displays limited knowledge and skills related to the learning task.
3 - Developing	Student displays a developing level of content and concepts related to the learning task.
4 - Commendable	Student displays functionally adequate attainment of the content and concepts related to the learning task.
5 - Accomplished	Student displays mastery of the content and concepts related to the learning task.
6 - Exemplary	Student displays a novel or personal level of mastery of the content and concepts related to the learning task.

Note. This rubric meets some of the tenants of rubric design, but from this rubric, the student would not have sufficient information about the knowledge gaps but just that he or she has gaps. To improve the rubric one could replace the words *knowledge and skills or content and concepts* with specific knowledge and/or skills necessary to the learning outcome.

Rubrics are an essential component of PBL that serve different purposes for those who are involved in the assessment process both at the stage of the rubric's development and its utilization during the evaluation. There are many stakeholders involved in the assessment process, and the whole group should have some level of responsibility in the development of rubrics, including students, peers, the supervisor (teacher), and possibly even external evaluators such as other content-area teachers, administrators, coaches, or interested community members. When all stakeholders are involved in rubric development, they not only understand the criteria but also own them.

The use of rubrics by students through teacher modeling can help them develop important self- and peer-assessment skills. However, in urban schools it is often difficult to enculturate self- and peer-assessments and teachers can find this to be time consuming to attain the positive impact these assessments are intended to achieve. However, some groups of students and or school cultures are less resistant and teachers can be surprised by how rapidly students take self- and peer-assessment. Sometimes students may be overly critical whereas at other times they are overly accommodating. It is important to model critical feedback (Falchikov, 1995) that is both honest and constructive. Students should understand that to identify a weakness without an accompanying suggestion for improvement does not foster intellectual development. To foster the development of self- and peer-assessment, which are important skills in life, it is important for students to (1) be involved in the development of rubrics, (2) be reflective by learning to self-assess, (3) receive critical commentary on their assessment skills, and (4) be responsible for critiquing others by learning to provide constructive assessment of peers.

The enhanced understanding of learning goals and assessment criteria help students to develop a metacognitive awareness of learning. Specifically, self-assessment improves metacognitive awareness and intrinsic motivation (Peckham & Sutherland, 2000). Students who regularly engage in PBL activities should be able to thoughtfully answer:

- How can I tell if I have learned _____ well enough?
- Does the learning serve my current needs?
- Did I learn it in a way that I will be able use it in the future?
- Will I be able to transfer this learning to new situations?
- Do I know what I do not know?
- Do I have the necessary foundation to learn more?

Self-Regulation

Explicit assessment helps students to self-regulate their behavior. Two different levels of self-regulation are present when students are integrally involved in the assessment process. The first level of self-regulation emerges as students co-develop rubrics for assessing various aspects of the PBL. Through involvement in the development of the rubrics, students establish ownership of the assessment model and a clear understanding of what aspects of the learning will be evaluated and how (Bray, 2001). This process will allow students to decide the degree to which Figure 2 meets expectations. This thorough understanding of the rubric can guide students as they implement self-regulation to plan their learning activities to achieve the objectives of the rubric. At this first level of self-regulation, students become cognizant that a position of power (namely, the teacher) will evaluate their projects and that they need to achieve the rubric.

The second level of self-regulated behavior takes place when students learn peer- and self-assessment through the application of the rubrics they develop. As students do self-assessments, they get to know their areas of weakness and strength and allocate their effort to different areas of the learning objectives accordingly, thus holding themselves responsible. Students also start to align the requirements of the rubric with their learning process and desire to meet the requirements for their own benefit and purposes rather than to merely meet the requirements of the teacher. Peer-assessment adds another level to self-regulation because as students see the progress or the failure of their fellow students, they are more likely to reflect on those successes and failures and consequently adjust their learning behavior. This implementation of this second level of self-regulation may require several attempts and clarification by the teacher. Although the application of the rubric to assess a student's own learning and behavior may be difficult initially, repetition will lead to success, and the student will eventually develop an appreciation for the assessment and value for the learning task.

Figure 2

GUIDING THOUGHTS FOR TEACHERS ABOUT PBL ACTIVITIES AND ASSESSMENTS

- Think about the content you teach. Think about what makes your content area and the assessments you traditionally use distinct from assessments in other content areas. Consider the changes that PBL requires in both teaching practices and assessments (Moursund, n.d.).
- Think about how students learn. Much is known about the value of metacognition, self-assessment, and reflection on student learning. Do you think self-assessment is a valuable attribute for students who enter the workforce in a field related to your content area? How important is it in your content area or field to learn to assess one's own work and learning and that of peers or co-workers (Moursund, n.d.)?

– Think about your PBL. Critically examine your PBL and the lessons or activities that comprise it. Did the PBL cover the standards and objectives in your curriculum? Did you align assessment with your standards and objectives? Did you balance formative versus summative assessments? Think about providing useful formative feedback within the time constraints imposed by the length of your instructional time allotment. How will you ensure that feedback is timely so students' effort can reflect this information before the next assessment occurs (Moursund, n.d.)?

– Think about PBL versus traditional instructional practices. Consider the substantive adaptations or modifications you need to make in the structure of your curriculum and teaching practice. What aspects of PBL attract you to make the effort and go through these changes (Moursund, n.d.)? If you are satisfied with the results of your current teaching practices, then one reason to implement PBL is to infuse the social responsibility so prevalent in PBL. Perhaps you are ready to try something new that will provide you a new challenge and add rigor to your activities to build on previous successes. You may have considered that times have changed and students will need to be prepared to thrive in a STEM world where the ability to creatively solve problems in dynamic and fluid situations abound. Regardless, students who are preparing to enter college will benefit from their experiences with PBL, and those students who do not participate in post-secondary education will develop a deeper and more salient understanding of the working world that they will enter. All students will have the opportunity to develop the cooperation and collaborative skills that are in demand regardless if they become factory workers or engineers. Recall Figure 1 where the task was customized to provide a suitable task or one group of students, it is important to remember that students at the other end of the continuum also require a degree of customization. As an example of scaling up rigor and PBL task customization Figure 3 shows the added rigor for another group doing the same PBL as shown in Figure 1.

PBL SAMPLE AND ASSESSMENTS

In the "Who Killed Bob Krusty?" PBL (Appendix A), the scenario contains all the salient information a student needs to successfully engage the problem. The activity integrates calculus and science with a forensic science and criminology spin. There are important aspects that need to be assessed before the start of the project and then again after the completion of the project. In this PBL, students are given the same assessment form before and after the activity. The pretest serves as one formative assessment. It provides students with a structure about what they are expected to be able to do upon completion of the PBL. For the teacher, the assessments provide insights about students' strengths and weaknesses so that the teacher can adjust the PBL process to meet students' needs, such as providing whole-group instruction on specific topics. The posttest provides a direct measure of how much improvement was achieved through the PBL. Another summative assessment may include, but of course is not limited to, daily journal entries where students reflect on their learning, record their thought processes during the PBL, and discuss what mathematics they need to employ or learn more about.

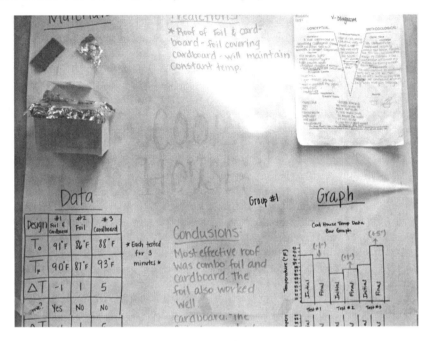

Figure 3

This activity can facilitate incorporation of knowledge from other disciplines. A drawing of the crime scene could be useful to determine if the conditions present were aligned with falling from the window or being thrown. This aspect would involve the engineering or CAD design teacher. This could incorporate geometry and trigonometry as well as physics and chemistry. It is also essential to incorporate the scientific process that medical examiners employ during a death investigation. That is, they rule out causes of death based on death scene characteristics, medical history, and other factors, and whatever is left that cannot be ruled out is in fact the cause of the death. Additionally, in real life, coroners, forensic examiners/investigators, and police officers author reports; therefore, within this activity students should also be expected to write reports to meet learning objectives, thereby facilitating connections to the language arts class. At periodic intervals during the activity for a check on learning, students should provide forensic reports that rule out possible causes of death. The final report should incorporate these preliminaries and provide a detailed hypothesis and a conclusion, so students can demonstrate a clear explanation incorporating the mathematical and scientific processes supporting the hypothesis and the conclusion.

UNDERSTANDING PBL

Given that this chapter is on assessment, it is important to connect the discussions in this book through an assessment model. The following PBL Refresher Quick Quiz should be considered formative. Some answers are not obvious initially from just reading this book. In fact, PBL is much like riding a bicycle. No matter how many technical manuals one reads about riding a bike, one must still get on, fall off, and reflect on both actions and suggestions in order to master the task. What makes riding a bike so complex? It is not just one task. It is composed of many small tasks that must be mastered to enjoy success. You must be able to balance, coordinate peddling and steering, remember that balance is easier as long as you are moving forward, remember how to brake, and understand that loose gravel can result in a painful lesson. Just like riding a bike, PBL is not just one task but the interaction of several smaller tasks including choosing learning outcomes, planning content, determining a scenario, writing the scenario, developing formative assessments, planning rubrics, and creating a summative assessment. Then, once the PBL starts, two new tasks arise: managing the materials and students. Therefore, as one reads and then implements PBL, one will gradually be more confident about the answers to the PBL Refresher Quick Quiz. It is only the iterative process of reading about PBL and then implementing it in the classroom that will make it second nature. Only through practice is it possible to perfect one's teaching because it is the teacher's own experiences and reflections on them that offer the best opportunities to improve student achievement.

WHO KILLED BOB KRUSTY? A DYNAMIC PROBLEM-SOLVING EVENT

Contributed by Christopher Romero, Calculus Teacher, Dallas, Texas

At 3:15 a.m. on a night in 2006, Ms. Fine, a maid who worked in the home of multimillionaire Bob Krusty was awoken by the sound of a loud thud outside her window. She got out of bed to discover that her employer had apparently "fallen" from one of his mansion's three balconies; Bob Krusty was dead. There were balconies located on the 2nd, 3rd, and 4th floors of his mansion. Police arrived at 3:25 a.m. and immediately noticed that Mr. Krusty was more than 10 feet horizontally away from the end of the balconies. He has obviously been pushed and murdered.

Immediately, the police sequestered those who were in the house that night; all were suspects in the murder. Police contacted Mr. Krusty's secretary, who was not at the house that evening, and obtained his schedule from the day before. Mr. Krusty had had a dinner party the evening before. He had invited his former business partner and his wife, Mr. and Ms. Smith. The Smiths arrived at 2 p.m. and spent the hour between 3:30 and 4:30 alone with Mr. Krusty in a closed meeting over tea. Mr. and Mrs. Jefferson, Mr. Krusty's old friends, had arrived late to the dinner and for about an hour met with him privately over coffee when dinner ended at 7:45.

As the CSI team arrived, the police began to interview the maid, Ms. Fine. She told them that indeed Mr. Krusty hosted a dinner party that night. She had even prepared Mr. Krusty's favorite dessert, rhubarb pie. In addition to the Smiths and Jeffersons, Ms. Fine indicated that Mr. Krusty's son John had attended the dinner. John had arrived that morning. Mr. Krusty had brandy with his son from 10:30 to 11:30 p.m. and had read alone in his study between the meetings with his son and the Jeffersons.

According to Ms. Fine, Mr. Krusty's evening had not been very eventful. She has last seen him alive at 11:45 p.m. when she brought him his medication with a glass of water. At that time he was alone and was going to sleep. She also noted that Mr. Krusty had elected to sleep with the doors to his 4th floor balcony open despite the cool evening temperature of 62° Fahrenheit. Additionally, she indicated that the two couples slept that evening in guest bedrooms on the 2nd floor. John slept on a cot in his father's 3rd floor office, and she slept in the maid's quarters on the 1st floor.

Following Ms. Fine's interview, the CSI team told the detectives that it was definitely a murder; there were no bloodstains on the sidewalk where Mr. Krusty had landed. Given his injuries, they determined that he had hit the ground with a velocity of between 45 and 50 feet per second. (Assume that Mr. Krusty's fall can be modeled with the function: $d = -16t2$ where d represents vertical distance and t represents time.) After sealing off the house and sending Mr. Krusty to the morgue for further tests, the CSI crew left the mansion around 6:30 a.m. but left uniformed officers to monitor the guests until the detectives could return at 10:00 a.m. to question the suspects.

At 10:00 a.m. the investigators returned and told the suspects that toxicology results had left them puzzled. The medical examiner had estimated the victim's core body temperature at 83.3° Fahrenheit at 4:00 a.m. and 75.2° Fahrenheit when they loaded him into the hearse at 6:15 a.m. Body temperature at death can be modeled with the following integral equation

$$\int_a^b \frac{dT}{(T-62)} = \int_0^t -k_B dt$$

where T is the cooled body temperature after t hours and k-sub-b is a constant dependent on the victim's body weight and surface area. You may assume that the victim's body temperature at the time of death was 98.6 °.

The toxicology report indicated that 705 milligrams of some poison were present in Mr. Krusty's system and had been ingested sometime in the past 24 hours. (Hint: A person dies after absorbing the fatal dose of a poison and the amount of poison present at the time of death remains constant.) The rate at which a poison is absorbed by the body may be modeled with the equation

$$\frac{\partial y(t)}{\partial t} = k_p y(t)$$

where $y(t)$ is the amount of poison remaining in the body t hours after the poison was administered. You should assume that $y(0) = 705$. K-sub-p is the constant that is characteristic for a given poison, which may be any of the following:

3. Poison	4. K-sub-p	5. Fatal Dose (mg)
Acrylamide	-0.29500	1275
Aniline	-0.95200	2025
Arsenic	-0.09200	215
Cyanide	-2.42300	50
Methanol	-1.16700	790
Phenol	-0.00004	15
Strychnine	-0.07400	105

PBL REFRESHER

Quick Quiz—PROJECT-BASED LEARNING

In general, PBL is the creation of complex settings and environments where students develop important skill sets and apply prior knowledge in the creation of new flexible knowledge. The problem-solving approach is incredibly important to the PBL environment where mathematics, science, and engineering are key components.

1. Data collection *is* important.
   True ☐ False ☐
2. Numerical accuracy is an ***essential*** skill for a ***successful*** final product.
   True ☐ False ☐
3. Statistics is not ***important*** for making use of PBL.
   True ☐ False ☐
4. Ethics and education in ethics are ***NOT*** key components of Project-Based Learning.
   True ☐ False ☐
5. Peer assessment is an ***important*** and ***essential*** aspect of PBL.
   True ☐ False ☐

ASPECTS OF PBL:

Please check all that apply to the key aspects of a well-developed PBL. If you do not place a check in the box, cross out or write in the word or phrase that would allow you to place a check in the box.

Structure of PBL

❑ Problem solving is stressed.
❑ Projects should be irrelevant to students but closely address learning objectives.
❑ Teaching should be innovative with active learning.
❑ Learning objectives have no place in the design of PBL.
❑ Rigorous mathematics and science are integrated.
❑ Students work in groups.
❑ Team building is a secondary skill that should be addressed if everything else is working well.
❑ Exclusion from participation is a first line of behavior management.
❑ One group member selected at random presents the group's project.

Planning PBL

❑ ONLY one project per semester will result in the learning outcomes I expect, and the district will be satisfied.

❑ All the interpersonal, behavioral, and metacognitive skills students will need should be present before I try a PBL, or they should have them all when they finish the first PBL.

❑ Projects are set well in advance, and all the teachers and administrators are stakeholders in making this a success.

❑ Training is not important to planning and conducting a meaningful PBL.

❑ Administrators have a very important role in successful PBL, but they only need to give permission and provide supplies and have no other role.

❑ Teachers should develop a set of common resources used for the PBL.

❑ On-going collaborative meetings across and among all teachers involved are necessary for a PBL success.

Assessment in PBL

❑ Group work but individual accountability.

❑ Individual accountability for all summative assessments.

❑ On-going peer review only works when the teacher is completely in charge.

❑ Peer assessment.

❑ The use of culminating events like developing a marketing plan, conducting a trial, or developing a persuasive exposé can be used to explain, justify, or sell the PBL to investors, argue evidence, or prepare a news article are important to integration of writing and expressing ideas logically.

❑ Summative PBL reporting should be **only** in writing or **only** orally but ***NEVER*** both.

Student/Group Responsibility

❑ Students should develop a design notebook that details what they did and how their work crosses curriculum boundaries.

❑ Group members need to learn to engage in conflict.

❑ Conflict resolution is idiosyncratic and does not need to be taught or modeled.

❑ Individuals are responsible for their behaviors.

Benefits of Teams and Team Building for PBL

❑ Improved attendance

❑ More confusion for parents

❑ Improved engagement for teachers

❑ More community concerns

REFERENCES

Andrade, H. G. (2000). Using rubrics to promote thinking and learning. *Educational Leadership, 57*(5), 13–18.

Andrade, H. G. (n.d.). *Understanding rubrics.* Retrieved June 1, 2008, from http://learnweb.harvard.edu/ALPS/thinking/docs/rubricar.htm

Boaler, J. (1998). Open and closed mathematics approaches: Student experiences and understandings. *Journal for Research in Mathematics Education, 29*, 41–62.

Bray, B. (2001, April). Student achievement needs to drive the professional development program. *OnCue Newsletter.*

Brophy, J. (2004). *Motivating students to learn* (2nd ed.). Mahwah, NJ: Erlbaum.

Falchikov, N. (1995). Peer feedback marking: Developing peer assessment. *Innovations in Education and Teaching International, 32*, 175–187.

Kulm, G. (1994). *Mathematics assessment. What works in the classroom.* San Francisco, CA: Jossey-Bass.

Moursund, D. (n.d.). *Part 7: Assessment.* Retrieved June 1, 2008, from http://www.uoregon.edu/~moursund/PBL/part_7.htm

Peckham, G., & Sutherland, L. (2000). The role of self-assessment in moderating students' expectations. *South African Journal for Higher Education, 14*(1), 75–78.

Secretary''s Commission on Achieving Necessary skills. (2000). *What work requires of schools: A SCANS report for America 2000.* Washington, DC: U.S. Department of Labor.

Solomon, G. (2003, January). Project-based learning: A primer. *Technology & Learning, 23*(6), 20–30.

Zimmaro, D. M. (2004). *Developing grading rubrics.* Retrieved June 1, 2008, from the University of Texas at Austin, Division of Instructional Innovation and Assessment Web site: http://www.utexas.edu/academic/mec/research/pdf/rubricshandout.pdf

Robert M. Capraro
Department of Teaching, Learning and Culture,
Texas A&M University

Z. Ebrar Yetkiner
Department of Teaching, Learning and Culture,
Texas A&M University

OVERVIEW FOR THE DESIGN OF STEM PBLS

WELL-DEFINED OUTCOME AND AN ILL-DEFINED TASK

Our definition for a PBL drives all of the design and implementation decisions discussed in this book. Therefore, a quick deconstruction of our definition is useful prior to reading through our sample PBLs or designing of your own PBLs.

Well-defined outcome – The well-defined outcome comes from the dual influence of the engineering design process and high-stakes accountability and standards. An engineer always starts with an end in mind (e.g., span this river, minimize fuel consumption, etc.) and in today's high stakes testing environment so should designers of instruction. Our STEM PBL design process always begins with a measurable objective in mind and typically includes the design of summative assessments prior to instructional design to ensure that the students will in fact meet the objective. In the best case scenario, these summative assessments will include open-ended assessments that look a great deal like the learning activities from the PBL and multiple choice questions that are similar in style and content to local, state, and national assessments that students will be taking in the future. This is NOT teaching to the test, it is designing to the objective.

Because the majority of our work is in the state of Texas, we have chosen to use Texas state standards (http://www.tea.state.tx.us/teks/) to model our design process but other local, state, or national standards that guide your instruction would be the beginning of your *well-defined outcome*. All of our STEM PBLs start with a well-defined outcome (could have been labeled as the primary objective). The well-defined outcome was developed through the integration of the secondary objectives and it is the integrated well-defined outcome that initiated the design process, informed our summative assessment design and all subsequent instructional design decisions. The secondary objectives are crucial as they define the integration and provide the STEM for our PBL. Group planning is also encouraged by including substantive secondary objectives. Secondary objectives are assessed to varying degrees (formative and summative) depending upon the intent of their inclusion. Please resist the temptation to pull a single concept out of a secondary objective and implement the PBL with that as the primary objective. If you change the well-defined outcome, you will need to change the PBL.

Ill-defined task(s) – The ill-defined task(s) are essential to the inquiry process. Too often, hands-on activities are verification of known – or at least taught – concepts. The ill-defined nature of STEM PBL requires higher order thinking skills, problem-solving, and increased content learning. One misconception about PBL in general is that it is chaotic or haphazard. Nothing could be further from the truth. Ill-defined is not ill-designed. The teacher must design tasks that allow for student investigation, multiple solutions, and engaging contexts all of which converge in a common understanding of the well-defined outcome.

Putting it all together in a STEM PBL classroom – As a teacher, you and your students will need practice and support as you transition to STEM PBL tasks and learning. A simple suggestion which may hasten the transition is an extended 5-E model of instruction. We have chosen to use the 5-E model to communicate our design, but recognize that there are other appropriate inquiry models that can be modified to fit STEM PBL. Resist the temptation to tell the students what they are going to learn, let them learn it! But plan to let your students talk, plan to talk yourself, just don't talk first, last, or the most. We have included a limited number of examples of STEM PBLs that we have used in the past and recommend as well-tested exemplars for you as you learn to design and implement STEM PBLs. This is not a comprehensive list and we do not think that providing one would dramatically improve your chances of implementing STEM PBL. Your local and state standards are different, your resources are different, you potential partners are different . . . and thus your STEM PBLs should be different. Good luck!

NON-NEWTONIAN FLUID MECHANICS

Well-defined outcome

The student will be able to use the general form of functions (including comparison of linear and quadratic) to describe the effect of % water on viscosity of silly putty and apply the general form of the quadratic parent function to explain non-linear flow of a non-Newtonian fluid (silly putty).

Secondary objectives:

Mathematics (Algebra I)
1) The student understands that a function represents a dependence of one quantity on another and can be described in a variety of ways.
A) The student describes independent and dependent quantities in functional relationships.
B) The student gathers and records data, or uses data sets, to determine functional (systematic) relationships between quantities.
C) The student represents relationships among quantities using concrete models, tables, graphs, diagrams, verbal descriptions, equations, and inequalities.
D) The student interprets and makes inferences from functional relationships.

2) The student uses the **properties and attributes of functions**.
A) The student **identifies** and sketches the **general forms** of linear ($y = x$) and **quadratic ($y = x^2$) parent functions**.
B) For a variety of situations, the student identifies the mathematical domains and ranges and **determines reasonable domain and range values for given situations**.
C) In solving problems, the student collects and organizes data, makes and interprets scatterplots, and models, predicts, and makes decisions and critical judgments.

Science (Integrated Physics and Chemistry)

IPC 7A) **investigate** and identify properties of fluids including density, **viscosity**, and buoyancy;
IPC 8A) **distinguish** between **physical** and **chemical** changes in matter such as oxidation, digestion, changes in states, and stages in the rock cycle;

Materials

4% Borax solution (premixed)	Elmer's Glue
Plastic cups Timers	
Meter Sticks	Baggies
Markers Funnels	
Stirrers	
Graph paper/overheads/pens	

Safety Notes

Use safety glasses and gloves when mixing the Borax solution and do not allow students to access to the dry powder. The Borax solution is a **mild** bleaching agent and is thus basic, so students should wash their hands after the lab. The silly putty product is non-toxic and can be taken home by the students.

Engagement (As close as we get to stating the ill-defined task)

Day 1 (5-15 minutes)
1. Play with a large "ball" of silly putty as the students walk into class.
2. Answer questions about what you are playing with. Be ready to ask if it is a solid or a liquid if that is not asked.
3. Guiding Question - What effect does %water have on the viscosity of silly putty . . . and how can the general forms of functions help us interpret this relationship?

Exploration

Day 1 (30-60 minutes – the rest of the period!)
The students will explore the Internet or other resources to find suitable recipes for silly putty (teachers may substitute similar products such as GAK or slime, but be aware that slime requires the purchase of poly vinyl alcohol in advance from a chemical supplier such as Flynn Scientific . . . it is also harder and more expensive to make). The students will then write up a procedure to make and test the viscosity of the chosen material. School based silly putty is typically created my mixing equal amounts of a 4% Borax solution and Elmer's Glue™, although some web-based resources recommend diluting the glue or altering the 1:1 mixing ratio – hence the inquiry! HINT: Their original design might not work – that is a good thing! Don't "perfect" their designs for them – that is the purpose of doing the PBL!

Day 2 (45-90 minutes)
Make some silly putty and test it. Students need to be prompted to keep good notes on different trials for their write-up and they may eventually need some hints to get data which answers the question(s).

Explanation

Day 3
The Math – In the activity, students will construct a scatterplot that shows a definite nonlinear relationship that – when the domain and range are properly controlled – appears to be quadratic in nature. Vocabulary that needs to be reviewed and or discussed include: dependent/independent/control variables, linear/ nonlinear/quadratic, domain and range, functions/parent functions. HINT: Use REAL student data in the explanation/discussion.

The Science - The glue contains a polymer called polyvinyl acetate resin. We changed the polymers' behavior twice in this activity; once when we added water to the Elmer's glue and the second time when we added borax. What did the borax actually do? The borax is called a cross-linker. It chemically "ties together" the long strands of the polyvinyl acetate. This tying together changed the viscosity of the glue. It increased the viscosity because the new cross-linked chains interfere with the ability of the solution to flow. As a result the silly putty is "stiffer" It is not a solid though. How do we know this? If we leave the silly putty alone on a table it will flatten out. It is also not a liquid because we can form it into a shape. So what is it?

Many fluids exhibit a ***non-linear*** response to stress, and are called non-Newtonian fluids. Such fluids fall halfway between being a solid (where the stress depends on the instantaneous deformation) and Newtonian fluids (where the stress depends on the instantaneous rate of change in time of the deformation). For such 'soft solids' or 'elastic liquids', the stress depends **nonlinearly** on the history of the deformation (Institute for Non-Newtonian Fluid Mechanics - http://innfm.swan.ac.uk/ innfm_updated/content/about/glossary.asp?index=4).

Read more about Non-Newtonian fluids on the Internet. We recommend http://antoine.frostburg.edu/chem/senese/101/liquids/faq/non-newtonian.shtml at General Chemistry Online for a good conceptual answer, or a more detailed; but understandable explanation at Wikopedia - http://en.wikipedia.org/wiki/Non-Newtonian_fluid.

Extension

Day 3 or 4 (depending upon available time)
What would the data for a Newtonian fluid look like?
Do all viscous materials flow nonlinearly?
Are there other common nonlinear fluids?
Could this test be used to identify Non-Newtonian fluids?
How do engineers take advantage of nonlinear flow?
What kinds of problems does nonlinear flow create for engineers?

Evaluation

Day 4 (or homework depending upon available time)

<u>Formative assessment I</u> will focus on questioning individuals and small groups relative to dependent/independent/control variables, linear/ nonlinear/quadratic, domain and range, functions/parent functions while they are working on the PBL.

<u>Formative assessment II</u> will be whole group discussion of the above vocabulary and science concepts PRIOR to students finishing their write-ups.

<u>Formative assessment III</u> will be a formal write-up answering the initial question(s). Require the students to answer at least one Extension question in the write-up.

<u>Summative assessment</u> will be a traditional paper and pencil exam with a combination of open-ended questions that are similar to the design activities and multiple choice questions that are similar to the state exam that the students will take. One example from a previously administered TAKS test (The Texas accountability exam) is provided below. The correct answer for the sample question is the F, which represents a linear function instead of a nonlinear function like the example in the test to test for transfer.

Identify the graph that best represents the relationship between the number of gallons of gasoline Mr. Johnson purchased at $1.49 a gallon and the total cost of his gasoline.

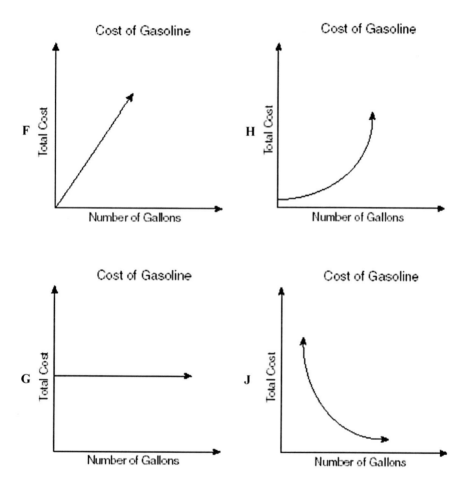

Figure 1. Multiple choice question.

Previously administered TAKS exams are available at
http://www.tea.state.tx.us/student.assessment/resources/release/).

EXPONENTIAL GROWTH

WELL-DEFINED OUTCOME:

The student will be able to analyze data and represent exponential growth of humans to evaluate the significance of genetic manipulation of DNA to extend human life expectancy as they develop a PowerPoint presentation on "should scientists be researching genetic pathways to extend human lifespan?"

Secondary objectives:

Mathematics (Algebra I)

ALG I 3C) The student **analyzes data** and **represents situations** involving **exponential growth** and decay using concrete models, **tables, graphs,** or **algebraic methods**.

Science (Biology)

Biology 3C) identify and illustrate how **changes in DNA** cause mutations and **evaluate the significance** of these changes;

Materials

Internet
Safety Notes

NA

Engagement

Day 1 (15- 30 minutes)
Read any article that discusses expanding the life span of non-human animals (typically nematode worms and mice are used as models) through genetic engineering.
Examples can be found at:
1. http://query.nytimes.com/gst/fullpage.html?sec=health&res=9907E0D6103FF
930A25756C0A96F958260&n=Top%2fNews%2fScience%2fTopics%2fDNA
%20Deoxyribonucleic%20Acid
2. http://www.sciencedaily.com/releases/2005/07/050725065410.htm
3. http://query.nytimes.com/gst/fullpage.html?sec=health&res=9D01E2D9153FF
936A2575BC0A961958260

Ask the question:

> Should scientists be researching genetic pathways to extend human lifespan?

Allow for short discussion and follow with:

> How can mathematics help us answer such a question?

Exploration

Day 1 (30-60 minutes – the rest of the period!)
The students will explore the Internet or other resources to find more in depth information on genetic engineering and human population growth. End day one with students recording the world population from one of the world population clocks online (see explanations for acceptable sites if students do not find on their own).

Day 2 (45-90 minutes)
Record the new world population. The students will select appropriate data from various online resources and calculate the equation that represents the growth rate of the data. Students will be prompted to look at countries with differing life spans to compare growth rates.

Explanation

Day 3
Overall - Counter-intuitively, extending the life-span of humans would not dramatically affect world population. This shows up dramatically in the activity in several ways: 1) the math - the most important factor in predicting future human populations is the compounding rate, which is unaffected (see 2); 2) natural selection increases fitness for reproduction, increasing the life-span doesn't increase the number of off-spring; and 3) in verification of point 2, a simple investigation of current trends in population growth supports the notion that living longer actually decreases off-spring (probably because extending life-span of humans normally follows better education related to health and health infrastructure, which also accompanied by a change from an agrarian lifestyle which rewards large families)

The Math – In the activity, students will work with exponential growth using the formula ($y = a^x$), where a = population and x = rate of growth. A particular point of emphasis in this activity is that extending the life-span doesn't change x (the rate of growth) and has only a one-time minor effect on a (the population) and thus extending the life span of humans would not noticeably change the world population. The students will also be interpreting graphs, tables, and use various algebraic methods to determine the effect of extending life span of different populations from Wikipedia website on human population and US Census bureau.

The Science – Evolutionary biologist don't generally predict a life-span gene because 1) life span is a multifactorial phenomenon (many factors contribute to aging); 2) natural selection favors retention of characteristics and behaviors which increase fitness up to reproduction and not beyond, because just living longer doesn't produce extra off-spring (a very important point in our activity); and 3) increasing life-span increases the number of post-reproductive organisms which would compete with their own off-spring for resources (food etc.).

Read more about genetic engineering and extension of the human life span on the Internet. We recommend:
1. http://ibgwww.colorado.edu/tj-lab/ (One of the labs that does the research and as such includes current links to professional and popular press publications relevant to genetic engineering and the extension on human life spans.)
2. http://en.wikipedia.org/wiki/World_population
3. http://www.worldometers.info/population/ One of several world population clocks on the web.
4. http://www.census.gov/ US Census bureau, which includes links to entire world population.

Extension

Day 3 or 4 (depending upon available time)
Are there other pathways to extending life-span in humans?
Are there other genetic "treatments" that are beneficial to man (e.g., cure an illness)?
Is genetic engineering of humans ethical?
Is genetic engineering of any living species ethical?
What factors have to occur for exponential decay in population growth to occur? Is this currently happening in any countries?
Is the destruction of rain forests an example of exponential decay?
Can you write a generalized from for an exponential decrease or increase?
How is exponential change related a Fibonacci sequence? Unlike?

Evaluation

Day 4 (or homework depending upon available time)
Formative assessment I will focus on questioning individuals and small groups relative to dependent/independent/control variables, linear/ nonlinear/quadratic, domain and range, functions/parent functions while they are working on the PBL.
Formative assessment II will be whole group discussion of the above vocabulary and science concepts PRIOR to students finishing their PowerPoint presentations.
Formative assessment III will be an evaluation of the PowerPoint presentations formal answering the initial question(s). Require the students to answer at least one Extension question in the presentation.
Summative assessment will be a traditional paper and pencil exam with a combination of open-ended questions that are similar to the design activities and multiple-choice questions that are similar to the state exam that the students will take.

WHO KILLED BOB KRUSTY?

A DYNAMIC PROBLEM-SOLVING EVENT

Well-defined outcome:

The student will be able to use functions and integrals to analyze the data within scenario to make predications about who killed Bob Krusty.

Secondary objectives:

– work with functions represented in a variety of ways: graphical, numerical, analytical, or verbal. They should understand the connections among these representations.
– understand the meaning of the derivative in terms of a rate of change and local linear approximation and they should be able to use derivatives to solve a variety of problems.
– understand the meaning of the definite integral both as a limit of Riemann sums and as the net accumulation of change and should be able to use integrals to solve a variety of problems.
– understand the relationship between the derivative and the definite integral as expressed in both parts of the Fundamental Theorem of Calculus.
– communicate mathematics both orally and in well-written sentences and should be able to explain solutions to problems.
– model a written description of a physical situation with a function, a differential equation, or an integral.
– use technology to help solve problems, experiment, interpret results, and verify conclusions.
– determine the reasonableness of solutions, including sign, size, relative accuracy, and units of measurement.
– develop an appreciation of calculus as a coherent body of knowledge and as a human accomplishment

– (College Board, 2008) found at:
– http://www.collegeboard.com/student/testing/ap/sub_calab.html

Science (Chemistry)
Chemistry 5A) identify changes in matter, determine the nature of the change, and **examine the forms of energy involved**; and
Chemistry 5B) **identify** and **measure energy transformations** and exchanges involved in **chemical reactions**.

Materials

Bob Krusty Scenario   Graphing Calculator

Safety Notes

NA

Engagement

Day 1 (15-30 minutes)
From the original scenario: At 3:15 a.m. on a night in 2006, Ms. Fine, a maid who worked in the home of multimillionaire Bob Krusty was awoken by the sound of a loud thud outside her window. She got out of bed to discover that her employer had apparently "fallen" from one of his mansion's three balconies; Bob Krusty was dead. There were balconies located on the 2nd, 3rd, and 4th floors of his mansion. Police arrived at 3:25 a.m. and immediately noticed that Mr. Krusty was more than 10 feet horizontally away from the end of the balconies. He has obviously been pushed and murdered.

Have students work in groups to discuss why it is obvious that it was murder and what evidence they will need to solve the murder. Share group discussions.

Exploration

Day 1 (30-60 minutes – the rest of the period!)
From the original scenario: Immediately, the police sequestered those who were in the house that night; all were suspects in the murder. Police contacted Mr. Krusty's secretary, who was not at the house that evening, and obtained his schedule from the day before. Mr. Krusty had had a dinner party the evening before. He had invited his former business partner and his wife, Mr. and Ms. Smith. The Smiths arrived at 2 p.m. and spent the hour between 3:30 and 4:30 alone with Mr. Krusty in a closed meeting over tea. Mr. and Mrs. Jefferson, Mr. Krusty's old friends, had arrived late to the dinner and for about an hour met with him privately over coffee when dinner ended at 7:45.

    As the CSI team arrived, the police began to interview the maid, Ms. Fine. She told them that indeed Mr. Krusty hosted a dinner party that night. She had even prepared Mr. Krusty's favorite dessert, rhubarb pie. In addition to the Smiths and Jeffersons, Ms. Fine indicated that Mr. Krusty's son John had attended the dinner. John had arrived that morning. Mr. Krusty had brandy with his son from 10:30 to 11:30 p.m. and had read alone in his study between the meetings with his son and the Jeffersons.

    According to Ms. Fine, Mr. Krusty's evening had not been very eventful. She has last seen him alive at 11:45 p.m. when she brought him his medication with a glass of water. At that time he was alone and was going to sleep. She also noted that Mr. Krusty had elected to sleep with the doors to his 4th floor balcony open despite the cool evening temperature of 62° Fahrenheit. Additionally, she indicated that the two couples slept that evening in guest bedrooms on the 2nd floor. John slept on a cot in his father's 3rd floor office, and she slept in the maid's quarters on the 1st floor.

Following Ms. Fine's interview, the CSI team told the detectives that it was definitely a murder; there were no bloodstains on the sidewalk where Mr. Krusty had landed. Given his injuries, they determined that he had hit the ground with a velocity of between 45 and 50 feet per second. (Assume that Mr. Krusty's fall can be modeled with the function: $d = -16t2$ where d represents vertical distance and t represents time.) After sealing off the house and sending Mr. Krusty to the morgue for further tests, the CSI crew left the mansion around 6:30 a.m. but left uniformed officers to monitor the guests until the detectives could return at 10:00 a.m. to question the suspects.

At 10:00 a.m. the investigators returned and told the suspects that toxicology results had left them puzzled. The medical examiner had estimated the victim's core body temperature at 83.3° Fahrenheit at 4:00 a.m. and 75.2° Fahrenheit when they loaded him into the hearse at 6:15 a.m. Body temperature at death can be modeled with the following integral equation

$$\int_a^b \frac{dT}{(T-62)} = \int_0^t -k_B dt$$

where T is the cooled body temperature after t hours and k-sub-b is a constant dependent on the victim's body weight and surface area. You may assume that the victim's body temperature at the time of death was 98.6°.

The toxicology report indicated that 705 milligrams of some poison were present in Mr. Krusty's system and had been ingested sometime in the past 24 hours. The rate at which a poison is absorbed by the body may be modeled with the equation

$$\frac{\partial y(t)}{\partial t} = k_p y(t)$$

where y (t) is the amount of poison remaining in the body t hours after the poison was administered. You should assume that y(0) = 705. K-sub-p is the constant that is characteristic for a given poison, which may be any of the following:

Why is the CSI team confused?

Poison	K-sub-p	Fatal Dose (mg)
Acrylamide	-0.29500	1275
Aniline	-0.95200	2025
Arsenic	-0.09200	215
Cyanide	-2.42300	50
Methanol	-1.16700	790
Phenol	-0.00004	15
Strychnine	-0.07400	105

Explanation

Day 2
Overall - Prepare a PowerPoint presentation identifying the killer of Bob Krusty. Include **all** evidence and address all testimony.

The Math – Discuss the importance of learning calculus and it uses in solving seemingly complex real-world problems. Many real-world phenomena can be explained through calculus. Discuss functions and the using integrals to solve problems, and demonstrate the interpretability of integrals. . Therefore, discuss the information obtained by doing integrals instead of focusing on the algorithmic processes.

Science – The rate of change in temperature of an object is proportional to the difference between the object's original temperature and the temperature of the surrounding environment – or Newton's Law of Cooling. Therefore, with a few basic assumptions and two measurements of a dead person's temperature, we can determine fairly accurately the time of death (see equation above). A person dies after absorbing the fatal dose of a poison and the amount of poison present at the time of death remains constant because cellular metabolism has ceased.

Extension

Day 2 or 3 (depending upon available time)
Which assumptions in the scenario are most likely not to be true?
What effect would the temperature of the room have on the calculation?
What effect would the person having a temperature have on the calculation?
What effect would the medium (air vs. floating in a body of water) have on the calculation?

Evaluation

Day 3 or 4 (or homework depending upon available time)
<u>Formative assessment I</u> will focus on questioning individuals and small groups relative to energy transformations in chemical reactions, integrals, functions, fundamental theorem of calculus, and half-life while they are working on the PBL.
<u>Formative assessment II</u> will be whole group discussion of the above vocabulary and science concepts PRIOR to students finishing their PowerPoint presentations.
<u>Formative assessment III</u> will be an evaluation of the PowerPoint presentations formal answering the initial question(s). Require the students to answer at least one Extension question in the presentation.
<u>Summative assessment</u> will be a traditional paper and pencil exam with a combination of open-ended questions that are similar to the design activities and multiple-choice questions that are similar to the state exam that the students will take. (Sample Attached)

PRE AND POST ASSESSMENTS FOR WHO KILLED BOB KRUSTY?

Throughout this test, this function will be referenced as $Z(x)$:

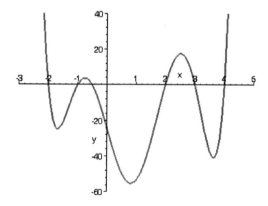

I. True/False (A=True, B=False)
   a. If $x=c$ is a critical number of a function, $f(x)$, then it is also the critical number of the function, $g(x) = f(x) + k$, where k is some constant.
   b. If $f'(x)>0$ for all real number values of x, then $f(x)$ increases without bound.
   c. If $f'(c)=0$ for some real number c, then the function must either be switching from increasing to decreasing or decreasing to increasing.
   d. If $f(x)$ is a continuous function on $[a,b]$ and differentiable on (a,b) and there exists k in (a,b) such that $f'(k)=0$, then $f(a) = f(b)$.
   e. There exists a function $f(x)$ such that $f(1)=-2, f(3)=10$, and $f'(x)>0$ for all x.
   f. If $f'(x)=g'(x)$, then $f(x)=g(x)$.
   g. If $f(x)$ has three x-intercepts on a particular interval, then $f(x)$ must have two critical points.

h. The derivative of $Z(x)$ (the function graphed above) equals 0 at 6 different values of x.

i. There exists a function $f(x)$ such that $f(x)>0$, $f'(x)<0$, and $f''(x)>0$ for all x.

COMPUTATIONAL INTEGRALS TEST

Due End of Class! 10 Integrals – 5 points per prompt – 60 total points

Take Home: You may use any inanimate source. You may not discuss the problems with each other. This test is meant to be challenging. Do not freak! All problems are solvable with concepts covered in both class and the book/handouts. Please be extremely neat! If I cannot read or understand your work, I cannot give you credit for it.

Section I – Basic Integrals

a) $\displaystyle\int 8x^3 + 3x^2\,dx$

b) $\displaystyle\int_0^1 x^2 \cos x^3\,dx$

c) $\displaystyle\int e^x \sin x\,dx$

d) $\displaystyle\int x^2 \ln x\,dx$

e) $\displaystyle\int_{-\infty}^0 (1+x)e^x\,dx$

f) $\displaystyle\int_0^\pi \frac{x\sin x}{1+\cos^2 x}\,dx$

g) $\displaystyle\int \cot x\,dx$

h) $\displaystyle\int \sec x\,dx$

ORIGINAL WHO KILLED BOB KRUSTY SCENARIO

At 3:15 a.m. on a night in 2006, Ms. Fine, a maid who worked in the home of multimillionaire Bob Krusty was awoken by the sound of a loud thud outside her window. She got out of bed to discover that her employer had apparently "fallen" from one of his mansion's three balconies; Bob Krusty was dead. There were balconies located on the 2nd, 3rd, and 4th floors of his mansion. Police arrived at 3:25 a.m. and immediately noticed that Mr. Krusty was more than 10 feet horizontally away from the end of the balconies. He has obviously been pushed and murdered.

Immediately, the police sequestered those who were in the house that night; all were suspects in the murder. Police contacted Mr. Krusty's secretary, who was not at the house that evening, and obtained his schedule from the day before. Mr. Krusty had had a dinner party the evening before. He had invited his former business partner and his wife, Mr. and Ms. Smith. The Smiths arrived at 2 p.m. and spent the hour between 3:30 and 4:30 alone with Mr. Krusty in a closed meeting over tea. Mr. and Mrs. Jefferson, Mr. Krusty's old friends, had arrived late to the dinner and for about an hour met with him privately over coffee when dinner ended at 7:45.

As the CSI team arrived, the police began to interview the maid, Ms. Fine. She told them that indeed Mr. Krusty hosted a dinner party that night. She had even prepared Mr. Krusty's favorite dessert, rhubarb pie. In addition to the Smiths and Jeffersons, Ms. Fine indicated that Mr. Krusty's son John had attended the dinner. John had arrived that morning. Mr. Krusty had brandy with his son from 10:30 to 11:30 p.m. and had read alone in his study between the meetings with his son and the Jeffersons.

According to Ms. Fine, Mr. Krusty's evening had not been very eventful. She has last seen him alive at 11:45 p.m. when she brought him his medication with a glass of water. At that time he was alone and was going to sleep. She also noted that Mr. Krusty had elected to sleep with the doors to his 4th floor balcony open despite the cool evening temperature of 62° Fahrenheit. Additionally, she indicated that the two couples slept that evening in guest bedrooms on the 2nd floor. John slept on a cot in his father's 3rd floor office, and she slept in the maid's quarters on the 1st floor.

Following Ms. Fine's interview, the CSI team told the detectives that it was definitely a murder; there were no bloodstains on the sidewalk where Mr. Krusty had landed. Given his injuries, they determined that he had hit the ground with a velocity of between 45 and 50 feet per second. (Assume that Mr. Krusty's fall can be modeled with the function: $d = -16t2$ where d represents vertical distance and t represents time.) After sealing off the house and sending Mr. Krusty to the morgue for further tests, the CSI crew left the mansion around 6:30 a.m. but left uniformed officers to monitor the guests until the detectives could return at 10:00 a.m. to question the suspects.

At 10:00 a.m. the investigators returned and told the suspects that toxicology results had left them puzzled. The medical examiner had estimated the victim's core body temperature at 83.3° Fahrenheit at 4:00 a.m. and 75.2° Fahrenheit when they loaded him into the hearse at 6:15 a.m. Body temperature at death can be modeled with the following integral equation

$$\int_a^b \frac{dT}{(T-62)} = \int_0^t -k_B dt$$

where T is the cooled body temperature after t hours and k-sub-b is a constant dependent on the victim's body weight and surface area. You may assume that the victim's body temperature at the time of death was 98.6 °.

The toxicology report indicated that 705 milligrams of some poison were present in Mr. Krusty's system and had been ingested sometime in the past 24 hours. (Hint: A person dies after absorbing the fatal dose of a poison and the amount of poison present at the time of death remains constant.) The rate at which a poison is absorbed by the body may be modeled with the equation

$$\frac{\partial y(t)}{\partial t} = k_p y(t)$$

where $y(t)$ is the amount of poison remaining in the body t hours after the poison was administered. You should assume that $y(0) = 705$. K-sub-p is the constant that is characteristic for a given poison, which may be any of the following:

	K-sub-p	Fatal Dose (mg)
Acrylamide	-0.29500	1275
Aniline	-0.95200	2025
Arsenic	-0.09200	215
Cyanide	-2.42300	50
Methanol	-1.16700	790
Phenol	-0.00004	15
Strychnine	-0.07400	105

HEAT ENERGY

Well defined outcome:

The student will be able to determine the optimum roofing materials which will keep a model house cool by testing various materials, collecting, measuring, and graphing heat energy conducted and radiated into the house and representing and explaining the meaning of linear functions in the real-world.

Secondary Objectives:

Mathematics (Algebra I)
1) The student recognizes the various **representations of linear functions**
A) The student **makes connections** between **graphical and verbal descriptions of linear functions.**
B) The student **collects and records data to compare ratios** of heat absorption
2) The student **determines relationships** between various materials to **identify the slope and intercepts in the graph to calculate rates** of absorption.
A) The student makes **interpretations and inferences** to determine the functionality of linear functions as these apply in the real-world
B) The student will be able **to investigate and demonstrate** the effects of changes in heat transfer through various materials.

Science (Integrated Physics and Chemistry)

1. The student understands the importance of **heat energy in everyday life.**
A) The student applies the **law of conservation of energy.**
B) The student makes inferences and tests various materials to determine which material is the **least conductor of heat.**
C) The student **collects data** and makes inferences as to which pair of materials are optimum to promote **conduction, convection and radiation.**
D) The student **graphs heat temperature to compare** materials to determine the optimum radiation of heat and its relationship to R-values.
E) The student **explains results by providing evidence** as to why homes should be well insulated – real world applications

Materials

Index cards	fabric material
Cellophane tape	paper (various colors)
Aluminum foil	Stopwatch
Styrofoam	Balsa wood

Shingles		Overhead transparencies
Cardboard	Data sheet	
Fabric material	Graph paper	

Testing station materials

Extension cord	Light bulb 100 watt frosted, incandescent
Ring stand and clamp lamp	Thermometer or Heat probe
Cup with water at room temperature	Stopwatch

Safety Notes

Use safety glasses to protect your eyes when reading the thermometer. Do not touch the light source when it is on because its temperature may cause burns to your hands. Wait until the light bulb has cold off to remove it.

Engagement (As close as we get to stating the ill-defined task)

Day 1(30-45 minutes) class period.
Walk into class with a large heavy coat, gloves, insulated hat, and a scarf. Discuss when and where to wear such an outfit and why it is appropriate for those situations. Next ask the following guiding questions before the activity: What is heat energy? How does heat energy work? Explain how. What may happen if you are exposed to high amounts of heat energy? Why? How do we protect ourselves from heat energy? These questions will get students engage in thinking of possible sources and uses of heat energy and how this type of energy is beneficial of harmful. After students have responded to the questions, present students the following scenario. "You have been shipwrecked on an island. You washed up the beach along with materials the ship was carrying including a large crate with no top (packing materials, cardboard, etc.) Ask students to brain storm ideas on how to use the crate as a shelter and construct a roof that will protect them from the sun harmful rays and high temperatures. Encourage students to bring their own materials to design and test for the roof. Before students test the roof materials ask students to predict which materials will keep the house the coolest and why? Students should take notes and answer the questions in their journal.

Day 2(30-45 minutes) class period.
Students build a 3x5 index cards house with a 3x 5 window made of a piece of the transparency sheet. This side of the house will be used as a window to view the temperature of the thermometer. Students can also use a heat probe attached to a calculator to collect the temperature and graph the results.

Exploration

Day 3(30-55 minutes) class period.
Set up the testing station on the designated table (test the station before the students use it). Mark an area on the table where the house should be placed. Set up the lamp or heat source to shine 9 inches from the marked area. The designed house should be under the heat lamp for 3 minutes. Ask students to cut a 3 x 5 piece of five individual materials to be used as the roof of the house. Remind students to record the temperature of the house before and after the heat light is on. Record the temperatures on the data sheet provided (if using the thermometer, do not forget to cool it off after each reading by dipping it water at room temperature).

Day 4 (30-55 minutes) class period.
Students will be testing combinations of materials they found to be the most efficient in keeping the temperature of the house temperature down. Materials should be layer down in pairs. Students should repeat the same procedure used to test selected pairs of materials (5 pairs).

Explanation

Day 5 (30-55 minutes) class period.
The Math – In the activity students will record initial temperature on a data sheet every 30 seconds for 3 minutes for each pair of materials tested. Calculate ΔT, record the difference in temperature. Graph results to determine y intercept, slope and equation. Students should be able to explain the results using dependent and independent, control and variables. Students will be able to visualize meaningful uses of linear functions by identifying the slope and intercepts of the graph and the effects of changes in parameters of linear functions in real-world and mathematical situations.

The Science – After testing, conducting calculations, and graphing results students can compare their predictions to the results obtained. Ask students to explain why they think their prediction did or did not work. Ask the following questions to review concepts such as convection, conduction, radiation, insulators, conductors, R-values: Explain why some of the materials they use kept the temperature high or rising? Why did the temperature decrease? What is the difference between a conductor and an insulator? How are these materials used in everyday life? Why? How do the results obtained inform them about insulators use to keep their homes cool in the summer time and warm in the wintertime? Ask student to research on the internet other real world applications of insulators and conductors.

Extension

Day 6 (30-55 minutes) class period.

Based on availability of time students could design their own roof using the most optimum materials. Two or three different designs may be tested to determine whether or not the type of roof reduces the amount of heat entering the house. In addition students could investigate different types of roofs, the best types of insulators, etc.

Evaluation

Day 6 or 7 (30-55 minutes) class period.

Formative assessment I will focus on the guiding questions that can be used in conjunction with a Know-Want to Know-Learned (K-W-L) chart to guide student thinking and make their learning visible in the learning community. These questions may also be used to identify students' prior knowledge in relation to heat energy and to build connections to everyday life. Student journal entries should provide the teacher with written evidence of conceptual understanding.

Formative assessment II will focus on student performance, student-student interactions, but most importantly problem solving strategies. Students engage in constructing scientific knowledge though discussion and collaboration within their group. Students record and compare predictions to findings.

Formative assessment III will focus on students' responses to essential questions. Students' explanations provide the teacher with the opportunity to determine whether or not students are able to make connections between the science and mathematics concepts and their application in a new situation.

Summative assessment will focus on student evidence of understanding and application of science and mathematics concepts in everyday life. Students will be asked to present their findings by explaining the y intercept in their graphs and what this means to them. Student explanations should include an explanation as to the relationship between the materials tested and the increase or decrease in temperature using the terms conduction, convection and radiation. Student explanations should be supported by data collected and graphed to support their conclusions.

Summative assessment will be a traditional paper and pencil exam with a combination of open-ended questions that are similar to the design activities and multiple-choice questions that are similar to the state exam that the students will take.

NOTE: Adapted from Challenges in Physical Science: Solar House Project sponsored by the Harvard-Smithsonian Center for Astrophysics with funding from the National Science Foundation and additional support from the Smithsonian Institution. Published by Kendall/Hunt Publishing Company. Dubuque, Iowa 52002.

RUBRIC SAMPLES

Group Skills Rubric-Peer Evaluation	
Points:	**Criteria**
4 Par 5 out of 6	This group member contributed equitably to the group as well as: • took a leadership role when needed and was a good follower when appropriate. • demonstrated knowledge of the topic, concepts, and principles needed to complete the task or took the initiative to develop them. • communicated effectively with **ALL** team members. • made **ALL** team members feel comfortable, competent, and capable. • took action in dealing with group members who were not fully engaged in the task. • accepted responsibility for an equitable portion of the task and completed **ALL** his or her own portions of the task independently.
3 Par 4 out of 6	This group member: • accepted leadership when asked. • was an adequate follower when appropriate. • demonstrated limited or adequate knowledge of the topics, concepts, and principles but did not go above and beyond to assist the group. • communicated effectively with a subset of the group but was not hostile to the rest of the group. • used a preponderance of effort in discordant activity as contrasted by consensus building. • accepted responsibility for an equitable portion of the task, had difficulty meeting his or her responsibility or failed to accomplish the task as set out by the group, or the finished portion was not representative of work of the group as a whole.
2 Par 4 out of 6	This group member: • accepted leadership reluctantly. • followed strong leaders or a clique within the group. • communicated on a limited basis, just the facts, or just enough to get the job done. • demonstrated limited knowledge of the topics, concepts, and principles or did not go above and beyond to learn more. • accepted responsibility reluctantly or accepted responsibility for a much smaller proportion of the task than other group members but took leadership of his or her assigned task even

	if it was not complete.
	• failed to complete his or her task or another group member(s) or did some portion of the task.
1 Par 3 out of 7	This group member: • did not accept leadership or did not accept leadership for his or her own task. • communicated ineffectively with at least one group member. • made only minimal contributions to designing the task or contributing ideas. • followed no one or worked independently outside group consensus. • prevented consensus without offering substantive positive suggestions. • completed a task that either did not fit with group or was substandard or caused the group to receive a lower score because of discontinuity. • did not complete his or her own task.
0	Failed to meet the group at originally agreed upon times or provided only unsuitable times for group meetings.
/4	Total Group Skills mean score *25= Individual score

Name_____
    Evaluator_____

Project_____
    Date_____

Created by Dr. Robert M. Capraro, 2008

SELF-ASSESSMENT PROBLEM SOLVING RUBRIC

Mathematical Language (My math words) --
Level 1☐   Level 2☐   Level 3☐

I didn't use math words.   I used some math words in a few parts
I used math words correctly for all of my solution.

Mathematical Representation (My graphs, plots, charts, tables, models, diagrams) ------------
Level 1   Level 2   Level 3
I didn't use any...   I tried to use ...   I accurately used ...
_____ graphs   _____ graphs   _____ graphs
_____ plots   _____ plots   _____ plots
_____ charts   _____ charts   _____ charts

_____ tables	_____ tables	_____ tables
_____ models	_____ models	_____ models
_____ diagrams	_____ diagrams	_____ diagrams

Documentation (My explanations) --

Level 1 ☐	_Level 2_ ☐	_Level 3_ ☐
I have no clear parts in my solution. - _or_- I have work that is incorrect.	I have some clear parts in my solution. - _or_- I have a few math mistakes.	I have a solution that is clear and easy to understand. - _or_- My math is correct.

Approach and Reasoning (My ideas) --

Level 1	_Level 2_	_Level 3_	_Level 4_

I don't get it. I can do part of it. I understand the problem. I found a rule.

My approach didn't work. I got part of it my way. My approach worked.

I solved the problem in more than one way. I solved it in a special way.

Connections (My thinking) --

Level 1	_Level 2_	_Level 3_	_Level 4_

I started the problem I explained some of it. I need to explain better. I clearly explained my work. I explained most of it.

Solution (My work) --

Level 1	_Level 2_	_Level 3_

I didn't solve the problem. I solved part of the problem correctly. My answer is correct an my work supports my answer

Presentation Rubric-Not requiring PowerPoint®	
Points:	**Criteria**
25 Max	Organization (hierarchy) 25 well-organized, complete and factual, correctly formatted, displays a theme, properly identified, evidence of shared work and collaboration—Each person knows what is happening; each person has an important role and all group members closely support each other during the presentation. 20 fairly well-organized, mostly complete and factual, no format errors and easily navigable 15 fairly well-organized, mostly complete and factual, a few errors in format, navigation difficulties, some shared work and collaboration, some members show evidence of the events, members show limited support, limited assistance in managing the participants 10 poorly organized or lacking significant information but extensive technology is incorporated 5 poorly organized, lacking significant factual information, several errors in format, little evidence of collaboration or group presentation
25 Max	Mechanics 5 presentation flows naturally with all members playing an essential role 5 easy to navigate, few spelling errors in the required handouts 5 linear (not scattered) 5 engaged the audience, provided for audience participation and involvement (more than interesting) 5 evidence of group work through interactions among group members 0 No Score: numerous spelling/grammatical errors, some confusion because groups members not supportive or actively involved in maintaining engagement while others are presenting
25 Max	Content Relevancy 25 good examples of coursework, lessons related to teaching experiences 20 general information relevant to the course, examples of sound pedagogy, lessons, mathematical accuracy and precision 15 general information and somewhat relevant to course, varied delivery that addresses the mathematics presented or being represented

	10 mostly cursory information or no relevance to coursework or chapter or syllabus 5 only cursory information without explanation or examples
25 Max	Theme 5 well organized and planned 5 necessitates or merits group work 5 presentation follows in a natural progression that communicates the theme to the participants 5 challenging and represents the contents of the course 5 presented in a manner in accordance with the requirements of the syllabus 0 No score: no theme represented or communicated
/100	Total Presentation
/100	Individual Score
/100	Overall Score= mean of the two previous scores

Rubric

Points:	Criteria
4 Par 5 out of 6	This group member contributed equitably to the group. • took a leadership role when needed and was a good follower when appropriate • demonstrated knowledge of the topic, concepts, and principles needed to complete the task or took the initiative to develop them. • communicated effectively with **ALL** team members • made **ALL** team members feel comfortable, competent, and capable • took action in dealing with group members who were not fully engaged in the task • accepted responsibility for an equitable portion of the task and completed **ALL** his or her own portions of the task independently
3 Par 4 out of 6	This group member: • accepted leadership when asked • was an adequate follower when appropriate • demonstrated limited or adequate knowledge of the topics, concepts and principles but did not go above and beyond to assist the group. • communicated effectively with a subset of the group but was not hostile to the rest of the group • a preponderance of effort used in discordant activity as contrasted by consensus building • Accepted responsibility for an equitable portion of the task, had difficulty meeting his or her responsibility or failed to accomplish the task as set out by the group or the finished portion was not representative of work of the group as a whole.
2 Par 4 out of 6	This group member: • accepted leadership reluctantly • followed strong leaders or a clique within the group • communicated on a limited basis, just the facts, or just enough to get the job done • demonstrated limited knowledge of the topics, concepts and principles or did not go above and beyond to learn more. • accepted responsibility reluctantly or accepted responsibility for a much smaller proportion of the task than other group members but took leadership of his or her assigned task even if it was not complete • Failed to complete his or her task or another group member(s) did some portion of the task

The first row of the table is titled **Group Skills Rubric-Peer Evaluation** (spanning Points and Criteria columns).

1 Par 3 out of 7	This group member: • did not accept leadership or did not accept leadership for his or her own task • communicated ineffectively with at least one group member • made only minimal contributions to designing the task or contributing ideas • followed no one or worked independently outside group consensus • prevented consensus without offering substantive positive suggestions • completed a task that either did not fit with group or was substandard or caused the group to receive a lower score because of discontinuity. • did not complete his or her own task
0	Failed to meet the group at originally agreed upon times or provides only unsuitable times for group meetings
/4	Total Group Skills mean score *25= Individual score

Name_____**Evaluator**_____

Project_____**Date**_____

Presentation Rubric-Not requiring PowerPoint®	
Points:	**Criteria**
25 Max	Organization (hierarchy) 25 well-organized, complete and factual, correctly formatted, displays a theme, properly identified, evidence of shared work and collaboration - Each person knows what is happening, each person has an important role and all group members closely support each other during the presentation. 20 fairly well-organized, mostly complete and factual, no format errors and easily navigable, 15 fairly well-organized, mostly complete and factual, a few errors in format, navigation difficulties some shared work and collaboration, some members show evidence of the events, members show limited support, limited assistance in managing the participants 10 poorly organized or lacking significant information but extensive technology is incorporated 5 poorly organized, lacking significant factual information, several errors in format little evidence of collaboration or group presentation
25 Max	Mechanics 5 presentation flows naturally with all members playing an essential role 5 easy to navigate, few spelling errors in the required handouts 5 linear (not scattered) 5 engaged the audience, provided for audience participation, and involvement (more than interesting) 5 evidence of group work through interactions among group members. 0 No Score: numerous spelling/grammatical errors, some confusion because groups members not supportive or actively involved in maintaining engagement while others are presenting
25 Max	Content Relevancy 25 good examples of coursework, lessons related to teaching experiences 20 general information relevant to the course, examples of sound pedagogy, lessons, mathematical accuracy and precision 15 general information and somewhat relevant to course, varied delivery that addresses the mathematics presented or being represented 10 mostly cursory information or no relevance to coursework or chapter or syllabus 5 only cursory information without explanation or examples
25 Max	Theme 5 Well organized and planned theme 5 Theme necessitates or merits group work 5 The presentation follows in a natural progression that communicates the theme to the participants 5 The theme is challenging and represents the contents of the course 5 The theme is presented in a manner in accordance with requirements 0 No score: No theme represented or communicated.
/100	Total Presentation
/100	Individual Score
/100	Overall Score= mean of the two previous scores

SELF-ASSESSMENT PROBLEM SOLVING RUBRIC

Mathematical Language (My math words) ---------------->
Level 1 ☐   Level 2 ☐   Level 3 ☐

I didn't use math words.   I used some math words in a few parts   I used math words correctly all the.   of my solution.

way through my solution

Mathematical Representation (My graphs, plots, charts, tables, models, diagrams)

Level 1 I didn't use any...   Level 2 I tried to use ...   Level 3 I accurately used ...

Level 1	Level 2	Level 3
___ graphs	___ graphs	___ graphs
___ plots	___ plots	___ plots
___ charts	___ charts	___ charts
___ tables	___ tables	___ tables
___ models	___ models	___ models
___ diagrams	___ diagrams	___ diagrams

Documentation (My explanations) -------------
Level 1 ☐   Level 2 ☐   Level 3 ☐

I have no clear parts in my solution.	I have some clear parts in my solution.	My solution is clear and easy to understand
- or -	- or -	- or -
I have work that is incorrect.	I have a few math mistakes.	My math is correct.

Approach and Reasoning (My ideas) -------------

Level 1	Level 2	Level 3	Level 4
I don't get it.	I can do part of it.	I understand the problem.	I found a rule.	I solved the problem in
My approach didn't work.	I got part of it my way.	My approach worked.		more than one way.

217

Connections (My thinking) ----------------------------------

Level 1	Level 2	Level 3	Level 4
I started the problem and stopped.	I explained some of it. I explained most of it.	I need to explain better.	I clearly explained my solution.	I solved it in a special way.

Solution (My work) ----------------------------------

Level 1	Level 2	Level 3
I didn't solve the problem.	I solved part of the problem.	I solved the problem correctly.	My answer is correct and my work supports my answer.

Business Plan Poster Rubric

	Advanced 4	Proficient 3	Basic 2	Minimal 1	Score
Interview	All of proficient level and included relevant follow-up questions.	Relevant and appropriate number of questions. Complete and edited answers.	Most questions are relevant. Basic number of questions. Complete answers, not fully edited.	Few relevant questions. Answers are incomplete and unedited.	
Survey	Questions are extremely well organized, clear and relevant. Information is gathered completely and orderly.	Questions are well organized, clear, and relevant. Information is administered and gathered completely.	Most questions are organized, clear and relevant. Not all information is administered or gathered.	Questions are unclear, disorganized. Information either not administered or gathered.	
Statistics	Statistics are accurate, and displayed in a very professional, striking manner. Statistical display used is appropriate.	Statistics are mathematically accurate and displayed in a professional and attractive manner. Statistical display used is appropriate.	Some inaccuracies. Display is somewhat professional and attractive. Display not used appropriately.	Many inaccuracies. Unattractive. Inappropriate display.	
Written Expression	Mechanically stupendous. Fewer than 2 grammatical errors.	4 or fewer grammar errors.	6 or fewer grammar errors.	More than 6 grammar errors.	
	Content is superb. All information presented in logical, appropriate manner. All facets of project are reflected.	Content is good. Most facets of project reflected and presented in logical manner.	Some facets of project are reflected. Not presented in appropriate manner.	Many facets missing. Presented in illogical manner.	
	Design is extraordinary. Wonderful use of sounds, fonts, graphics, and transitions.	Design is good. Fine use of sounds, fonts, graphics, and transitions.	Acceptable design. Use of sounds, fonts, graphics, and transitions are reasonable	Poor design. Weak use of sounds, fonts, graphics, and transitions.	

Business and Marketing Plan

	Advanced 4	Proficient 3	Basic 2	Minimal 1	Score
Service Plan or Prototype	Service plan is extremely inventive, very workable and well thought out.	Service plan is workable and well thought out.	Some kinks in plan. Not well thought out.	Plan not thought out. Very impractical	
	Prototype is exceptionally imaginative, workable, cost-efficient and striking.	Prototype is workable, cost-efficient and attractive.	2 of the 3 requirements. (Workable, cost-efficient, attractive.)	Unusable.	
Financial Plan	Plan is extremely well laid out, showing cost per material, marketing costs, and profit. Very easy to read and follow. Realistic and feasible.	Plan shows cost per material, marketing costs, profit in easy to follow visual format. Is realistic and feasible.	Plan shows most of costs per material, marketing costs and profits. Realistic and possible.	Non-realistic and not possible.	

Presentation Rubric

	Advanced 4	Proficient 3	Basic 2	Minimal 1	Score
Business Plan Presentation (may use PowerPoint®)	Outstanding delivery of persuasive speech. Speaker had superb attention-getter, thesis, points, support, and conclusion. Maintained good eye contact, used loud, clear voice, proper gestures.	Good delivery of speech. Had attention-getter, thesis, points, support, and conclusion. Good eye contact, voice and gestures.	Delivery is acceptable. Had some of previous requirements. Lacking eye contact, loud, clear voice. Inappropriate gestures.	Poor delivery. Many requirements missing. Improper body language and gestures.	
	Mechanically stupendous. Fewer than 2 grammatical errors.	4 or fewer grammar errors.	6 or fewer grammar errors.	More than 6 grammar errors.	
	Content is superb. All information presented in logical, appropriate manner. All facets of project are reflected.	Content is good. Most facets of project reflected and presented in logical manner.	Some facets of project are reflected. Not presented in appropriate manner.	Many facets missing. Presented in illogical manner.	
	Design is extraordinary. Wonderful use of sounds, fonts, graphics, and transitions.	Design is good. Fine use of sounds, fonts, graphics, and transitions.	Acceptable design. Use of sounds, fonts, graphics, and transitions are reasonable	Poor design. Weak use of sounds, fonts, graphics, and transitions.	

Participation and Cooperation Rubric

	16	12	8	4	Score
Cooperation	Students worked extremely well together, demonstrating extensive time and effort. Accomplished all goals. Shared responsibilities, and compromised when needed.	Students worked well together. Compromised when needed. Shared responsibilities, time and effort equally.	Some cooperation problems arose. Did not always compromise well. All did not share responsibilities, time and effort equally.	Many problems within group.	
	Students used extremely supportive language, encouraged each other.	Students used supportive language, encouraged each other.	Some students were supportive occasionally using supportive language and providing some level of encouragement.	Evidence of competitiveness among group members, use of negative motivation or encouragement.	
Prompt & Attending	Student is always prompt and regularly attends classes and/or group meetings.	Student is late to class once every two weeks and regularly attends classes and/or group meetings.	Student is late to class more than once every two weeks and regularly attends classes and/or group meetings.	Student is late to class more than once a week and/or has poor attendance of classes and/or group meetings.	
Engagement*	Student proactively contributes to class by offering ideas and asking questions more than once per class.	Student proactively contributes to class by offering ideas and asking questions once per class.	Student rarely contributes to class by offering ideas and asking questions.	Student never contributes to class by offering ideas and asking questions.	

* may be reworded to specifically refer to the group or the group can be held responsible for the behavior of its members.
This rubric can be amended to accommodate listening skills, behavior, and preparation.

Robert M. Capraro
Department of Teaching, Learning and Culture,
Texas A&M University

Scott W. Slough
Department of Teaching, Learning and Culture,
Texas A&M University

Christopher Romero
Calculus Teacher,
Dallas, Texas

Teresa Jimarez
Department of Teaching, Learning and Culture,
Texas A&M University

LaVergne, TN USA
25 November 2009

165278LV00001B/81/P